Many Shades of Red

Many Shades of Red

State Policy and Collective Agriculture

Mieke Meurs

ROWMAN & LITTLEFIELD PUBLISHERS, INC.
Lanham • Boulder • New York • Oxford

ROWMAN & LITTLEFIELD PUBLISHERS, INC.

Published in the United States of America
by Rowman & Littlefield Publishers, Inc.
4720 Boston Way, Lanham, Maryland 20706

12 Hid's Copse Road
Cumnor Hill, Oxford OX2 9JJ, England

British Library Cataloguing in Publication Information Available

Library of Congress Cataloging-in-Publication Data

Meurs, Mieke.
    Many shades of red : state policy and collective agriculture / Mieke Meurs.
        p. cm.
    Includes bibliographical references and index.
    ISBN 0-8476-9038-5 (alk. paper). – ISBN 0-8476-9039-3 (paper : alk. paper)
        1. Collectivization of agriculture—Case studies. 2. Agriculture and state—
    Communist countries—Case studies. I. Title.
    HD1492.A3M48   1999
    338.7'683'0947—dc21   98-41936
                                                                      CIP

Printed in the United States of America

⊖™ The paper used in this publication meets the minimum requirements of American
National Standard for Information Sciences—Permanence of Paper for Printed Library
Materials, ANSI Z39.48–1984.

Contents

Acknowledgments

This collection is a product of collaborative work over the period 1991-1995, supported by a grant from the MacArthur Foundation Grant for Collaborative Studies. Early versions of the chapters in this volume were presented at a conference in Hungary in 1991, where Phillip Huang, Teodor Shanin, Ivan Szelenyi, and Michael Watts served as discussants on these papers. Work on most of the chapters then continued through 1996. Over this period, a number of students at American University worked on the manuscript. Kelly Aleksejuk, my undergraduate research assistant from 1991-1994, worked many hours collecting and organizing data. Graduate students Genna Miller, Monique Morrissey, Joe O'Connor, and Jeff Strohl all contributed editorial assistance. Yvon Pho, also a graduate student at American University, worked extensively on the final draft. Without her work, the book would have taken many more years to complete. Finally, Carmen Diana Deere offered immeasurable moral and political support, without which the collaborative project would never have been possible.

1

The Continuing Importance of Collectivization

Mieke Meurs

Why Reexamine Collectivization Now?

With the collapse of the Soviet Union, the debate over the benefits of collective forms of agriculture may appear closed. To counter such conclusions, the analysis developed in this volume seeks to address two popular misconceptions about the experience of collectivized agriculture: that the process can be characterized as the global application of a single, Soviet-defined model of collective agriculture, and that the experience should be understood as an unqualified failure.

Socialist states did legitimize their agricultural policies by referring to universal "Marxist" theoretical principles and to the Soviet model. Nonetheless, agrarian policies were also strongly influenced by diverse histories, geographies, and political conditions of the countries in which collectivization was implemented. As a result, governments encouraged smallholders to pool their land into collective forms of production in quite different ways, on different timetables, with different consequences. The five cases examined here, Russia, Bulgaria, Hungary, Cuba, and China, illustrate some of these differences.

In some cases, official encouragement of collectivization quickly changed to force, and the collectivized property was brought under tight control by the central government. In other cases, governments relied to a greater extent on incentives and compromise to encourage smallholders to pool their land and left more decisions in the hands of local farm management. Occasionally, the new farms were ruthlessly exploited to provide a surplus for the central government's use in industrialization, and famine resulted. In his examination of the Chinese case,

Justin Lin reports that an excess of 30 million peasants may have starved, while Victor Danilov estimates 3 to 5 million hunger-related deaths of Russian peasants during the collectivization process. In other cases, however, subsidies flowed from the central state to the collectives, permitting the mechanization of backbreaking agricultural labor and the improvement of rural living standards.

A careful reexamination of this diversity of collective experiences is important for more than clarifying the historical record. In much of the world, agrarian reform and reorganization of production remain burning issues. About three-quarters of the world's population works in agriculture. Many of these producers have inadequate access to land, and fragmented holdings and limited technology are linked to low levels of agricultural productivity and poverty. Many small producers and rural advocates still look to various forms of agricultural cooperation as a means of increasing access to capital, consolidating land, raising productivity, and improving the conditions of agricultural workers. A careful comparison of the varied experiences with collective production under socialism has much to contribute to the ongoing debate about the role of cooperative forms of agriculture in rural development.

In addition, a reexamination of collectivization offers insights important for many of the recent and current processes of decollectivization and post-communist transformation. The top-down radical restructuring under way in East Central Europe and the former Soviet Union mirrors the earlier process of collectivization in its disregard of local conditions and the peasants' own evaluations of the benefits of varying forms of agricultural organization.[1] A reexamination of the collectivization experience may suggest more appropriate ways of promoting rural reform and development in formerly centrally planned economies as well.

The case studies included in this volume draw on a variety of new material, including new life history interviews and survey data, and newly available archival sources gathered with funding from the MacArthur Foundation from 1991 to 1996. The countries included, while all underdeveloped agrarian economies at the time of collectivization, provide a diversity of contexts in which to examine collectivization. The Soviet and Chinese cases provide two examples of collectivization in large nations with strong central states but quite different agricultural geographies. While Hungary and Bulgaria are small economies with similar agricultural geographies, they also provide interesting contrasts—in rural class structure and interests prior to collectivization and in different eventual paths of collective agriculture. The Cuban case offers an example of late collectivization, in which private producers were not urged to pool land until industry was relatively well developed, and significant amounts of capital could be provided to the new cooperatives. Drawing on the new materials, the cases studies presented here illustrate some of the wide diversity of experiences with collective forms of agriculture under state socialism.

Recent work in new institutionalist economics provides one framework in which to examine changes in peasants' interests in collective agriculture as conditions and policy vary, a framework that I draw upon in this introductory overview. Clearly, factors other than peasant interests influence the viability of collective agriculture. But an analysis of peasant interests is central to an evaluation of potential for voluntary collectivization as a means of improving rural conditions. Little empirical work has been done to date examining the relationship between historical and institutional conditions, peasant interests, and the potential political and economic viability of collective forms of agriculture.

Viewed through this framework, the case studies in this volume highlight the path-dependent nature of the collectivization process. Conditions in agriculture prior to collectivization, including land scarcity, social relations, and political organization, structure peasant interests and state policy in distinct ways and play an important role in the subsequent dynamics of collectivization. Outcomes vary widely even where the initial conception is based on the same or a similar "model." This finding complements work on collectivization by Joan Sokolovsky, which focuses on the impact of varying historical conditions in generating distinct state behaviors during collectivization in Poland and Hungary, and Fred Pryor's findings that government capacity and the form of organization prior to collectivization played an important role in defining the various strategies of land reform and collectivization across socialist countries.[2] It also offers a strong argument against attempts to define and impose blueprints for "optimal" forms of agricultural organization in contemporary agrarian reforms. Some institutional frameworks will be unacceptable or unsustainable in particular historical contexts, even while they stimulate economic growth in others. Varying adaptations will result.

Despite the diversity of the experiences, taken together the cases also generate a number of conclusions about factors that have contributed to the moments of success and failure in the experience with collective forms of agriculture. The cases suggest that collectives must be able to offer significant technical benefits over individual production; in most cases, the benefits of consolidating small parcels are not sufficient to offset incentive problems that arise in the collective organization of work. Specific institutional parameters also contributed to more successful collective organization by reducing incentive costs. The organization of small to medium-sized production units, farmed by a stable group that exercised some degree of local control and financial independence, emerges as a particularly important factor. Where the majority of these conditions was met, significant numbers of peasants voluntarily pooled their land into collective forms of production. Forced collectivization was generally associated with disastrous production results, including widespread starvation. But some government pressure to collectivize, for example through some regulatory increase in the problems faced by private farmers, did not preclude improvements in agricultural growth rates and living standards.

Why Collectivization?

A number of good reviews of Marxist theories of agrarian development and collectivization have already been written, and this literature will not be reviewed again here.[3] Still, an understanding of why governments might promote collective forms of agricultural production and why peasants might accept these will be central to both an understanding of policy developments and an evaluation of the success or failure of these policies. A brief review of some of the main arguments follows.

It may be helpful to begin by defining the term *collectivization*. In literature on socialist agriculture, collectivization is frequently defined as the pooling of small privately held parcels into larger-scale agricultural enterprises.[4] To distinguish collectivization from cooperativization, collectivization is often understood to occur under state guidance that limits the independence of the new units or the rights of peasants to remain in private, individual production. In all the cases examined here, the process of moving from smallholder to large-scale state-guided agriculture occurred in stages: early encouragement of a wide variety of collective endeavors (machine sharing, collective tilling, and processing cooperatives, for example), promotion of loose forms of independent agricultural production cooperatives, and, at some stage, pressure to adhere to a state-approved form of agricultural production cooperative under state guidance.

All of the varying levels of collective organization, from collective labor in parts of the production process through fully collectivized property and labor under state guidance, will be referred to here as collectivization. But to distinguish between the various stages, organizational forms that retain significant independence will be referred to as cooperatives, while the state-dominated organizations will be called collective farms. Because our interest is in the conditions under which independent producers may willingly and beneficially pool their land into collective forms of production, state farms will not be included in our analysis of collectivization. For the same reason, many of the case studies included here focus on the period in which the collective farms retained at least some degree of autonomy, distinguishing them from state farms.[5]

Marxist scholars such as V. I. Lenin and A. V. Chayanov were among those who argued that peasants would find benefits in pooling their land and efforts. In chapter 2, Victor Danilov outlines the positions of these Russian authors in support of peasant cooperatives. While there were important differences in their perspectives, Danilov notes that both authors believed that economies of scale existed in important agricultural tasks and that peasants would benefit from working collectively on these tasks. Agricultural productivity would increase and, in combination with the nationalization of land, inequalities in rural incomes would be reduced. Chayanov maintained, however, that small-scale family production could also offer productive advantages in certain sectors, and that "labor cooperative peasant farms" should not uniformly replace family organization.

Somewhat later, Stalin, too, emphasized the benefits of scale economies and technological change that could be achieved by pooling land, while Mao emphasized the benefits of labor pooling, which would permit the production of irrigation structures and other public goods.[6] Others such as E. O. Preobrazhensky highlighted the benefits of cooperatives in centralizing surplus for the "primitive accumulation" that would precede industrialization. More recently, scholars have suggested that cooperatives may offer additional economic benefits to peasant producers, including risk sharing and improving access to resources when markets are imperfect.[7]

In the countries under examination here, which were relatively poor and heavily agrarian at the time socialist governments came to power, economic arguments no doubt had an influence on government policy. But economic considerations went beyond simply raising agricultural productivity and incomes. The new socialist governments were committed to rapid economic development and industrialization, which required both the freeing of labor from the countryside and the extraction of a surplus for industrial investment and feeding industrial labor. If collective forms of agricultural organization could replicate some of the dynamics that underlay the industrial revolution in the West, by raising agricultural productivity and increasing the agricultural surplus available for industrialization, this was an important additional argument in their favor. In Russia and China, such considerations appear to have been particularly important.

But political arguments for collectivization were also important in the cases examined here. In countries where rural interests were important in resisting the consolidation of the socialist governments at a national level, the organization of rural producers into collective farms facilitated the identification and control of opposition members (real or imagined). At the same time, collective farms could facilitate the transfer of resources to the countryside while ensuring that the resources would be used for government-approved purposes (mechanization or road building, for example). Resulting improvements in working and living conditions could help consolidate government support among poor peasants, while improved food delivery could consolidate support among urban workers. Finally, at certain points countries faced strong pressure from the Soviet Union to apply the collectivized model to agriculture, and international political considerations influenced government choices. In Hungary, Cuba, and Bulgaria, political factors may have played a central role, although both the Hungarian and Bulgarian experiences were also characterized by a significant "freeing" of the rural population for work in the industrial work force. The varying weight of each consideration may do much to explain the distinct policies pursued by the different governments over time and thus the viability of collectivized agriculture.[8]

The Task of this Book

The case studies included in this book reexamine the process of collectivization, highlighting the changes over time and evaluating the potential of various forms of land and resource pooling to improve agricultural performance under varying conditions. Other authors have undertaken similar evaluations. In the 1970s, a number of books provided empirical evaluations of the performance of socialist agriculture as a whole, including both collective and state farms. Contrary to popular conceptions, the majority of this work points to a link between collectivization and agricultural growth, at least into the 1970s.[9]

Carmen Diana Deere examined socialist collectivization experiences in small peripheral countries. Her study revealed that the majority of these countries have relied heavily on state farms to organize agriculture. But she found that peasants have voluntarily collectivized their land in a number of cases and that "the most salient feature of voluntary collectivization is that it must make economic sense to the peasantry."[10]

More recently, Fred Pryor has provided a comprehensive overview of Marxist collectivization experiences, focusing mainly on conditions and performance in the 1980s and the outlook for subsequent reforms.[11] Pryor details the wide variety of organizational forms that occurred under the general rubric of collective agriculture and notes their link to the specific historical conditions in different countries. Pryor finds that, in the 1970s and 1980s, socialist and non-socialist countries had similar rates of growth in semigross agricultural output, regardless of whether "socialist" was defined by the Marxist nature of the government or the degree of agricultural collectivization. Total factor productivity, however, generally grew at a slower rate in socialist agriculture during this period than in market economies.

Pryor offers an excellent discussion of problems in both the overall system of central planning and the organization of collective farms that may have undermined the productivity of socialist agriculture. However, his empirical analysis focuses only on macro-organizational factors that played a role in performance, such as the Marxist nature of the state, the degree of collectivization, and the level of countries' development. The data in his aggregate study are not sufficiently detailed to link variations in the organization of collectives to performance differences across countries and over time or to examine the micro-organizational factors that underlay the periods of strong growth. Other literature has offered richer descriptions and analysis of particular cases, but the focus on a single experience reduces the usefulness of these studies in drawing general conclusions about the conditions under which collectives can successfully foster gains in agricultural productivity.[12]

Perhaps most important, empirical work to date has generally not examined the conditions under which peasants voluntarily pooled land at the beginning of the collectivization process. A large body of theoretical work has attempted to address this question, however, offering insights into the conditions under which collective agriculture may be politically and economically viable. Putterman and Carter examine conditions under which peasants might voluntarily pool their land, assuming that peasant households will compare the return to collective farming with that possible as independent producers.[13] These authors note that independent producers may be faced with a large number of problems that undermine their productivity and even survival—land fragmentation, lack of capital, poor markets, and so on.

Collective endeavors may offer some benefits in dealing with these problems—pooling of land and capital to attain mechanization and economies of scale, risk sharing. But the benefits of collective organization must be substantial if voluntary collectivization is to be successful, because they will be weighed against the costs inherent in collective organization. These costs can be understood as the result of a classic collective action problem: each collective member would prefer that all others work hard in the collective and that the farm perform well, but would also prefer to do less work herself, unless pay can be perfectly linked to individual performance (usually an impossible task). The literature suggests that this danger can be reduced by keeping group size small, and through adequate pay structures and supervision, so the costs of collective production vary across organizational forms.[14]

In examining conditions under which pay structure and supervision will be more adequate, a number of writers emphasize the importance of democratic control by members.[15] Since members' incomes depend on the adequacy of pay structure and supervision, and since they have good information on the labor process, they are more motivated and more able to design good structures than are outsiders. Members are also more likely to be committed to the rules they participate in making and to work harder to make sure that they are enforced. Economies of scale or other technological benefits of cooperation are also essential. Adequate work effort will be impossible to ensure if there are not real benefits to be gained from cooperation.

Recent theoretical work also suggests that "soft" factors, such as trust or social cohesion among members, may be important in ensuring appropriate levels of collective work and good farm performance.[16] Trust can increase a member's willingness to contribute work when it reduces the member's fear that others will not also work. The origins of trust are difficult to define, but trust appears related to potential for effective punishment of cheaters.[17]

Effective punishment, in turn, may be enhanced by a number of local conditions. The existence of a stable community increases the potential for punishment by linking members in a complex of potential future interactions. If the collective generates significant benefits relative to private farming, this may also increase the potential for punishment, since a retaliatory decrease in the efforts of some could undermine the entire collective endeavor. If members can freely join and leave the cooperative, those not working can also be threatened with expulsion or with the withdrawal of others.

This theoretical work suggests that variations in the political and economic viability of collective forms of agriculture may be closely linked to the changing political and economic contexts of the farms. Drawing on the detailed institutional descriptions included here, the remaining sections of this chapter examine this relationship. The analysis highlights ways in which institutions that are successful in motivating collective work and raising productivity in one context may be unacceptably costly in another. But the analysis also offers support for a number of the theoretical propositions about the conditions under which collective forms of agriculture might be expected to provide a viable alternative to private farming.[18]

To say that collective forms of agricultural production are viable in a specific place at a certain point in time is not to claim unlimited sustainability of this form of organization, however. As the economy develops or other changes occur in the economic and political context of the farms, the relative benefits of private and collective agriculture may change, requiring institutional adaptation. Collectives provide a solution to a particular set of historically defined problems, but they may not provide the best solution to others.

Brief Overview of the Cases

The cases are examined in detail in the chapters that follow. Here, I offer only some broad comparisons of the experiences and suggest aspects of their path-dependent relationship with local conditions. In the following section of this introductory chapter, I develop the conclusions about the viability of various collectivization strategies outlined above.

All of the cases here proceeded through three basic stages of rural reform. In all five countries, long-standing rural demands, severe rural poverty, or agricultural stagnation resulted in the implementation of basic land-to-the-tiller reforms prior to any attempt at collectivization of small producers. With the exception of the Bulgarian and Chinese cases, the reforms addressed a situation in which latifundia coexisted with extensive landlessness. Large producers, even when linked to the global capitalist economy, depended on cheap labor and extensive production methods rather than modernization, and productivity stagnated. Hungarian agricultural production rose by well under 1 percent per year over the period 1915-1938 (starting from its average in 1911-1915).[19] Imre Kovach, in chapter 4 on Hungary, points out that this slow growth was outstripped by population growth, resulting in a decline in per capita agricultural output. In Cuba and China, too, per capita agricultural production declined in the decade before the revolution, while technology and total output stagnated.[20] Bulgaria escaped severe maldistribution of land, but annual growth rates of cereal output remained around 1 percent and modernization was limited—one metal plow was available for three farms in 1934.[21] Russian agriculture grew at the respectable rate of 3 percent per year from the turn of the century through 1913, but the inefficiencies and costs imposed on the peasantry by the unequal land distribution and the strip farming system are well documented.[22]   Table 1.1 summarizes land distribution and growth figures. The poverty and underdevelopment produced demands for reform in all five countries.

As will be seen below, in the precollectivization land reform, governments set varying upper limits on the permissible size of holdings and distributed varying amounts of land to peasants, landless tenants, and agricultural laborers, depending on local conditions. But in all cases the initial reforms expanded the class of private landholders. In Russia, land was nationalized prior to distribution, and new farmers were granted usufruct rights to as much land as could be farmed with household labor. Victor Danilov, in chapter 2 on Russia, argues that the nationalization of land responded to peasant demands; however, nationalization had been a popular demand during 1905-1907, as a strategy for radicalizing the limited proposals of the Stolypin reforms.

A second common stage of reform was the spontaneous emergence of a wide variety of forms of collective labor and production immediately after the land reform. Small groups of peasants and intellectuals, inspired by increased access to land, the magnitude of problems faced by smallholders, and the sea of social change, experimented with forms of collective production, mutual assistance, joint seed growing, machine sharing, and the like. Danilov reports that in Russia in 1927, prior to the forced collectivization and while dissatisfied cooperative members could still leave cooperatives, cooperative farms of various sorts incorporated well over 10,000 households on 2 percent of agricultural land (see table 1.1). In chapter 3 on the Bulgarian case, Meurs reports that 7 percent of agricultural land was collectivized by 1948, prior to any real pressure from the central government, and Kovach reports that 96,000 Hungarian peasants remained in cooperatives even when they were officially encouraged to leave in 1956. In chapter 6 on Cuba, Carmen Diana Deere argues that peasant households continue even today to exercise real choice over joining cooperatives, as seen by the 123,500 peasants who continued to farm 82,200 private holdings in the later 1980s, earning significantly more than state farm workers, and the resignation of several thousand members from cooperatives in each year for which data are available. Still, cooperative membership increased from negligible levels in 1977 to 82,600 in 1983 (the peak membership year). In chapter 5, on the China case, Lin reports that there, too, millions of rural smallholders joined loose production associations voluntarily. These diverse experiments were characterized by local control, autonomy from the state, and voluntary participation.

Some of these early organizations thrived and have survived even into the present. More often, lacking resources or training, they quickly collapsed. Still others survived for a time but were taken over or crushed in the next common stage of collectivization: the imposition of a single, government-sanctioned model of collective farm.

In all the cases examined in this volume, some degree of force or government pressure was eventually used to increase the share of agricultural land farmed collectively, and collectives were at some point forced to adopt organizational structures designed by the central government. In Russia, despite the arguments of agricultural economist A. V. Chayanov that large-scale cooperatives should exist symbiotically with "those sectors of the economy in which small-scale family production was technically more suitable," uniform collective farm organization was extended ruthlessly in the 1930s.[23] Those peasants who, while committed to collective forms of organization, refused to adopt the state-sanctioned model were imprisoned or killed.[24] Bulgaria also stands out for its early insistence on a single, "correct" model of collective agriculture, without regard to local production conditions or social relations. China during the Great Leap Forward is perhaps the most extreme case, however—even land allocated to individual households for subsistence was eliminated for a few years, and all communes were urged to attempt self-sufficiency in grain, regardless of local climate and conditions.

In Hungary and Cuba, this universalizing tendency was diminished somewhat by peasant resistance. In Hungary after 1958, a single model of collective was officially approved. But local collective farms were often permitted to elect officials without interference from central authorities, and in practice, many farms allowed individual households to sharecrop on collective land, especially in cases where production was particularly labor intensive.[25]

In Cuba in the early 1980s (twenty years after the revolution) pressure was exerted on all remaining peasant smallholders, including those in areas apparently better suited to small-scale, family farming, such as mountainous areas specializing in tobacco and coffee growing, to integrate their land into cooperatives. Peasant resistance and Castro's refusal to force resisters into collectivizing their land combined to limit homogenization, however. Private producers, like those in cooperatives, must meet delivery quotas at state-set prices, but over 80,000 private farms remained in 1990. Within the cooperative sector, state policy in the late 1980s supported extensive homogenization of organization, including the extension of centrally determined work norms and borrowing limits to all cooperatives and closer integration into central planning. This policy was scaled back in the 1990s, however, and Deere reports that the Cuban cooperatives continue to exhibit a relatively high degree of organizational diversity and autonomy.

Despite similarities in the overall dynamic of collectivization exhibited in the cases reviewed here, the case studies illuminate a great diversity in the pace of collectivization and the resulting scale and organization of farms. Local historical and geographical conditions contributed to significant differences in the land-to-the-tiller reforms and their ability to solve the agrarian question. By influencing the viability of smallholder production and thereby also the appeal of the collective alternative, these reforms affected later peasant responses to state-supported collectivization.

In Bulgaria, land scarcity and a relatively equal postwar land distribution limited the potential of the land-to-the-tiller reform to ease economic pressures on the peasantry. Landholdings were limited to 30 hectares (ha) (20 ha in intensive farming areas), but only 7 percent of arable land was distributed in the reform, in

Table 1.1 Comparative Overview of Land Reform (LR)

	Bulgaria	Hungary	Russia	China	Cuba
Prior to LR					
Growth (% p.a.)	1 [a,b]	1 [a,b]	3 [c]	1 [a,d]	1 [e]
Land Distribution (% holdings)	1934	1935	1905		1946
Under 5 ha	63	88			39
Over 50 ha	0.2	1	14 [k]		15
Under 50 ha (% land)	30	19			3
Over 50 ha	2	48	62 [k]		80
LR Limit (ha)	30	114	Work Self		67
After LR	1946	1949	1927	1954	1963
Land Distribution (% holdings)					
Under 5 ha	69	87		52 [h]	
Over 5 ha	0 [l]	1		3 [h]	
Under 5 ha (% land)	38	39	84 [i]		
Over 5 ha	1	21	0.5 [j]		
Average		4			14
Voluntary Coop (% arable)	7	17 [f]	2 [g]		13

[a] 1911-1915 to 1938
[b] grain only
[c] 1897-1901 to 1909-1913
[d] 1931-1937 to 1957
[e] 1950-1958
[f] 1956
[g] 1927

[h] Chinese data use the categories "poor" and "rich" farmer
[i] less than 4.35 ha.
[j] more than 11 ha.
[k] noble landholdings of all sizes, as share of private holdings and land
[l] 0.2 %

Sources: Dwight H. Perkins, *Agricultural Development in China* (Chicago: Aldine Publishing Co., 1969); Doreen, Warriner, *Economics of Peasant Farming* (London: Frank Cass and Co., 1964); Paul Gregory, "The Russian Agrarian Crisis Revisited," in *The Soviet Rural Economy* ed., Robert Stuart (Totowa, N.J.: Rowman and Allanheld, 1984); Arthur MacEwan, *Revolution and Economic Development in Cuba,* (London: Macmillan Press 1981); Ivan Volgyes, "Dynamic Change: Rural Transformation 1945-1975," in *The Modernization of Agriculture: Rural Transformation in Hungary 1948-1975,* ed., Joseph Held (New York: Columbia University Press, 1980); Rositsa Stoyanova, "A Periodization of the Bulgarian Collectivization, Part I: Pre-War Background and Early Collectivization (1960)," paper prepared for MacArthur Conference on Collectivization and Its Alternatives (Budapest, 1992); Brian Pollitt, "Some Problems in Enumerating the 'Peasantry' in Cuba," *Journal of Peasant Studies* 4, no. 2 (1977): 162-80; R. W. Davies, "From Tsarism to NEP" in introduction to *From Tsarism to the New Economic Policy,* ed., R.W. Davies (Ithaca, N. Y.: Cornell University Press, 1990); also all relevant chapters in this volume.

plots averaging 1 ha. Holdings under 5 ha, unlikely to furnish their households with an adequate income, continued to make up more than half of holdings.[26] (See table 1.1.)

In addition, Bulgarian peasants had prior experience with such reforms. A populist peasant government had implemented a land reform in the 1920s, redistributing 4 percent of arable land and providing strips of state land for sharecropping by poor households. While total crop production rose slowly to 134 percent of pre-World War I levels by 1930, about one-third of the farm population still could not meet subsistence needs and few of the new small farms were able to accumulate the capital necessary for modernization.[27] Many peasants alive in 1945 could recall the poor results of this effort at land reform. Results of the postwar land reform confirmed their expectations: output in 1948 barely exceeded 1939 levels.[28]

In Hungary, in contrast, prewar land distribution was the most unequal in East Central Europe. Lacking a strong political party, the Hungarian peasantry had not been able to force any radical prewar redistribution of land. Radical land reform may thus have held substantial appeal to peasants as a means of spurring rural growth. The postwar land reform was rather tentative, however, limiting ownership to 100 holds (about 57 ha), or 200 holds (114 ha) in the case of certain productive wealthy peasants.[29] The state distributed an average of 3 ha to 660,000 of 730,000 applicants, but the majority of agricultural workers, dwarfholders, and smallholders received nothing, and the reform produced little change in the overall structure of landholding (see table 1.1). The main effect was to increase the number of households with 0-3 ha, and increase the number and share of households with total holdings of 3-6 ha. Those households receiving land lacked access to the machinery or credit needed to farm the new land.[30] Imre Kovach argues that by increasing the number of smallholdings, the reform actually decreased the number of units likely to provide more than bare subsistence to their owners. As a result, nearly as many recipients had sold their land to the state or others by 1949 as had received land, and agricultural productivity remained 15 percent below 1938 levels in 1948.[31]

In contrast to the cases discussed above, in the Cuban and Russian cases the land-to-the-tiller reform created a potentially more viable class of small producers. In Cuba, the government set a limit of 67 ha on private holdings, granting every tenant, sharecropper, and squatter the right to claim up to that amount from the land they worked. Deere reports that this reform essentially created a landholding class from among a highly proletarianized agricultural work force, with private smallholders claiming an average of 14 ha after the reform (see table 1.1). The majority of these new landholding households continued to farm their land privately through the late 1970s, with many earning more than workers in the socialized sectors. Even after tripling the number of landholding peasants through reform, the state continued to hold 70 percent of the agricultural land, which it managed in state farms. This freed the state from dependence on peasant producers as a source of agricultural surplus.

In Russia, Danilov reports, although the distribution of nationalized land did not eliminate landless and land-poor households (some localities simply had too little land to distribute), the reform resulted in 24,000-25,000 peasant farms. Households took an average of 4-5 ha (see table 1.1) and had some agricultural capital with which to work the land: on average, one horse and one or two cows. Only 15 percent of farms had any machines and 28 percent of farms had no horse (an old Russian saying asserts that "without a horse one is not a proprietor"), but various forms of cooperatives developed quickly to provide machinery and support input purchases for the majority of peasant farms. Output grew modestly, with gross agricultural production for the period 1925-1929 averaging 7-8 percent over the level of 1909-1913, an annual growth rate of under 1 percent.[32]

Other problems undermined agricultural growth. Land continued to be distributed in traditional fragmented strips, complicating the implementation of modern farming methods and requiring peasants to spend substantial amounts of time getting to and from plots.[33] Further, Danilov argues here that while Soviet claims of kulak domination were exaggerated, strong feudal traditions did result in the rapid reemergence of a class of moneylenders and middlemen. These accounted for only about 4 percent of farms in the late 1920s, but they owned most of the agricultural capital. Their power disrupted village relations and skewed capital accumulation away from the smaller farmers. Still, Danilov argues that continued growth would have been possible following the model of combining private and cooperative production.

As in the Bulgarian case, land reform in China resulted in a highly egalitarian distribution of land. Despite an early commitment to meet the needs of the poor peasants without jeopardizing the middle peasantry, land scarcity and lack of capital limited the potential of land reform alone to reduce rural poverty. Lin reports that after the land reform was completed in 1952, 52 percent of peasants were still classified as poor (see table 1.1). Only 36 percent of poor peasant households owned a plow and only half owned draft animals.[34] Emerging forms of cooperation helped these households gain access to more capital, but the peasant sector remained unable to quickly provide the state with the surplus to finance industrialization.

Diverse patterns of collectivization followed these diverse beginnings. The mixture of incentives and pressure used in each case to promote collectivization of private land is detailed in the chapters that follow. Here we note only the main differences in pace and outcome.

In Russia, collectivization actually began very slowly. Although there was some pressure on households to collectivize during the first two years after the 1917 revolution, this policy was quickly dropped in favor of promoting service and limited production cooperatives to support individual production. Under this model, leaders expected peasants to voluntarily "grow into" increasingly collectivized labor as they saw the benefits of collective activity, although the optimal amount of eventual collectivization remained subject to debate. Some

10,000 households did choose to form various forms of production cooperatives in this period, but they were a minority. Danilov reports that ten years after the Bolsheviks took power, only 2 percent of agricultural land was in collective or state farms.

By 1929, Danilov reports, government impatience with the rate of generation of agricultural surplus and changes in government leadership resulted in radical increases in pressure to collectivize. Brutal pressures resulted in a rapid increase in collective farming: by 1929-1930, 50 percent of farms had been collectivized, rising to 69 percent by early 1934.[35] In 1960, collective farms included 56 percent of agricultural land, but their share fell to 32 percent by 1978, as state farms expanded.[36]

As collectivization proceeded in the 1930s, the government ordered the consolidation of land into increasingly large production units. Average collective farm size grew from 97 ha and 17 households in 1927, to 1,534 ha and 76 households in 1937 (an average of 20 ha per household), to 6,100 ha and 420 households in 1965 (15 ha per household) (see table 1.2).

In Bulgaria, the Bulgarian Workers' Party began to encourage collectivization almost immediately after forming its first government in 1945. Meurs reports that government pressure for collectivization was not significant until the 1950s, but then, with a few short setbacks (especially after local outbreaks of peasant resistance in 1951-1952 and Stalin's death in 1953), government pressure resulted in steady increases in collectivization. By 1958, the process was "complete," and in 1960 collective farms accounted for 80 percent of agricultural land. The farms grew from 266 ha in 1948 to 1,264 ha in 1958 and reached a peak of 4,865 ha in 1963. State farms accounted for another 11 percent of agricultural land, while private plots accounted for 9 percent. In the 1970s, the Bulgarian government eliminated collective farms, merging them into the state farms to form state-run agro-industrial complexes, averaging near 30,000 ha.[37]

As in Bulgaria, the Hungarian government began to encourage collectivization immediately after the consolidation of the Hungarian Communist Party after 1947. Hungarian collectivization did not proceed as smoothly as in Bulgaria, however. The first postwar Hungarian government was led by Matyas Rakosi, who appears to have enjoyed the honor of being "Stalin's best pupil," and substantial pressure was exerted on peasants to collectivize as early as 1949.[38] By 1955, nearly 300,000 peasants had joined collective farms. Other households resisted fiercely, however, and many who had joined remained uncommitted to collective organization. Kovach notes that when the government softened policies in the aftermath of the 1956 uprising, permitting and even encouraging peasants to leave the collective farms, 157,000 members did so. Many members stayed on, however, in 1,600 collectives.

A new Hungarian government policy that combined substantial compromises with private landholders with continued pressure for collectivization resulted in about half of agricultural land being incorporated into collective farms by 1960.

Another 12 percent of land was held in state farms and the rest in private plots, mainly plots belonging to collective farm members. By 1978, the share of land in collective farms had risen to 70 percent, largely at the expense of private plots, but Hungarian collective farms continued to be distinguished from those in Russia and Bulgaria by the compromises made with smallholders.[39] The farms retained greater local control over organization, and Kovach emphasizes the rights of cooperatives to form on the basis of local social groupings, to farm substantial amounts of collective farmland in family units under sharecropping arrangements and as sideline production, and the farms' liberty from state production quotas. Hungarian farms also remained smaller than Bulgarian or Russian farms, averaging only 747 ha in 1960 and 1,658 ha in 1970. By 1978, farm size had increased to 3,097 ha, but Hungarian farms never reached the size of Russian or Bulgarian farms at their peak.[40]

Agricultural cooperation in various forms had been promoted in the liberated zones of China during its civil war (1945-49). These were extended throughout the country simultaneously with the land reform. Lin emphasizes that, as in the early Russian cooperatives, these were loose groupings of private property holders at this point, organized in mutual aid teams and a variety of other flexible forms. Peasants shared draft power but faced little pressure to collectivize production further. By 1954, however, peasants had already begun to protest increasing state requisitions, and Lin emphasizes that as state industrialization plans were hindered by insufficient grain deliveries,[41] the state responded with a shift to a rapid, forced development of massive, uniformly organized communes beginning in 1958.

The communes averaged 4,000 ha (less than Russian and Bulgarian farms) but, because of land scarcity in China, included an average of 5,000 households (compared to 450 households in Russia), providing less than 1 ha per household. Nearly all agricultural land was farmed under this system, and farmed under strict central guidelines that required all regions to attempt grain self-sufficiency. After the famine of 1962, however, the communes were broken down into relatively small production teams, made up of 20-30 neighboring households (see table 1.2). Like the communes, these smaller units still faced strict production guidelines. This structure persisted until the partial decollectivization after 1979.

Collectivization proceeded most slowly in the Cuban case, where the process did not begin until 1977, almost twenty years after the revolution. Deere reports that beginning in 1977, a substantial package of incentives was offered to encourage peasants to join cooperatives, and by 1983, one-third of private agricultural producers had joined cooperatives. The incentive package has declined over time, and the Cuban government has resisted any temptation to force the remaining two-thirds of private producers into cooperatives. Collectivized agriculture thus controls only a small share of agricultural land in Cuba, where state farms dominate and a significant private sector continues to exist. Deere argues that the cooperatives retain a relatively high degree of managerial independ-

Table 1.2 Comparative Dynamics of Collective Agriculture

Bulgaria	Farm Size end yr ha	Investment (% total)	Collective (% land)	Force	Local Control	Finan Indep	Growth (% p.a.)
1946-1948	266	6	7	no	fully	fully	below prewar
1948-1953	932	13	59	pressure	significant	significant	3
1953-1958	1264	18	90	yes	some	significant	3
1958-1963	4865	25	90		little	some	5
1963-1968	4,340 a	22	90		no	little	1
Hungary	Farm Size ha	Investment (% total)	Collective (% land)	Force	Local Control	Finan Indep	Growth (%p.a.)
1949-1953	221	10 b	18	pressure	some	fully	1 h
1953-1956	450	15 b	20	pressure	some	significant	-1
1956-1960	747	18	45	pressure	significant	significant	3
1960-1968	1391	16	68		some	significant	2
1968-1982	3,525 c	15 d	70 c				3
Russia	Farm Size arable ha	Investment (% total) d	Collective % peasant hhs	Force	Local Control	Finan Indep	Growth (%p.a.)
1917-1925		minimal	2	no	fully	fully	0
1925-1929	97 d	20	4	no	fully	fully	1
1929-1932		18	62	yes	some	some	-5
1932-1937	1,534 e	20	93	yes	no	no	7
1937-1941	3450	15			no	no	1
China	Farm Size hhs	Investment	Collective % peas hhs	Force	Local Control	Finan Indep	Growth
1949-1952	6		50 f	no	fully	fully	7 g
1952-1957	153	7	97	little	fully	fully	3
1957-1962	5000	11	100	yes	little	some	-3
1963-1965	30	18	100		little	some	5
1965-1978	30	10	100		little	some	3
Cuba	Farm Size	Investment mill. peso	Collective % priv. land	Force	Local Control	Finan Indep	Cost/peso
1979-1983	637	43	67	no	significant	fully	0.68
1984-1987	689	71	72	no	significant	significant	0.8
1987-1990	639	57	60	no	some	significant	0.75

a 1970
b an estimated 2/3 of this amount went to state farms
c 1975-1980 only
d 1927
e agricultural land
f percent in mutual aid teams
g 1950-1953

Sources: Victor Danilov, *Rural Russia under the New Regime* (Bloomington, Ind.: Indiana University Press, 1988); Frank Durgin, "The Relationship of the Death of Stalin to the Economic Changes of the Post-Stalin Era" in *The Soviet Rural Economy*, ed., Robert Stuart (Totowa, N.J.: Rowman and Allanheld, 1984); Mieke Meurs and Simeon Djankov, *Privatizing the Land*, ed., Ivan Szelenyi (London: Routledge, 1998); Peter Nolan, "Collectivization in China: Some Comparisons with the USSR" *Journal of Peasant Studies* 2, no.3 (1976); Mark Selden, *The Political Economy of Chinese Development* (Armonk, N.Y.: M. E. Sharpe, 1993); Nigel Swain, *Collective Farms Which Work?* (New York: Cambridge University Press, 1985); Vienna Institute, *Comecon Data, 1988,* (Westport, Conn.: Greenwood Press, 1989); Karl-Eugen Wadekin, *Agrarian Policies in Communist Europe,* (London: Allanheld, Osmun, 1982); S. G. Wheatcroft, "A Reevaluation of Soviet Agricultural Production in the 1920s and 1930s," (Totowa, N.J.: Rowman and Allanheld, 1984); also relevant chapters in this volume.

ence, despite their integration into central planning. These relatively new cooperatives are much smaller than collective farms that evolved in the other cases examined here. In 1990, they averaged 639 ha and 48 members (see table 1.2).

The cases reviewed here suggest a number of path-dependent relations between local histories of landholding and productive organization and subsequent institutional evolution. Where the size of private landholdings and availability of production support through service cooperatives facilitated private production after land reform, as in Russia and Cuba, peasants were more resistant to pooling their land than in Bulgaria, where private producers faced significant production difficulties. Deere's detailed comparative study of three municipalities in Cuba offers the most careful development of this path-dependency argument by comparing three distinct regional histories with private and cooperative production. In Hungary, where producers also faced serious production difficulties due to land shortages and lack of capital, the (limited) tradition of upward mobility through capitalist agriculture and the limited experience with the trials of small-scale private agriculture described by Kovach may have contributed to peasant attachment to smallholder production. How states responded to resistance to collectivization also varied, with the strong, centralized Russian and Chinese states responding with brutal force while the Cuban and Hungarian states responded with compromise.

Traditional forms of rural organization may also have affected collectivization paths. Meurs argues that in Bulgaria collectivization was facilitated by a strong, egalitarian tradition of collective labor organized at the village level (especially in haying and logging) and widespread participation of peasants with small landholdings in prewar cooperative networks. Kovach notes that Hungary's rural population, on the other hand, was divided along many lines, including agricultural workers from large estates, servants supplementing their meager incomes, smallholders, dwarfholders, and those still holding over 100 ha after the postwar reform. These groups had little history of interaction or collective action. In the plains regions, where collectivization might have offered the greatest advantages from increased mechanization, farming households traditionally lived in dispersed homesteads and were highly self-reliant. Collective labor (beyond the family) was foreign to these dispersed households. Collective labor thus had to be organized from scratch and often offended existing social norms. Similarly, Cuban peasants traditionally lived in dispersed dwellings and were highly self-reliant, with little history of collective labor. The Russian experience differed somewhat from this pattern. Village land was held collectively and strong local institutions existed for organizing the period redistribution of this land according to established guidelines. These traditions may have contributed to peasants' willingness to experiment with varied forms of cooperation, but it did little to increase acceptance of state-imposed collective farms.

The Viability of Collective Agriculture: What Lessons Can Be Drawn?

Like its organization, the performance of collective agriculture has also varied greatly across time and place. There is no doubt that collectivization and collective agriculture resulted in significant losses of productivity, output, and living standards in some periods and some places. In the cases of China and Russia, declines resulted in widespread famine. At the same time, the studies presented here reinforce previous findings that collectivization sometimes also contributed to rapid growth in agricultural output. In so doing, the collectives contributed to the government goal of rapid industrialization and sometimes to substantial improvements in living standards. The case studies in this volume, combined with the theoretical framework outlined above, suggest some conclusions regarding the general conditions that contribute to the viability of collective agriculture and its appeal as a solution to problems of peasant agriculture.

Karl-Eugen Wadekin, looking at East Central European agriculture at the beginning of the 1980s, found that "growth on the whole has been continuous."[42] At the same time, he noted that growth was "less than soils permit and less than earlier aspirations aimed at." These findings were echoed by Pryor.[43] The studies included here also report periods of strong growth under collective organization, while noting that the stage of *forced* collectivization, combined with other policies discussed below, often contributed to substantial declines in output and undermined overall performance.[44]

More detail on performance is provided in the individual chapters, but a brief overview will serve to illustrate the variation. During the period from 1949 to 1956, Hungarian agricultural output grew slowly. From 1953 to 1956, growth rates were negative, falling about 1 percent per year, about the prewar rate. From 1956 to 1968, however, Kovach reports that output grew steadily at the respectable rate of about 3 percent per year. In Bulgaria, gross agricultural production rose 3 percent per year over the first decade of collectivization (from 1948 to 1958). Growth rates accelerated further from 1958 to 1963, reaching 5 percent per year before falling to a disappointing 1 percent for the period 1963-1968 (see table 1.2). Rural living standards also improved rapidly in Bulgaria in the 1950s, as agricultural labor was mechanized and household subsistence production was supplemented with goods from the collective farm. Meurs cites one life history informant recalling this as a period of living "like kings."

In Russia and China, where collectivization was particularly brutal, performance variations were particularly dramatic. Slow but positive growth resulted in Russia under the combination of private agriculture and rural cooperatives during the New Economic Policy (NEP), with grain output rising less that 1 percent per year from 1925 through 1929. Yields on the new collective farms were consistently higher than on the average of peasant farms, but collective farms continued to control only a very small share of the arable land.[45] Growth collapsed during the forced collectivization, falling a massive 5 percent per year from 1929 through 1934, and resulting in rural starvation in the early 1930s. Growth did not recover until the mid-1930s: annual growth of agricultural output averaged 7 percent from 1932 to 1937 as Russia recovered from the famine, but only 1 percent per year from 1937 to 1941 (see table 1.2).

In China, the combination of land reform and emerging simple forms of cooperation contributed to rapid increases in grain production of over 7 percent per year from 1942 to 1952.[46] Lin reports that gross grain output grew 3 percent per year as loose and varied forms of collective production continued to expand from 1952 to 1958. Total factor productivity and peasant consumption also grew. Growth ended with the forced reorganization of various production associations into communes, however. Output fell 3 percent per year from 1952 to 1957, before recovering to 3 percent growth from 1957 to 1962 and increasing to 5 percent from 1962 to 1965 (see table 1.2).

The performance of collective agriculture is harder to evaluate in the Cuban case, as separate production data are not published for the collectivized sector. Improvements in the performance of the private sector as a whole (including both privately and cooperatively farmed land) did accompany collectivization. Nonstate agricultural production grew 4.1 percent per year from 1980 to 1985 (when an average of 48 percent of private land was farmed in cooperatives), after falling 2.5 percent per year between 1975 and 1980 (by which time only 15 percent of private land was collectivized).[47] In addition, Deere notes that cooperative costs of production have consistently been below those on state farms. By this measure, cooperatives performed best from 1979 to 1983, when costs per peso of production averaged .68. Costs rose to .80 for the period 1984 to 1987, before falling back to .75 from 1987-1990 (see table 1.2). In addition, 36 percent of cooperative members interviewed in the early 1990s reported that their living standards improved after joining the cooperative. Reported incomes of cooperative members did not differ significantly from those of private farmers, but many members gained improved access to infrastructure—11 percent reported that they gained access to electricity for the first time.

Variations in the performance and appeal of collective agriculture may be partly explained by recalling that the early theorists expected collectivization to boost agricultural production by permitting the realization of scale economies. Variations in the resistance to collective agriculture across regions of individual countries suggest that such technical benefits do affect the appeal of collectives. In the Bulgarian case, collectivization proceeded relatively smoothly in the grain-growing plains regions, where mechanization promised immediate benefits, but was met with strong resistance and ultimately performed poorly in the mountainous regions. In Cuba, too, Deere reports, the strongest resistance, slowest collectivization, and weakest performance came in the mountainous and semimountainous regions, where producers specialize in labor-intensive crops such as tobacco, coffee, and cacao.

Similarly, attempts to build collectives among the poorer peasants, who had little land to contribute, produced weak collective farms. Meurs reports that early cooperatives in Bulgaria, for example, could offer members only about 2 ha per household. With such high labor/land ratios, mechanization made little sense, and collectivization offered few benefits to farm households. Not surprisingly, the collectives performed dismally in the period 1946-1948, and the government was forced to call a temporary halt to collectivization. In Hungary, where early government policy explicitly targeted poor but not middle or rich peasants for collective membership, performance on the land-poor farms was again so disappointing—with cooperatives producing 20 percent less per ha than private farmers—that the strategy had to be abandoned. Danilov reports that many early Russian collective farms suffered from the same land shortage and related weak production results.[47]

Of course, the realization of economies of scale, even in the plains regions where labor/land ratios were low and mechanization was possible, depended on financing for the mechanization. (An important exception to this is seen in the Chinese case, where Lin suggests that the benefits of reduced fragmentation of land alone were substantial, so that increased scale of production yielded productivity gains even where mechanization was extremely limited.) Collectivization does not ensure mechanization, as the African collectivization experiences have shown.[48] Still, in the cases studied here, collectivization appears to have played an important role in facilitating state investment in agriculture and infrastructure and in providing a political motivation for such investment, by allowing greater state control over returns on the investment. Once collectives were in place, substantial investment often followed. In Bulgaria, for example, 13 percent of state investment funds from 1949 to 1952, and 18 percent of investment from 1953 to 1957, went into agriculture, mainly into collective farms. As a result, Meurs reports, fertilizer and chemical applications rose to over ten times 1939 levels by the mid-1950s, and the number of tractors in use rose from 1,000 to 11,200.[49] Available tractors doubled again by 1965. Under these conditions, collectivization did produce scale economies and productivity increases, contributing to the smooth collectivization and the steady 3 percent annual growth of agricultural output noted above.

In Cuba, too, collectivization was accompanied by significant increases in investment into the nonstate agricultural sector. Resources invested in the private sector tripled between 1979 and 1983, with 62 percent of the investment going to the new cooperatives.[50] Deere argues that the ability of the Cuban state to provide this investment was central to the political and economic success of the cooperatives in areas where mechanization was possible. She also points out, however, that too much investment, especially if it is not well targeted, can sink the cooperative under an excessive debt burden.

Where the flow of modernizing investment was not forthcoming, as in the early years of the Russian and Hungarian experiences, the collectives performed poorly and could not attract voluntary members. In Hungary, for example, Kovach reports, 10-15 percent of total investment allocated to agriculture prior to 1956 (see table 1.2) was channeled mainly to state farms. Fertilizer applications per ha did not increase at all over 1938 levels by 1950, and only increased by about 50 percent by 1956. Although the number of tractors in use rose substantially, from 7,000 to 22,300, the increase was much less than in Bulgaria.[51] The underequipped collectives performed poorly and provided few incentives to join, and only 17 percent of agricultural land was in collective farms in 1956.[52] Agricultural output fell. After 1956, however, investment in agriculture was increased to 18 percent of total investment and more was allocated to the growing number of collective farms. Available tractors increased to 48,000 by 1960 and 100,000 by 1968.[53] Output grew, achieving a steady 3 percent per year through 1960 and 2 percent through 1968 (see table 1.2).

In Russia, collective farms benefited from some investment in the NEP years and by the mid-1920s they had significantly more machinery than peasant farms.[54] Still, most collective farms continued to rely on groups of peasants producing side by side with traditional technology. Despite 20 percent of annual state investment being directed to agriculture from 1925 to 1929 (see table 1.2), Danilov reports that less than 1 percent of spring sowing area was plowed by tractors in 1928. Some productivity improvements were obtained in Russia without mechanization, as the consolidation of small and dispersed plots allowed peasants to implement the crop rotation, but the potential gains from this innovation alone were limited.[55] Output grew slowly through 1929 (see table 1.2).

The Russian government failed to recognize or heed the connection between mechanization and output growth, increasing its demands on agriculture and forcing expansion of collectivization in the absence of any technological rationale or ability to supply machinery to the mushrooming collective farm sector. As collectivization accelerated in 1929, agriculture's share of fixed capital and equipment investment fell to about 18 percent. Investment shares continued to fall through the collectivization process, reaching a low of about 15 percent in 1937 (see table 1.2). Low levels of investment turned to disinvestment by 1929 as even seed grain was stripped from the countryside.

This disinvestment resulted in a collapse in gross agricultural production, with output falling by 5 percent per year from 1929 through 1932 (see table 1.2). Danilov cites a letter from Russian writer Mikhail Sholokhov to Stalin: "The poorer peasant is starving, personal property, even samovars and strips of land are being sold . . . by the average peasant." Only after the disaster was mechanization substantially increased in 1932-1937, so that by 1937 nine-tenths of all farms had tractors, and output growth resumed.

In the Chinese case, too, state investment funds for agriculture were initially very limited. While early discussions of collectivization in China had emphasized the importance of mechanization in making production cooperatives viable, the state found itself unable to supply capital without first achieving the industrialization that collectivization was meant to finance.[56] As a result, Lin reports, state investment funds for agriculture accounted for only 7 percent of the capital construction budget for 1953 to 1959 and 11 percent from 1959 to 1963 (see table 1.2). To maximize its impact, the state focused the investment mainly on labor-intensive infrastructure construction. Some intensification of production did occur as well, as Lin reports that chemical fertilizer applications rose from 2 kg/ha in 1952 to 11 kg/ha in 1957 and the area cultivated by tractor power rose from 0.1 percent of agricultural land in 1952 to an almost equally insignificant 2.4 percent in 1957. The mobilization of labor and increase in fertilizer use in small to medium-sized farms coincided with strong growth of 3 percent per year for grain from 1952 to 1957. But once large-scale collective production was enforced after 1958, the low-investment strategy ceased to ensure results. Production plummeted, falling below 1952 levels. Only after China increased agricultural investment to 18 percent of the capital construction budget following the disastrous famine of 1961-1962 did collective production begin to recover. Lin reports that area plowed by tractors rose from 2 percent in 1957 to 15 percent in 1965, while chemical fertilizer rose from 11 kg/ha to 62. Output responded accordingly, returning to 1957 levels by 1965 and growing 4 percent per year until 1978.

Even where production benefits did derive from collectivization, the empirical studies presented here highlight the way in which these could be undermined by incentive problems inherent in the collective organization of production. Factors exacerbating these problems include the large size of the farms, pay structure that failed to tie pay to farm performance, and weak social relations underlying the collective structures.

Meurs, in examining the Bulgarian case, emphasizes the interactive role of several of these factors in the performance of the agricultural collectives. When the village-based collective farms were consolidated into multivillage, 4,000 ha collectives in the 1960s, the size of production units made it increasingly difficult to tell who was working and who was not. In addition, production units were no longer made up of neighbors, against whom social pressures and village networks might be effectively used to limit free riding. Supervision by state-appointed officials could provide only a poor substitute for member policing in the context of dispersed and uneven agricultural work. The problem was exacerbated by state policies in the late 1960s that reduced the link between individual's pay and farm performance, further reducing motivation for quality collective labor. As state investment in agriculture fell and incentive problems grew simultaneously in the 1960s, the benefits of collective agriculture were reduced. This was reflected in weakening farm performance after 1963 (see table 1.2).

In looking at the Chinese case, Lin argues that incentive problems were linked to the involuntary nature of collectivization. He emphasizes that, even where collectives provide real benefits to members, members must be able to credibly threaten to quit and thus bring down the entire endeavor to ensure that others honor their commitment to work. When state-imposed collectivization eliminated the possibility of leaving the collectives in the late 1950s, effective retaliation against shirkers became impossible. Unable to pressure others to work, each member then also chose defensively to work less, and effort levels settled at a low level. The Chinese state attempted to address this problem over the years with mechanisms linking pay to individual productivity, and such efforts did coincide with a return to agricultural growth prior to 1978. Lin argues that these efforts were ultimately unsuccessful, in that growth and productivity remained below that of comparable Asian countries.

In analyzing the Russian case, Danilov has argued that the early collective farms retained significant financial and organizational independence and voluntary membership into the late 1920s.[57] Combined with benefits from the consolidation of scattered plots and the small, familiar nature of the farms (17 households in 1929), self-reliance helped to stimulate good cooperative performance. Farm leaders made little attempt to link individual pay to labor effort in this early period, however, which may explain the collapse of many farms even while others succeeded—abandoning the farm may have been the main recourse against lazy fellow members.[58]

In his chapter in this volume, Danilov also focuses on the negative impact that the subsequent forced collectivization and the central imposition of a single form of organization had on members' work incentives. He argues that after 1928, the state expanded collective agriculture mainly to facilitate the rapid extraction of resources for industrialization. With little investment in new technology and even the stripping of seed grain from the collective farms, hard work could yield few benefits. Incentives for collective labor collapsed. Further problems were created by the campaigns of "dekulakification," which resulted in the displacement and destruction of over a million households. Despite the attempts of many peasants of modest means to defend their "kulak" neighbors, detailed by Danilov, the experience substantially reduced trust among villagers. Later, when violence had ceased and investment had somewhat restored the economic viability of the farms, mergers and the inability of members to leave cooperatives reduced potential means of punishing unproductive workers and kept growth rates down through World War II (see table 1.2).

In Cuba, where households have retained the right to leave cooperatives, Deere argues, this has indeed played a role in cooperatives' economic success. Although members cannot take their land with them when they leave the cooperative, many households have been willing to leave poorly functioning cooperatives to take jobs in other areas of the economy. This has greatly increased the labor shortage faced by weaker cooperatives, threatening members' incomes. Threats of departure may thus provide a real incentive for others to work appropriately. Deere also emphasizes the role of increasing state control over the cooperatives in the late 1980s in reducing the stability of membership and weakening the link between members' actions and farm performance. Performance weakened. As state interference was again reduced in the 1990s, local initiative and member stability increased, and performance improved. The relatively small size and close social relations in many Cuban cooperatives may also play a role in their general economic viability, by allowing members to pinpoint the source of performance problems and address these effectively. Cooperatives where large numbers of members came from outside the local area or outside of agriculture performed worse than those characterized by close kinship relations.

Like Deere, Kovach highlights the benefits of local control and flexible organization in his evaluation of the Hungarian case. In the earliest years (1949-1953), the lack of investment resources was exacerbated by substantial state pressure to collectivize and organize farms along lines defined centrally. Later, however, Hungarian collectives were characterized by a relatively high degree of local control and differentiation. Neither as large as the Russian or Bulgarian collectives, nor as small as the Cuban cooperatives or the post-1963 Chinese production teams, the middle-sized Hungarian farms relied on varied combinations of collective production and subcontracting to households and small work groups. This strategy increased the likelihood that collective production would be undertaken mainly in those areas where it offered some real advantages, improving incentives in both collective production and in household production. At the same time, the small size and local control of farms helped to ensure that supervision and pay would be more adequately structured in collective work. The cooperatives contributed to the steady annual agricultural growth of 3 percent through 1968.

Kovach argues that after the 1970s, when farms grew in size, investment fell off, and the link between cooperative performance and individual pay gave way to a system of simple wage labor, incentive problems were reduced by the transfer of many labor-intensive tasks to household production. Easier-to-monitor tasks, such as mechanized grain production, remained in the collectives, where economies of scale and heavy machinery remained important. This flexibility may have helped sustain the 3 percent growth rate into the 1980s (see table 1.2).

Taken together, the case studies suggest a list of variables that play an important role in the viability of collective production. The collectives generally performed better where physical conditions permitted the consolidation of land and investment supported mechanization. In addition, collectives performed better when they were small to medium-sized units, farmed by a stable group that exercised some degree of local control, and when income was effectively linked to individual work. Under these conditions, significant numbers of peasants voluntarily joined cooperative production arrangements. When collectivization resulted from severe repression, when resources for investment were not forthcoming, and when control and income determination shifted outside the farm, however, performance appeared to lag.

Some of the cases described in the chapters that follow present exceptions to these patterns. In addition, a definitive study of the link between conditions and performance would require econometric tests on more complete data than are included in this collection of case studies. Nonetheless, these patterns emerge clearly across the five cases presented and provide preliminary support for a broad group of theories on conditions under which collective action can be successful.

The Waning of Collectivization

While collective agriculture produced rapid growth over certain periods and under certain conditions, agricultural performance declined uniformly as the experiences "matured." On the one hand, as state-supported modernization of agriculture achieved technological "catching up," the benefits of collectives as a means of channeling investment into agriculture and achieving mechanization and economies of scale declined. In many cases, investment was reduced. On the other hand, as noted above, most states gradually consolidated the collective farms into larger units and extended control over them. Problems with labor efficiency mounted in turn. Over time, the potential benefits of collective farming declined, and these offered a decreasingly attractive alternative to more individual forms of organization.

In China, Lin argues, despite positive agricultural growth of about 2 percent through the late 1960s and 1970s, these rates were disappointing to government officials in that they fell below those achieved in other Asian countries. In Bulgaria, growth rates fell steadily from a peak of 5 percent per year from 1960 to 1965 to a negative 2 percent per year for the period 1982-1989.[59] Collective farms were merged with state farms in the 1970s in an attempt to achieve ever-greater economies of scale and integration with central planning, so that further declines in the performance of Bulgarian agriculture do not relate directly to our discussion of collective farms. They do, however, provide the prelude to later attempts at decentralization, and individualization slowed slightly in the late 1960s, prompting a general decentralization that opened space for increasing private agricultural production. In Russia, agricultural output stagnated badly after 1976, growing only 1 percent by 1982.[60] Rapidly increasing investment failed to boost growth. The exception to the general growth slowdown in collectivized agriculture is the younger Cuban experiment, where cooperatives continued to perform well through the end of the 1980s. Private-sector (that is, cooperatives and private farmers) sales to the state grew 4 percent per year from 1986 to 1988.[61] In 1990, the dissolution of the Soviet Union and massive disruption of the Council for Mutual Economic Assistance (CMEA) trading bloc sent shock waves through the Cuban economy. Although economic data has not been published since then, Deere reports that the cooperatives have continued to perform well enough to attract new members.

Partly as a result of the widespread stagnation, the 1970s and 1980s were characterized by a gradual shift away from collective agriculture and toward more limited forms of cooperation across centrally planned economies. In some cases, the initiative came from the collective farm management and collective members themselves. In the Chinese case, for example, Lin argues that the shift to the household responsibility system of subcontracting began secretly at the local level, and was only sanctioned by the government later, once positive production results were seen. In Hungary, decentralization increased after the economic reforms of 1968, but Kovach argues that the rural households pushed the limits of permissible household production as a means of raising incomes and consumption. Continued loosening of regulations facilitated further expansions of household production. In contrast, in Bulgaria and Russia, the push for greater decentralization appears to have come from the central state. In all these cases, the new forms of production continued to rely on collective ownership of assets and selective use of large-scale production, but increasingly subcontracted labor-intensive work out to small local or family-based groups. In Cuba, where cooperatives have remained small and somewhat autonomous, they have not been restructured. Instead, the cooperatives have served as a model for the reorganization of the large, centrally run state farms, which have been hurt by the loss of subsidized inputs from the Soviet Union.

The specific forms that subcontracting took varied across countries. In the case studies presented here, only the Hungarian and Chinese cases document this process of decentralization. In China, Lin argues, the process began in the mountainous and hilly regions, where collective agriculture could offer the fewest productive benefits. Households pushed for subcontracting of production to the household level. Once the state began to support this policy after 1978, the state also made additional efforts to improve production incentives. A price reform improved returns to labor and uniform mandatory production quotas were eliminated, so that households could specialize in products most suitable to their region. Depending on location, household production still depended on a variety of collectively organized production supports from the central and local governments, but rapidly increasing amounts of production were organized by the household and produced with household labor. Lin reports that growth rates improved under these reforms, reaching 7 percent per year from 1978 to 1984, before falling back to 4 percent per year from 1984 to 1987.[62]

In the Hungarian case, Kovach argues that the labor-intensive vegetable and livestock production was increasingly taken over by individual households in the 1970s and 1980s, leaving the highly mechanized grain production to the cooperatives. By the mid-1970s, a larger share of Hungarian households was producing agricultural goods for market than ever before. Agricultural growth rates improved slightly, rising above 3 percent per year from 1968 to 1982. This decentralization was also not a final solution to the "agrarian question," however, as growth rates collapsed in 1982, with output falling 0.3 percent per year through 1989. Kovach argues that the stagnation resulted from continued state restrictions on the allocation of resources and production between the two sectors, which prevent households from choosing the best mix of production scales and organization.

In the Russian and Bulgarian cases, implementation of decentralizing reforms was more limited and results are less clear. In Russia, a system of contract brigades was extended to small groups of collective farmers beginning in 1984. By 1985, about half of all farm workers were organized in this way. The contract brigades attempted to recreate some aspects of cooperative agriculture: groups were small, averaging 22 people and 419 ha in the late 1980s, the group's income depended on net revenues from the contracted work, and each member's income depended on the work of the other group members. Unlike the earlier cooperatives, however, the contract teams received all their services and inputs from the state and often faced interference from party functionaries in contracting or organizing production. As would be expected given the analytical framework presented here, the contracting agreements produced greater productivity gains in labor-intensive production than in the highly mechanized products such as grain.[63]

In Bulgaria, little land was freed from the state farms prior to 1989, but the state ordered Soviet-style subcontracting of production to small groups or families after 1987.[64] By 1988, 78 percent of those working in agriculture worked under such subcontracts. As in the Soviet case, a variety of services and capital goods were still provided collectively through the state farm structure, but the contract groups were formally responsible for organizing production and controlled all net revenues from the contract. Perhaps this decentralization contributed to the slight improvement in agricultural production: output stopped falling and grew steadily from 1987 to 1989, albeit at only .03 percent per year.[65]

These partial "decollectivizations," by returning production to the control of the individual, family, or other small group, avoided many of the organizational costs associated with collective labor. The link between productive outcomes and pay was strengthened, while the small, familiar groups and interdependence of incomes encouraged effective enforcement of labor effort. At the same time, state and collective organs continued to offer varied levels of support to the small producers, including the provision of heavy machinery, stable purchasing arrangements, risk sharing, and the provision of public goods (such as irrigation works).

In combining collective and private forms of organization, the experiments of the late 1970s and 1980s mirrored the successful experiments with limited collectivization under the Russian NEP and the early Chinese mutual aid teams. The historical context of the recent experiments was quite distinct, however, in that they benefited from the prior consolidation of land into large, continuous plots, the mechanization of agriculture, and the industrialization of the economy. Whether agricultural production cooperatives could continue to offer benefits over private farming in this context is a question that will require further study.

In Russia, Hungary, and Bulgaria the experiments were interrupted by the overall economic transitions after 1989. But the transition period appears likely to offer further evidence on the issue as farmers, when given the freedom to choose, have chosen varying combinations of private and collective organization. In China and Cuba, this experiment continues, with some areas retaining aspects of collective cultivation and others moving to almost entirely private production. An analysis of the varying choices in the current period is the subject of a future volume.

Summary

As a comparative overview of the cases, this introduction has drawn on only a small part of the detail provided in the chapters that follow. It has attempted to provide one analytical framework for the comparison of the detailed case studies. Many others are certainly possible, and the rich detail of the case studies permits a reading through a variety of these. Four general findings emerge from the analysis presented here.

First, the close examination of the early years of collectivization experiences illustrates that a significant number of small- and medium-income farmers may voluntarily choose to collectivize some land and agricultural tasks into cooperatives as a means of solving problems they face in production and distribution. Their interest in doing so depends on the real benefits collectives offer over family farming. In particular, there must be technical benefits to collective organization, and these must not be outweighed by the costs of organizing and carrying out examined here. Labor mobilization or the consolidation of fields provided technical benefits without significant capital investment.

Second, the potential for collective organization to provide net benefits is closely linked to local conditions, that is, the rationality of such organization can only be determined locally. It will be strongly influenced by the specific needs of local peasants, the capacities and priorities of state structures, physical geography, and traditional cropping patterns. Where small-scale, labor-intensive agriculture generates large profits through specialized production for urban markets, for example, collective organization may have little appeal. On the other hand, where capital shortages keep grain-producing peasants at a bare subsistence level, and cooperatives provide a structure through which the state can and will increase support for mechanization, the potential appeal of collective organization will be much greater.

Third, incentive problems and thus organizational costs of collective production are influenced by more than pay structure. Clearly, pay structure is an important factor in reducing the incentives for collective members to free ride on the labors of others. In particular, the cases examined here illustrate a link between the dependence of members' incomes on farm performance and the viability of the farm itself. But incentive problems in collectives also appear to be affected by local social relations. Where rural households can draw on traditional structures of collective governance and labor, these may provide the mechanisms necessary to agree upon and enforce a commitment to collective labor. If collective labor can offer few real benefits, the agreed upon commitment is likely to be minimal, but where real benefits are expected to derive from collective labor, higher labor commitments may result. Where households have traditionally been highly self-sufficient, distrust of collective endeavors and a lack of institutions for determining and enforcing collective commitments will make collective organization more costly. The imposition of organizational forms by outsiders also consistently undermines delicate social agreements.

Finally, the cases examined here suggest that those concerned with rural development may do well to reexamine Chayanov's ideas on cooperative organization. Certainly there are serious debates on the potential of the NEP to modernize Russian agriculture over the long run.[66] Still, Danilov's case study suggests that the full potential of this form of partial collectivization into autonomous cooperatives was never realized in Russia. During the period in which peasant households could freely choose to collectivize part or all of agricultural production on the basis of the potential for collective organization to solve problems faced by private producers, collectives capitalized faster and out-performed private farms in many grain-producing areas of Russia.[67] Political commitment to rapid industrialization, rather than the poor performance of the collective-private mix, appears to underlie the Soviet decision to abandon this experiment.

In the late 1970s and 1980s, four of the five countries examined here experimented with forms of partial decollectivization. With the benefits of additional investment in agriculture falling and incentive problems mounting, the performance of many collective farms and cooperatives declined. Various aspects of production were decollectivized. Small groups and private households still benefited from the collective provision of certain capital services and infrastructure that they would probably not have been able to afford on their own. Rural households still were not allowed to choose freely which areas of production would benefit from continued collective organization. Such decisions were made by state officials, and that constraint may have ultimately limited the potential of partial decollectivization to spur growth. Still, the return of labor-intensive products to family or small group organization coincided with a burst in output and perhaps productivity growth in these areas.[68]

Taken together, these four findings remind us of the fallacy of a "one-size-fits-all" optimal form of agricultural organization. Collective organization has the potential to bring real benefits to peasant producers, but not under all conditions. The case studies presented here suggest that a flexible and fluid mix is likely to capture the most benefits from this form of organization, while avoiding excessive costs.

Notes

1. Gerald Creed, "The Politics of Agriculture: Identity and Socialist Sentiment in

Bulgaria," *Slavic Review* 4, no. 54 (1995): 843-68.

2. Joan Sokolovsky, *Peasants and Power: State Autonomy and the Collectivization of Agriculture in Eastern Europe* (Boulder, Colo.: Westview Press, 1990). Fred Pryor, *The Red and the Green: The Rise and the Fall of Collectivized Agriculture in Marxist Regimes* (Princeton, N.J.: Princeton University Press, 1992).

3. Pryor, *The Red and the Green.* Mark Selden, *The Political Economy of Chinese Development* (Armonk, N.Y.: M. E. Sharpe, 1993), 72-73, 83, 89. Carmen Diana Deere, "Agrarian Reform, Peasant and Rural Production, and the Organization of Production in the Transition to Socialism," in *Transition and Development: Problems of Third World Socialism,* ed. Richard Fagen, Carmen Diana Deere and Jose Luis Corragio, (New York: Monthly Review Press, 1986), 137.

4. Pryor, *The Red and the Green.* Selden, *The Political Economy,* 72-73, 83, 89.

5. State farms play very different roles in the agricultural sectors of the countries examined here, controlling 70 percent of agricultural land in Cuba after most collectivization was completed, but only 8 percent in Bulgaria. See Deere "Agrarian Reform, Peasant and Rural Production, and the Organization of Production in the Transition to Socialism," and Pryor, *The Red and the Green,* for a review of the role of various forms of organization in socialist agriculture.

6. Selden, *The Political Economy,* 72-73, 83, 89.

7. Michael Carter, "Risk Sharing and Incentives in Decollectivized Agriculture," *Oxford Economic Papers* 39 (1987). Mieke Meurs and Darren Spreeuw, "Evolution of Agrarian Institutions in Bulgaria: Markets, Cooperatives and Private Farming 1991 - 1994," in *The Bulgarian Economy: Lessons from Reform During Early Transition,* ed. Derek Jones and Jeffrey Miller, (Aldershot, U.K.: Ashgate, 1997).

8. Also see Sokolovsky, *Peasants and Power,* for a consideration of these issues.

9. Ivan Volgyes, "Modernization, Collectivization, Production and Legitimacy: Agricultural Development in Rural Hungary," in *The Political Economy of Collectivized Agriculture: A Comparative Study of Communist and Non-Communist Systems,* ed. Ronald Francisco, et al., (New York: Pergamon, 1979), 113. Karl-Eugen Wadekin, *Agrarian Policies in Communist Europe* (London: Allanheld, Osmun, 1982), 51, 85-87.

10. Deere,"Agrarian Reform, Peasant and Rural Production, and the Organization of Production in the Transition to Socialism," 137.

11. Pryor, *The Red and the Green.*

12. Selden, *The Political Economy,* 72-73, 83, 89. Ivan Szelenyi, *Socialist Entrepreneurs: Embourgeoisement in Rural Hungary* (Madison, Wis.: University of Wisconsin Press, 1988). Carmen Deere, Mieke Meurs, and Niurka Perez, "Toward a Periodization of the Cuban Collectivization Process: Changing Incentives and Peasant Response," *Cuban Studies* 22 (1992): 115-49. Alec Nove, *The Soviet Economic System* (Boston, Mass.: Allen and Unwin, 1986). Gerald Creed, "Economic Development Under Socialism: A Bulgarian Village on the Eve of Transition" (Ph.D. dissertation, CUNY, N.Y.: 1992).

13. Louis Putterman, "The Incentive Problem and the Demise of Team Farming in China," *Journal of Development Economics* (1987). Carter, "Risk Sharing and Incentives in Decollectivized Agriculture."

14. A. K. Sen, "Labour Allocation in a Cooperative Enterprise," *Review of Economic Studies* 33 (1966): 361-71. Louis Putterman and Marie Di Giorgio, "Choice and Efficiency in a Model of Democratic Semi-Collective Agriculture," *Oxford Economic Papers* 37 (1985): 1-21. Mancur Olson, *The Logic of Collective Action* (Cambridge, Mass.: Harvard University Press, 1965). Evsey Domar, "The Soviet Collective Farm as a Producer

Cooperative," *American Economic Review* 56 (1966): 734-57.

15. Elinor Ostrom, *Governing the Commons: The Evolution of Institutions for Collective Action* (Cambridge, Mass.: Cambridge University Press, 1990). Putterman and Di Giorgio, "Choice and Efficiency in a Model of Democratic Semi-Collective Agriculture," 1-21.

16. Michael Taylor, *On the Possibility of Cooperation* (New York: Cambridge University Press, 1987).

17. Robert Putnam, *Making Democracy Work: Civic Traditions in Modern Italy* (Princeton, N.J.: Princeton University Press, 1993). Paul Seabright, "Is Cooperation Habit Forming," in *The Environment and Emerging Development Issues,* ed. P. Dasgupta and K. G. Maler, (Oxford: Clarendon Press, forthcoming).

18. Of course, states can and did use policies biased against private production to artificially raise the relative benefits of cooperatives and thus encourage collectivization where it might not otherwise have been chosen. But such a strategy cannot ensure the economic viability of the cooperatives once they have been established.

19. Doreen Warriner, *Economics of Peasant Farming* (London: Frank Cass and Co., 1964), 47, 88.

20. Arthur MacEwan, *Revolution and Economic Development in Cuba* (New York: St. Martin's Press, 1981), 6.

21. Warriner, *Economics of Peasant Farming,* 47, 88. Dwight Perkins, *Agricultural Development in China* (Chicago, Ill.: Aldine Publishing Co., 1969), 30.

22. Paul Gregory, "The Russian Agrarian Crisis Revisited," in *The Soviet Rural Economy,* ed. Robert Stuart, (Totowa, N.J.: Rowman and Allanheld, 1984), 24. Victor P. Danilov, *Rural Russia Under the New Regime* (Bloomington, Ind.: Indiana University Press, 1988), 96, ch 2, 293-301. R. W. Davies, "From Tsarism to NEP," *From Tsarism to the New Economic Policy,* ed. R.W. Davies, (Ithaca, N.Y.: Cornell University Press, 1990).

23. A.V. Chayanov, *Fundamental Ideas and Forms of Organization of Peasant Cooperatives* (Moscow, 1919), 42.

24. *Memoirs of Peasant Tolstoyans in Soviet Russia,* edited by William Edgerton (Bloomington, Ind.: Indiana University Press, 1993), offers insights into the struggles of one collectivist group to maintain independent forms of organization.

25. Nigel Swain, *Collective Farms Which Work?* (New York: Cambridge University Press, 1985), 47.

26. John R. Lampe, *The Bulgarian Economy in the 20ᵗʰ Century* (London: Croom Helm, 1986), 125.

27. John Lampe and Marvin Jackson, *Balkan Economic History 1550-1950* (Bloomington, Ind.: Indiana University Press, 1982), 359. Warriner, *Economics of Peasant Farming,* 47, 88.

28. Gregor Lazarcik, "Bulgarian Agricultural Production, Output, Expenses and Net Product, and Productivity, at 1968 prices, 1939 and 1948 - 1970," in *Occasional Papers of the Research Project on National Income in East Central Europe OP-39,* ed. Thad Alton, (New York: Riverside Research Institute and L. W. International Financial Research, 1973), 8.

29. In 1948, the limit on private landholdings was further reduced to 40 holds or 23 ha, but the additional expropriated land was not distributed to individual households. See Peter Bell, *Peasants in Socialist Transition* (Berkeley, Cali.: University of California Press, 1984), 114.

30. Bell, *Peasants in Socialist Transition,* 106-7, 114.

31. Part of this decline can be attributed to damage and dislocation from World War

II, but since reliable production data was not collected during the war or in the first postwar years, it is impossible say what share of the decline is attributable to these causes. At the very least, it is clear that the land reform was unable to restore productivity quickly to its previous levels.

32. S. G. Wheatcroft, "A Reevaluation of Soviet Agricultural Production in the 1920s and 1930s," in *The Soviet Rural Economy,* ed. Robert Stuart, (Totowa, N.J.: Rowman and Allanheld, 1984), 47.

33. Danilov, *Rural Russia,* 96, ch. 2, 293-301.

34. Selden, *The Political Economy,* 72-73, 83, 89.

35. Eugene Zaleski, "The Collectivization Drive and Agricultural Planning in the Soviet Union," in *The Soviet Rural Economy,* ed. Robert Stuart, (Totowa, N.J.: Rowman and Allanheld, 1984).

36. Wadekin, *Agrarian Policies,* 51.

37. Wadekin, *Agrarian Policies,* 85-87.

38. Joseph Held, "Hungary on a Fixed Course: An Outline of Hungarian History," in *The Columbia History of Eastern Europe in the Twentieth Century,* ed. Joseph Held, (New York: Columbia University Press, 1992), 204-28.

39. Wadekin, *Agrarian Policies,* 85-87.

40. Wadekin, *Agrarian Policies,* 85-87.

41. Selden, *The Political Economy,* 72-73, 83, 89.

42. Wadekin, *Agrarian Policies,* 51, 85-87.

43. Pryor, *The Red and the Green.*

44. As Lin notes, many factors unrelated to agricultural organization also contributed to poor performance of collectivized agriculture. These factors included grain self-sufficiency policies and other government restrictions that prevented appropriate specialization in production, state-set prices, which left the agricultural sector with little surplus for independent investment, planning problems, which disrupted input delivery and selection, and restrictions on labor mobility, which sometimes keep excessive amounts of labor on farm accounts. These problems, while important, have been extensively discussed (see Alec Nove, *The Soviet Economic System.* Boston, Mass.: Allen and Unwin, 1986, for example) and will be ignored here in order to focus on a set of factors that has received less attention.

45. Danilov, *Rural Russia,* 96, ch. 2, 293-301.

46. Selden, *The Political Economy,* 72-73, 83, 89.

47. Comite Estatal de Estatisticas, *Annuario Estatistico de Cuba* (Havana: CEE, 1986), 280.

47. Ivan Volgyes, "Economic Aspects of Rural Transformation in Eastern Europe," in *The Process of Rural Transformation: Eastern Europe, Latin America and Australia,* ed. Ivan Volgyes et al., (New York: Pergamon Press, 1980), 118, 373.

48. Deere, "Agrarian Reform, Peasant and Rural Production, and the Organization of Production in the Transition to Socialism," 137.

49. Volgyes, "Economic Aspects of Rural Transformation in Eastern Europe," 118, 373.

50. Deere, Meurs, and Perez, "Toward a Periodization of the Cuban Collectivization Process: Changing Incentives and Peasant Response," 115-49.

51. Volgyes, "Economic Aspects of Rural Transformation in Eastern Europe," 118, 373.

52. Volgyes, "Modernization, Collectivization, Production and Legitimacy: Agricultural Development in Rural Hungary," 113.

53. Volgyes, "Economic Aspects of Rural Transformation in Eastern Europe," 118, 373.

54. Danilov, *Rural Russia*, 96, ch. 2, 293-301.

55. Danilov, *Rural Russia*, 96, ch. 2, 293-301.

56. Selden, *The Political Economy*, 72-73, 83, 89.

57. Also see William Edgerton, ed., *Memoirs of Peasant Tolstoyans in Soviet Russia* (Bloomington, Ind.: Indiana University Press, 1993).

58. Danilov, *Rural Russia*, 96, ch. 2, 293-301.

59. Michael Boyd, *Organization, Performance, and System Choice: East European Agricultural Development* (Boulder, Colo.: Westview Press, 1991).

60. Karl-Eugen Wadekin, "Agrarian Structures and Policies in the USSR, China, and Hungary: A Comparative View," in *Socialist Agriculture in Transition: Organizational Response to Failing Performance,* eds. Josef Brada and Karl-Eugen Wadekin (Boulder, Colo.: Westview Press, 1988), 55-74.

61. Carmen Diana Deere and Mieke Meurs, "Markets, Markets Everywhere? Understanding the Cuban Anomaly," *World Development* 20, no. 6 (1992): 831.

62. See Louis Putterman, *Continuity and Change in China's Rural Development: Collective and Reform Eras in Perspective.* New York: Oxford University Press, 1993, for a discussion of debates surrounding the calculation of this growth rate.

63. Elizabeth Clayton, "Economies of Small Scale in Soviet Agriculture: The Contract Collective," in *Communist Agriculture: Farming in the Soviet Union and Eastern Europe,* ed. Karl-Eugen Wadekin (New York: Routledge, 1990), 202-14.

64. A 1989 law ordered a decentralization of property back to the collective farms, but this was not implemented before the regime change in November of that year.

65. Boyd, *Organization, Performance.*

66. Mark Harrison, "Why Was NEP Abandoned?" in *The Soviet Rural Economy*, ed. Robert C. Stuart (Totowa, N.J.: Rowman and Allanheld, 1984).

67. Danilov, *Rural Russia*, 96, ch. 2, 293-301.

68. Increases in total factor productivity are difficult to measure, because of the lack of information on household inputs of labor.

2

Russia: Developing, then Crushing, Peasant Farming

Victor Danilov

In the former Soviet Union, researchers of the history of collectivization and of the collective farm it created have focused on the role of force as the decisive factor in the reorganization of agriculture, and the compulsory nature of the relationship between the collective and the government. There is no question that the collectivization of peasant farms was a real tragedy for the masses. It cost millions of lives and forcibly altered labor conditions and the way of life of the peasantry—its thoughts, moods, and customs. Therefore, when the dissolution of the socialist system began in the 1980s and 1990s, it seemed to many that the system of collective farming had run its course, and that there would be no opposition to its dismantling. Many heralded the anticipated revival of the peasantry, both as a social stratum and as a way of life.

However, to the great surprise of reformers, many peasants did not take advantage of the right to leave the collective farm with private land and property. On the contrary, many often openly opposed the dismantling of the collective farms, viewing decollectivization as the final step in the destruction of the peasant way of life. Certainly part of the reason lay with the character of the current agrarian reform, which turned out to be the same sort of bureaucratic "revolution from above" that collectivization had been. However, the peasantry may also have been responding to aspects of the kolkhoz system that have been ignored due to analysts' exclusive focus on the role played by physical force in its creation and preservation.

Until recently, the scientific study of the history of collectivization had been hindered by a lack of access to important documents kept in secret archives, as well as by stringent censorship that served to safeguard the official version of Soviet collectivization as a "revolution from above, with support from below." The declassification of secret materials, begun in the late 1980s, is, however, far from complete. Our society is just beginning to rethink what took place.[1]

Adding to the confusion has been the spread of historical myths, many of recent origin and with political overtones. These myths include claims that the Russian Revolution of 1917 was instigated with malicious intent by the Bolsheviks, that the prerevolutionary village was a flourishing community, that Russian agriculture in the 1920s had made miraculous advances, and that the concept of collective farming originated with the Bolsheviks.

These myths compel us, however briefly, to examine the agrarian development of the precollectivization period, the scale and nature of its real potential, and the problems that actually troubled the village at that time. As we will see, the precollectivization period in Russian agriculture was more complex than the myths suggest. The concept of collective farming did not originate with the Bolsheviks, but had deep roots in both the intellectual and peasant communities, as a response to serious problems that persisted in Russian agriculture before and after the revolution. Debate on how best to implement cooperative agriculture was cut short after 1929, however, and the forced collectivization was implemented by Stalin with disastrous results. Current changes reopen this debate.

The Russian Village before the Revolution

The backwardness of agriculture before 1917 and the poverty and ignorance then prevalent in rural areas are irrefutable. This underdevelopment was due, in the first place, to the system of landlord farming and to the tsarist autocracy that embodied Russian feudalism. In the second place, it is due to the fact that at the end of the nineteenth and beginning of the twentieth centuries, the Russian government implemented a plan of "catch-up" industrialization, which it paid for with agricultural exports at the expense of the rural population. At the time, 80 percent of the population was employed in agriculture or in related occupations, and agriculture was viewed as the primary source of material and human resources for the development of the country.

The latifundia system perpetuated a peasant class whose lives and farming methods had not changed markedly since the official abolition of serfdom in 1861. In 1917, out of 355.7 million hectares of agricultural land, 108.3 million hectares (or almost one-third) belonged to landlords, the tsar's family, the church, and the state.[2] Over half of the farmland owned by large landowners was rented out to peasants. Small-scale peasant farming—which was characterized by manual labor, primitive tools, and a three-field system of cultivation, as well as economic vulnerability and an orientation toward private consumption rather than the market—was the dominant mode of agricultural production. Meanwhile, an insignificant portion of the land was used in large-scale production. In European Russia, latifundia accounted for 8-10 percent of grain production, 1-10 percent of assorted industrial and oil crop production, up to 20 percent of the orchard and garden crops, and about 80 percent of sugar beet production. These farms also accounted for 5-6 percent of all livestock.[3]

Well-known economist N. D. Kondratiev compared Russian and U.S. agriculture in this period. On the eve of World War I, according to Kondratiev, annual investment in tools, livestock, and construction on a U.S. farm was approximately 4.3 times that on a European Russian peasant farm. The potential for productivity growth in agricultural production in Russia was, consequently, very limited, and American agricultural workers were approximately 4.8 times more productive than Russian workers.[4] Communal village lands, or *obshchina*, helped perpetuate peasant farming on a natural (rather than market) basis, and limited the scope of peasants' economic and social ties and relationships.

Under such conditions, poor harvests (an average of only 6.9 centners of grain per hectare in 1909-1913), frequent crop failures, and the weak development of industrial crops and livestock farming were unavoidable. Peasants led miserable lives in semistarvation, even while a significant portion of agricultural output was exported to Western markets. In a famous slogan, the tsarist government boasted: "We shall be underfed, but we shall export." Thus, peasant farms were poor not only because they were unproductive, but also because a significant portion of farm output was claimed by the state, landlords, and moneylenders.

It is instructive to examine how the successful grain harvest of 1913 was distributed. The gross output of grain was 765 million centners, of which 213 million centners made their way to markets outside the village. Had the rural population been free to choose how to dispose of the grain, approximately 300 million centners would have been consumed as food by the rural population. Another 130 million centners would have been kept for seed, 190 million centners for fodder, and at least 40 million centners would have been put aside as insurance against poor harvests in the future. The real marketable surplus in this case would not have exceeded 110 million centners.[5] Consequently, half of the marketed grain was involuntarily sold outside the village, to the detriment of the village population. Thus, even in a good harvest year, forced marketing condemned the peasantry to poverty and chronic starvation.

The hardships of World War I further devastated significant sectors of the peasantry. The war brought about a fall in agricultural production and engendered an acute food crisis. It is therefore not surprising that the demand "Bread for the Hungry!" was among the most popular slogans of both the February and the October (1917) Revolutions.

The Russian peasantry had already, in the course of the first Russian Revolution (1905-1907), advanced demands for the nationalization and transfer of all land to the cultivator. The landlords responded to the peasant strikes in 1905-1907 with the Stolypin agrarian reform, which tried to rescue the old system by modernizing it at the peasants' expense. The essence of this reform was the privatization of peasants' common landholdings (*obshchina* property) along with vacant state land that the landlords offered by way of a compromise. Note that the idea of transforming *obshchina* land into household plots dated back to the height of the tsarist bureaucracy in the 1880s, and the autocracy's sudden hatred for the *obshchina* was due not to a preoccupation with modernization and the future blossoming of Russia, but rather to the role played by *obshchina* local governments in organizing anti-landlord uprisings.

The Stolypin plan, had it been implemented, would have been a turning point in early twentieth-century Russian history. The plan was extolled as progressive because it contributed to the expansion of capitalism already taking place in Russia, and therefore to the weeding out of the "weak" in favor of the "strong" in peasant agriculture. Several million peasants would have been deprived of land as a sacrifice to new landlords. The Stolypin reform would have signaled the defeat of the peasantry in their struggle for land, and would have precluded the development of family farming along American lines, in favor of landlord capitalism on the Prussian model, and the pauperization of much of the rural population.

The Stolypin agrarian reform was incapable of modernizing the agricultural sector, because it was already too late. Rising social pressures left no time for reform. Moreover, the compulsory nature of the reform only kindled revolutionary fires. If the "weak" were driven from the countryside, they would go to the city, which could not provide work for hundreds of thousands of desperate rural refugees. The other option, resettlement in eastern Russia, often brought peasants complete ruin and a return to landlessness. The reform thus only exacerbated the resentment of the peasant masses against the landlords and against tsarism, and strengthened the peasant's hatred of private land ownership.

The Revolution and Its Aftermath

In 1917 the demand for the liquidation of private land ownership became the most important slogan of the peasant revolution then unfolding in Russia. This is attested to by the speeches of delegates at the First All-Russia Congress of the Soviets of Peasant Deputies, which took place in May 1917, and by the 242 peasant mandates delivered to the Congress from the provinces. These demands were combined under the title "Model Mandate" and published in August of that year. The entire mandate was permeated by the idea of the liquidation of private land ownership in favor of a system giving land rights to the cultivator, with periodic reallocation of land to correct inequities. "The right to private land ownership," announced the mandate, "is being abolished forever: land shall be neither sold, purchased, rented out or mortgaged, nor by any other means estranged. All land . . . without compensation to the landlord . . . becomes national property and is transferred to the use of all those who toil on it."[6]

The Bolsheviks supported this demand and brought it into being. The section of the mandate dedicated to the land issue was entirely incorporated into the text of Lenin's Land Decree and thus became law. The decree, the first act of the new government in the sphere of agrarian legislation, was ratified by the Second Congress of Workers' and Soldiers' Deputies on October 26, 1917. It abolished landlord property "swiftly, without any redemption fee," liquidated all types of private property, and implemented a virtual nationalization of land. All high-productivity farming was to be transferred to public and state institutions.

The legal recognition of the principle of "land to the tiller" extended to "all citizens (regardless of gender) of the Russian state, who wished to cultivate the land by their own labor, with the assistance of their families or in association, until such time that they no longer possess the strength to work."[7] Land would be periodically reallocated according to the number of workers and dependents in a given family. The peasant *obshchina* was also revived, though the peasant now had the option of leaving with land to form a farmstead or consolidated peasant smallholding, as well as the right to form a cooperative or other form of association with their land.

The ratification of the Land Decree was the culmination of the great agrarian revolution, which swept away the landlords and abolished most forms of private land ownership in favor of land nationalization and the transfer of most agricultural land to the peasantry for their free and unlimited use. By 1927, of the 355.2 million hectares of agricultural land, 314.7 million hectares were farmed by peasants, 36.1 million hectares were held by the state, and 4.9 million hectares were held by cities, institutes, and enterprises.[8] Only a very small number of latifundia were directly transformed into state farms or agricultural production cooperatives, which, ten years after the revolution, comprised no more than 2 percent of land under cultivation.

Both the land confiscated from private owners as well land owned by the peasants underwent an egalitarian redistribution. Many land-poor households, which had previously worked as hired labor, were raised to the level of independent small-scale producers. Relatively prosperous peasants, on the other hand, lost a large part of their land and their numbers consequently decreased.

The most important result of the land reform carried out over the course of the October Revolution was the conversion of the mass of the peasantry into middle peasants, and the creation of a nearly uniform system of small-scale producers. In 1927, a decade after the revolution, there were 24-25 million peasant farms in the country, each with an average of 4-5 hectares of arable land, one horse and one or two cows. With this, a peasant family had to feed five or six mouths, with two or three people working and no hired labor. In other words, even after the reform the average farm laborer was able to feed only one other person aside from himself or herself, or two in the case of a prime-age adult worker. Peasant labor remained manual labor, with few farm implements, and only 15 percent of farms had any sort of farm machinery. Wooden plows were still in use, and grain was often harvested with a sickle or scythe.[9]

The combination of the civil war and the closely preceding World War I caused a severe drop in agricultural production and led to the famine of 1921-1922 in the primary grain regions of the country—the Upper and Mid Volga, Kuban, Stavropol, and the Don, Ukraine. Despite this setback, peasants took advantage of their newfound independence, and agricultural production regained prewar levels within three years.

The following years show a continuing upward trend in agricultural productivity, with, however, substantial year-to-year fluctuations. From 724.6 million centners in 1925, grain production rose to 768.3 million centners in 1926, before falling to 723 million centners in 1927. Production rose again to 733.2 million centners in 1928, then fell back down to 717.4 million centners in 1929, finally rising to the unprecedented level of 835 million centners in 1930.[10] Livestock farming fared particularly well: the livestock count grew by roughly 5 percent per year from 1925 to 1928. In general, however, the unreliability of yields, which is typical of small-scale peasant farming, had an unfavorable effect on the rate of industrial development, which depended on agricultural production to fund investment.

Stalinist justifications notwithstanding, small-scale peasant farming did not exhaust its potential for development, and was not on the verge of collapse on the eve of the Stalinist forced collectivization drive of late 1929. The potential for continued growth in small-scale peasant farming was recognized by the authors of the first five-year plan, ratified in April-May of 1929, which predicted an increase in all types of peasant farm production. The anticipated growth would have accommodated the modest industrial development planned. This was not to be. The steady progress would shortly be undercut by forced collectivization, which led to a sharp fall in agricultural production, famine, and even interruptions in the industrialization drive.

The strengthening of peasant farms in the 1920s permitted a resumption in grain exports. In the early years, the state obtained grain for exports and internal markets through a system of tax in kind. The sale of grain remained compulsory (because even with some growth in agricultural productivity, grain production only met the modest needs of the peasantry), and the volume of exports was small. In 1913, out of 765 million centners of grain, 96.5 million centners were exported. By 1926 (after the country had recovered from the wars), the grain harvest was somewhat larger (768.3 million centners), but export volumes were much lower (21.8 million centners). During this period, the fall in exports reflected a relative leniency in the forced marketing of grain, which provided grain for internal and external markets at the price of rural malnutrition and lower fodder and grain reserves.

It has become fashionable to portray the village of the 1920s as a peasant's paradise, in which universal equality and a spirit of cooperation and contentment prevailed, and where only an inveterate idler or an out-and-out drunkard could have undermined the *mir* (communal) unity. In fact, substantial class differences had already begun to reemerge in villages. While increasing numbers of peasants were pauperized or worked as landless laborers, at the other end of the spectrum a rural bourgeoisie was emerging, mainly in the figure of the kulak. The old social structures in the village had not been fully eliminated by the nationalization and egalitarian distribution of land, and the potential for social stratification remained.

Statistics help illustrate the inequality that persisted in the village. In 1927, within the confines of Russia, 28.3 percent of all peasant farms had no draft animals, 31.5 percent had no plowing equipment, and 18.8 percent had no cows. (In Ukraine, 38.3 percent of peasant farms had no draft animals). Meanwhile, about 6 percent of farms had three or more draft animals apiece. "Without a horse," went a common expression of the time, "a peasant is not a proprietor." The most prosperous 3-4 percent of peasant farms held 15-20 percent of the total capital and roughly a third of the agricultural machinery that was in the hands of the peasantry.

Poor peasants who could not sustain themselves through their private farms were forced to lease land to or to work as laborers for more prosperous peasants and kulaks. They also rented draft animals and equipment from the richer peasants and kulaks, frequently on onerous terms. (Renting draft animals was actually a more common transaction than leasing land or hiring labor.) These relationships, which were combined and intertwined with moneylending, were the basis for the growth of the kulak class in the village during the 1920s.

It is interesting to note the evolution of the term *kulak* in the Russian language. In V. I. Dal's *Concise Dictionary,* which reflects the usage of the first half of the nineteenth century, kulak is defined as "a speculator, a second-hand trader, a middleman, a fish-and-cattle wholesaler [or] a procurer . . . living through deceit, miscalculation and false measurement." Note that all of these personages are active in the market but not in productive activities. In the 1870s, however, A. N. Engelhardt used the term in his "Letters from the Country" to mean those engaged in exploitative practices in both the production and commercial spheres.[11] Kulaks were also understood to participate in both productive and commercial activities (during the epoch of "primary accumulation") in Lenin's *The Development of Capitalism in Russia,* which was written in the 1890s. According to Lenin, the kulaks lost many positions and declined numerically after the revolution, but did not disappear. In fact, the expropriation of some of their land may have led them to increase exploitation of poorer peasants.[12]

Concrete historical evidence indicates rather convincingly that the kulak of the 1920s was far from being an entrepreneur who organized commodity production on the basis of hired labor and machinery, but was rather to a significant degree simply a loan shark, or what Russians call a "bloodsucker." At the time of the anti-kulak campaigns, the process of evolution into capitalist entrepreneurs or farmers was not more than half complete.

Two examples will help illustrate the kulak method of exploitation. During periods of shortage, when not only the poorest, horseless peasants but even middle-level peasants did not have seed grain to plant the next crop, unlucky peasants would go to the kulaks for loans until the new harvest. The customary fee was "a pood for a pood" and "a ruble for a ruble," or 100 percent interest for the four to five months until the harvest. (A pood of grain equals 16.4 kg.) This rate made it impossible for the majority of debtors to repay a debt with grain or money, and peasants were then forced to provide labor to clear their debt, or lease the lender land at rock-bottom prices, or both. These exploitative practices were legitimized by traditional patriarchal norms. As Andrei Platonov's female peasant said: "Winter will come, and I will again humble myself before my neighbor . . . and at the home of the wealthy one, I will cry out in the vestibule. With some millet, I will be able to live on until the summer, but in the summer I will already be paying back what I owe with my own ruin—for one *meshok* (3 *poods*) a *meshok* and a half, and four days' labor, and five *meshoks* to honor him."

Another exploitative practice entailed lending horses to poor peasants at usurious rates. Payment for a horse was typically either a pood of grain per day, or the work of one peasant woman as a reaper for five days. Looking first at the rental cost of a horse in terms of grain, since twelve to fifteen days of draft-horse labor were required to fully cultivate one hectare, and the average harvest ranged from forty to fifty poods of grain per hectare, it is easy to see how one-third or more of the harvest could go to the owner of the horse. (Tenant farmers had poorer-than-average harvests, since work on tenant farms was done only after work for the landlords had been completed.) Furthermore, it was usually necessary to rent not only the horse, but also equipment, which raised the rent to half of the harvest.

Now we compare the rental cost of a horse in terms of grain with the cost in terms of labor: At the time, a pood of rye was worth 70-80 kopeks, and a pood of wheat was worth 1 ruble or 1 ruble, 10 kopeks. Since the rent could be either one pood of grain or five days' heavy labor, it follows that one day's labor was the equivalent of 15-20 kopeks. Hiring a farm laborer at market prices would have cost the employer five to six times that amount, which implies that peasant families who were forced to hire out their labor in exchange for draft animals were being exploited even more cruelly than those who could repay their debt in grain. In some cases, the rate charged for the loan of a horse (in terms of labor days) was not even stipulated beforehand, and the laborer did as much as he or she was called upon to do, at the mercy of the lender.[13]

Over the period 1925-1927, heated arguments erupted about the scale, character, and consequences of village stratification. Emotions especially flared regarding the question of who was a kulak. When should someone be designated a kulak—when they have eight hectares of tillable soil? Ten? Or twenty-five? The complexity of kulak characteristics gave rise to varying definitions for the amount of land that made up a kulak farm. Based on these different definitions, one estimate put the share of kulak farms at 4 percent at their peak in 1927.

While numerically a small group, the kulaks remained a real and growing social force in the village. It is reasonable to assume that, given the backwardness and exploitative practices that were characteristic of socio-economic relationships

Table 2.1 The Social Structure of the Village 1924/25 - 1926/27

Population Groups	Number of Individuals of the Independent Population (in '000s)			Proportion as a Percent		
	1924/25	1925/26	1926/27	1924/25	1925/26	1926/ 27
Proletariat	2,184	2,454	2,560	97.7	10.9	11.3
Poor Peasants	5,803	5,317	5,037	25.9	23.7	22.1
Average-Means Peasants	13,678	13,822	14,280	61.1	61.7	62.7
Kulaks	728	816	896	3.3	3.7	3.9

Sources: *Tiazhest' oblozheniia v SSSR: Sotial'nyi sostav dokhoy i nalogovye platezhi naseleniia Soyuza SSR v 1924/25, 1925/26, i 1926-27 godakh*. Doklad Komissii SNK SSSR no izucheniiu tiazhesti oblozheniia naseleniia Soyuza M. 1929. S. 74-77. *The Tax Burden in the USSR: Social Composition, Income and Tax Payments for the Population of the USSR in 1924/25, 1925/26 and 1926/27*. A Report of the USSR Commission for Studying the Tax Burden of the Population of the Union. Moscow: 1929, 74-77.

in the village, rural inequality would have worsened over time. If Russian agriculture had been left to modernize uninterrupted, then agriculture in today's Russia might be a combination of strip farming on several hundred large-scale enterprises, large landlord-owned farms descended from the old latifundia, and tens of thousands of smallholdings, with millions of peasant families still living in extreme poverty.

It has been often noted that Russian social thought in the mid-nineteeth century sought a means of avoiding capitalist development and preventing the "boiling down of the Russian *muzhik* [peasant] in the industrial boiler of capitalism." Both the autocratic and the revolutionary populist ideologies placed great importance on the communal village lands. The former saw the commons as a guarantee against the "pox of proletarianism," while the latter saw in the commons and the traditional cooperative an embryonic socialism and a ready-made mold for the creation of a system of collective farming. Despite the fact that the experience of the 1870s had shown that "capital and capitalist tendencies were encroaching upon [the communal lands] from without and destroying them from within, conservative hopes lasted until 1905. In their current form and under prevailing conditions, they could not swim against the tide of capitalism and all that was connected with it."[14]

Revolutionary populists pursued their hopes through early attempts to organize collective forms of farming, most notably following Tolstoy's example. Tolstoyism found expression in the socialization of virtually all aspects of farm life—from production to consumption. Generally, however, populist illusions of building socialism on the commons were shattered well before 1905.[15] In the early postrevolutionary period, the communes were incorporated into Soviet "communes" but preserved their internal independence until the 1930s.

The Cooperative Plan in Theory and in Practice

At the start of the twentieth century, particularly following the shocks caused by the First Russian Revolution (1905-1907), cooperativization was widely viewed as a means of surmounting the social obstacles to economic modernization in an agrarian economy. Drawing the peasantry into the market economy was viewed as a crucial step in the process of modernization. In the ten and a half years between 1902 and 1912, a network of consumer, credit and marketing, and cottage-industry cooperative societies sprang up. Whereas there were only 1,625 cooperatives registered in Russia in 1902, there were already 18,023 by 1912, and 35,200 by 1915. Rough estimates put membership in these cooperatives at 11-12 million members.[16] Since membership was usually by household rather than individual, this means that over 60 million people—well over a third of the population of the Russian Empire—were involved in cooperative societies.

As in other countries, cooperatives in Russia did not emerge spontaneously, but—from the very beginning—required a shift in the social consciousness of peasants. The activism of the advanced intelligentsia, the influence of scientific studies of the cooperative experience in England, Germany, France, and other countries, and the development of a general theory of cooperative societies all played important roles. The cooperativization of small-scale peasant farms was offered as a means of modernizing their organization and affording them the advantages of large-scale production, especially the benefits derived from science and technology—as well as remaking the farms on the basis of social justice.

The contributions of A. V. Chaianov—eminent agrarian and peasant-farming specialist, theorist and practitioner of Russian cooperative societies—were crucial in constructing a theory of peasant cooperatives. As early as 1908-1910, in a study of agricultural cooperatives in Italy and Belgium, he had observed that production on peasant farms took place as a series of separate technical processes, each of which was self-contained and could be separated from other tasks. This observation was the starting point for an analysis of the nature and socioeconomic significance of cooperative societies. The possibility of "singling out those economic processes in which large-scale production holds an undoubted advantage, permits the organization of these processes at the level of full-scale production" by a "merger with similar processes from among their neighbors into the cooperative," without, however, destroying the small family farm.[17]

The ideas set forth by Chaianov grew into a general theory of cooperatives and peasant farms, and into a plan of action for Russian cooperative societies. At the All-Russia Agricultural Congress in Kiev in September 1913, agronomists, economists, state agents, and entrepreneurs met to address the basic problems of agrarian development, including the problem of developing production coopera-tives. Among the first items on the agenda was a report by A. N. Minin that paid particular attention to addressing the problems faced by the poorest peasants: "The greatest numbers among the farming population . . . [farm] the smallest farms. The . . . material well-being of these groups is a question of first governmental importance [since] the development of a manufacturing industry provides no hope for a painless assimilation of the landless population." A resolution drafted by the Congress advised government agronomists and land-tenure officials that "a prominent place should be made for societies for joint land-use. The role of land-tenure regulation with regard to these societies should consist of apportion-ment, with the allotment of small land plots to a single site. The role of agronomy should be one of disseminating the very idea of associations, and of bringing this idea into being." The resolution also supported an expansion of land guarantees and the extension of broad credit and technical assistance to private farmers.[18]

Building on this tradition, the 1917 revolutions included the cooperative movement in the political struggle for agrarian reforms. The initial demand of a program for agrarian reform written by Chaianov was: "The labor cooperative peasant farm should be the basis for the agrarian structure in Russia, and to it should be transferred the lands of our homeland." The agrarian program included the most revolutionary demands of 1917, including the slogan "Land for the workers!" Moreover, the transfer of privately owned lands to the peasantry (especially those of large landowners) was viewed as the first step in agrarian reform, the final aim of which was immeasurably broader and more signifi-cant—the creation of a new agrarian structure and of a new agriculture. The two basic goals were to achieve: (1) "the greatest productivity of labor applied to the land"; and (2) "the democratization of the distribution of national revenue."[19]

While considering various "plausible systems of production relationships," Chaianov rejected not only capitalism but also "governmental socialism" and "anarchistic communism," even though he viewed both of these as ideally organized expressions of the principle of democratic distribution. The real task, in his opinion, was to "bring both organizational principles into a harmonic combina-tion." This was feasible only with cooperative societies, and he therefore determined that the future agrarian system should be a cooperative one.[20]

The economic and social values of the small peasant farm (in comparison with large-scale farms) were viewed as the basis for the planned cooperatives. Chaianov expected that cooperatives would bring to these small farms the advantages of market specialization and access to complex machinery and the achievements of science (the expertise of agronomists, improved livestock, for example). Basing his views on contemporary statistics, Chaianov argued that the nature of agricultural enterprise itself fixes the limits of the advantages of large-scale farming over small-scale farming, which "can never be particularly great." He concluded that joint cooperative societies would be able "to bestow all the advantages of large-scale farming to small peasant farms," and would even surpass them in productivity. "Through cooperative associations, the small peasant farm achieves a scale and strength to which even any sort of large-scale private farms cannot be compared."[21]

Agrarian reforms such as Chaianov's could possibly have been instituted in a country with a strong democratic tradition, but implementation of such reforms proved impossible because of the priorities of the new rulers, the weakness of the emerging democratic institutions, and the shortsightedness and political blindness of people who ended up at the head of these institutions. The peasant revolution in Russia had run its course. The revolution ruined the landlords and also, in general, private farming through direct seizure and transfer of property, which far exceeded the needs of the cooperative program.

As we shall see, the peasant revolution was displaced by the Bolshevik workers' revolution, which put the Communist Party into power and set in motion socialist reform through revolutionary methods. Though the number of cooperative societies continued to grow, there was an increasing move toward top-down control of the economy, which had an extremely detrimental effect on the functioning of the cooperatives. The cooperative societies were transformed into instruments for state procurement and distribution of agricultural products, and stripped of their spontaneous or voluntary—in other words, of their cooperative—nature.

To distinguish between cooperatives of the Chaianov model, which aided private farmers by allowing them to perform selected tasks collectively, and cooperatives on the eventual Bolshevik model, which replaced private farming, we shall adopt the Bolshevik name, kolkhoz, for the latter in the discussion that follows. Until the 1930s, a variety of forms of farming was supported by the Boshevik state, including associations of private farmers cooperating around limited production goals, such as mutual help associations, plowing land, or sprouting seedlings. While these "transitional forms" were sometimes referred to as kolkhozes by Soviet government officials, they were hardly distinguishable from Chaianov's cooperatives, except in the intention of the state to move them to a fully collectivized production cycle based on jointly owned assets. Once they had reached this "highest form" the kohkhozes would be the basis of large-scale, mechanized agriculture.

The growth of various forms of collective farming after 1917 was facilitated to a great degree by the prior nationalization of land and liquidation of the landowner holdings. Revolutionary enthusiasm, the striving of the poor to break free from the calamities of military collapse and starvation, and the strong support of the state all contributed to the growth of the kolkhoz movement. In a 1916 account of cooperative organizations, there were 107 farming cooperatives. By the end of 1918 there were 1,600, a number that grew to over 10,000 by 1920, bringing together 131,000—or 0.5 percent—of peasant households.[22] Although these figures were still not very high, for many in the Bolshevik ranks they served as evidence that it was possible to begin the conversion to universal collective farming.

Of course, even in the fall of 1918 there were those who urged caution, including Lenin, who argued the necessity of laying groundwork and using transitional stages: "(an) attempt to introduce by decrees and edict-making the public cultivation of land would be the greatest absurdity."[23] Lenin argued that the problem had to be resolved "patiently, with a series of gradual transitions, while awakening the consciousness of the working peasantry and progressing only at the rate of this awakening of consciousness."[24]

However, these arguments were not heeded. The leaders of the People's Commissariat of Agriculture were already envisioning the collectivization of the majority of peasant farms within three to four years, regardless of obstacles. These fervent goals, characteristic of "war communism," were echoed in the resolution of the All-Russia Congress of the Land Departments of the Committee of Poor Peasants and Communes of December 1918, as well as the "code of laws on the socialist land-tenure regulations and steps for the transition to socialist agriculture" adopted in February 1919.[25]

During the winter of 1918-1919, the violent and coercive measures employed by the state for forced collectivization of peasants in kolkhozes occasioned peasant protests and even armed uprisings. In the countryside, the slogan "Long live the Soviet Regime, but down with the commune!" gained widespread currency. The Eighth Bolshevik Party Congress in March 1919 resolutely condemned forced collectivization. Lenin made a remarkable speech at the Congress: "To act here through force means to ruin the whole business. At this point, what is required is work of protracted education. The task is not expropriating the peasant of average means, but rather—in order to account for the particular conditions of the life of the peasantry and to learn from the peasants the means for transition to the best system—we must not dare to dictate! Here is the rule which we have set for ourselves."[26]

The Congress demanded that those representatives of the Soviet regime who had used coercive tactics against the peasantry, whether direct or indirect, be called to account and suspended from work.[27] The Congress defined the fundamental principles of collectivization to be: voluntary membership, persuasion by practical example, and the creation of necessary material and cultural conditions. Another important cooperative principle—the principle of local initiative—was also mentioned: "The only valuable associations are those which have been put forward by the peasants themselves by free initiative, and the benefits of which are seen by them in practice."[28]

During this same period, A. V. Chaianov was engaged in a critical analysis of the first attempt at collectivization. His book, *Fundamental Ideas and Forms of Organization of Peasant Cooperatives*, published in 1919, developed and deepened earlier conclusions about the particulars of the organization of peasant farming and the capacity for dividing separate production functions. The book extolled the advantages of cooperatives, including the possibility "of singling out and organizing into large cooperative ventures those production functions where consolidation produced a noticeable positive effect, without destroying those sectors of the economy in which small-scale family production was technically more suitable than large-scale production." All production, therefore, could be organized according to the most suitable scale and social structure. Thus, large-scale collective enterprises could grow alongside peasant farms and partially replace them. Chaianov emphasized "the limits of collectivization of agriculture" and rejected "the cooperative socialization of all peasant farming as a whole." He also examined complex problems related to cooperative work incentives, labor organization, and management that are still unresolved today.[29]

Chaianov viewed his model of collectivization as the best, or even the only way of introducing the advantages of large-scale agriculture, industrialization, and state planning into peasant farming. Collectivization should be brought about on a voluntary basis and using economic incentives, almost "self-collectivization."[30] Chaianov did not reject the kolkhozes entirely, but advocacy of a combination of fully collectivized production cooperatives and other forms of peasant cooperative societies is what distinguished A. V. Chaianov's concept of cooperative collectivization.

The New Economic Policy (NEP), initiated in 1920, combined Lenin's views on the peasant path toward socialism with Chaianov's views and with lessons learned from long-standing cooperatives. Key elements of the NEP included the recognition of the peasant's right to the fruits of his own labor, and an awareness of the benefits of market relationships. Focused on the goal of socialism, however, Lenin viewed the NEP as a transition policy. The maximal development of cooperative societies to assist private farmers under the NEP would eventually result in their transformation into a universal form of social organization. He put forth this argument in an article "On Cooperative Societies" that set forth the task of achieving through NEP the participation of the entire population in cooperatives and came to the essentially new conclusion that under Soviet conditions, "the system of civilized cooperative members . . . is the system of socialism." Lenin saw the development of cooperatives as closely tied to a fundamental technical revolution in Soviet agriculture. As a result, he indicated no time line for the socialist reconstruction of peasant farms.[31]

The early years of NEP did result in a rapid growth of cooperatives. The greatest advances were made by consumer cooperatives, which allowed peasants to purchase goods at wholesale prices, affording them significant savings (cooperative members saved a total of 40.9 million rubles in 1923-1924 and 97.4 million rubles in 1924-1925). By 1927, a third of peasant households were active in consumer cooperatives, and half were active in 1929. Viewed from the point of view of the value of goods bought, consumer cooperatives appear even more important: approximately 53 percent of the retail value of goods in the villages were bought through consumer cooperatives in 1926-1927, a share that rose to 63 percent in 1928-1929.[32]

The number of agricultural service cooperatives (which supplied such things as credit, machinery, and marketing channels) also grew in the 1920s. There were

64,573 such agricultural societies belonging to local and national associations in October 1927 in the Russian territory, with a total membership of 9,468,200 peasant farms. An additional 13,767 or so "unofficial" cooperatives, with 620,100 member farms, did not belong to these associations. Allowing for some overlap (a single farm could belong to several different kinds of agricultural cooperative), the number of peasant farms belonging to various forms of agricultural cooperatives was roughly 8.1 million—about 32 percent of farms.

State legal and economic regulations promoted the access to cooperatives by the poor while limiting the access (and influence) of the richest farmers. The creation in 1926 of a special fund to found credit cooperatives for poor peasants played an important role. Census data from 1927 reveals that membership in consumer and agricultural service cooperatives was as follows: 17 percent of poor peasant farms belonged, as did 58 percent of middle-level peasant farms, 20 percent of well-to-do peasant farms, and 5 percent of kulak farms. (The share of these groups in the total farm population considered by the survey is 26.1 percent, 57.1 percent. 13.6 percent, and 3.2 percent, respectively.) The majority of cooperative members in the 1920s were thus middle-level and poor peasants.

Until the end of 1927, the largest category of agricultural cooperatives comprised those that supplied credit, farm implements, and other inputs, or served as marketing channels for individual peasant farms. There were 28,700 of these cooperatives, and they made up 44.5 percent of the total number. Furthermore, 90 percent of peasant farms that belonged to a cooperative belonged to this kind. These cooperatives did not directly engage in agricultural production, though a significant number were active in processing oil, fruits and vegetables, potatoes, and so on. Though many of these cooperatives rented machinery and milling equipment, cooperative members most often used this equipment individually, and the actual production of primary food products (milk, vegetables, potatoes) was done on individual farms.

Agricultural cooperatives became the primary conduit for production assistance to the peasantry, and it was through them that credit was supplied to peasant farms. In 1926-1927, agricultural cooperatives supplied 65 percent of peasants in Russia with machinery and other equipment, a share that rose to 86 percent in 1928-1929. Cooperatives also engaged in agricultural extension work.

Simple production cooperatives evolved from these credit, input, and marketing cooperatives, and introduced large-scale production techniques into peasant production activities. In October 1927, simple production cooperatives numbered 18,555. Of these, 10,347 were created for the joint ownership of machinery, 3,505 were for land improvement, 1,734 were for seed propagation, 1,880 were for cattle breeding, and 1,089 were resettlement associations. In all, over 700,000 peasant farms (8-9 percent of those in any form of cooperative) belonged to such limited production cooperatives. Together with "unofficial" associations, these exceeded 26,000 in number and had more than 900,000 members.

In higher forms of production cooperatives the primary assets were collectively owned, and production was on a large scale. In October 1927, there were 17,267 such kolkhozes created out of almost 400,000 peasant farms. Until the end of the 1920s, this was chiefly a movement of the poor peasantry, although others took part in it, including middle-level peasants and even kulaks. The predominance of poor peasants gave the movement its particular characteristics, such as leveling tendencies in distribution, and the role of state agencies in providing funds. These kolkhozes were neither very productive nor very prosperous, and failed to attract most of the peasantry, who preserved a lasting attachment to the individual family farm while eagerly participating in those forms of cooperative societies that were aimed at meeting the individual peasant needs, but only gradually reforming the individual farm's production structure.

The problems of the production cooperatives were related to a number of broader economic and social issues under discussion in the 1920s. A. V. Chaianov enriched and defined the concept of "cooperative collectivization" in the second edition of his book on peasant cooperative societies, published in 1926, in which the problem of ways and forms of organizing large-scale production received intense scrutiny. The organization of large-scale agricultural production by means of horizontal integration of one type of factory across a specific territory was compared with vertical integration of production processes. Chaianov supplemented his theoretical analysis with evidence from other countries. According to Chaianov, cooperatives that vertically integrated certain processes were capable of improvements in productivity and social progress, coexisting and cooperating with other forms and sizes of productive organizations—both cooperative and private—while horizontally integrated cooperatives would cause productivity slowdowns due to bureaucratic distortions, even when there was no element of coercion in their creation.[33]

In the long run, Chaianov thought cooperativization would lead to "an entire system being generated from the system of peasant farms, which cooperativized several functions into a system of public cooperative village farming, built on the basis of capital collectivization and leaving the implementation of certain processes up to private farms of its members."[34] Though Chaianov generally preferred vertical to horizontal integration, he did not entirely dismiss the option of concentrating all agricultural production into optimal areas of 300-800 hectares. He underscored that this should not "in any way affect our basic system of purchase-credit-marketing and production cooperative societies, which would remain organized just as they were before. The one difference would be in the fact that instead of the small-scale peasant farms, collective farms would be members of the primary cooperative societies."[35] But such cooperatives would have to be voluntarily created by peasants on their own initiative and in their own interest.

Chaianov believed that the preservation of the "basic system" of cooperative societies was of primary importance. The issue was not only the cooperatives' effectiveness in serving the needs of rural areas, although this was significant. The chief point was something else: the cooperatives were by their very nature self-governed organizations, and their preservation under conditions of general collectivization of peasant farms would guarantee the cooperatives the organizational ability to confront state violence.

N. I. Bukharin also made an outstanding contribution to the defense and development of the cooperative program. In turning to his works, we note especially that he examined the potential for cooperative societies as part of a realistic plan for socialist reformation in a peasant country. While reiterating the basic tenets of "cooperative collectivization," he wrote that "small-scale peasant farms, hampered by their small size . . . would, supported by the proletarian state regime, solve this problem by means of their own cooperative organizations, and would thereby gain the advantages enjoyed by all types of large-scale associations, while using these advantages and profits obtained from cooperation in their own struggles against the private kulak economy."[36]

Bukharin viewed cooperatives under the NEP as a means of drawing an ever-wider segment of peasant farms into contact with the socialized sector of the national economy (state industries, banks, and other organizations), thereby encouraging their own socialist transformation. Furthermore, in the process of developing cooperative societies "for the organization of trade . . . and the organization of local production," the peasantry would be transformed. The transformation to "an ever more social form of management" was seen as a very lengthy process due to the necessity of technically re-equipping peasant labor, and it would "obtain its fullest expression" only after the scale of production expanded with the electrification of agriculture.[37] Bukharin believed that a diverse array of cooperatives—industrial, trade, and credit—should be fostered and should interact at all stages of the reform process. The cooperativization of peasant farming would then take on the character of an organic process, that is, something that developed out of the internal needs of the peasant farms.

There was much dispute over Bukharin's construct of "cooperative ladders," which linked forms of cooperatives with social strata of the village: fully collectivized production cooperatives with the poorer peasants; marketing cooperatives with the average-means peasants; and credit cooperatives with the kulaks. From here also followed a proposal for forming "kulak cooperative nests" (groups), which would be drawn into the socialist economic system and gradually reformed by it.[38] Since kulak farms represented only 3-4 percent of all farms, and 20-30 percent of the village was cooperativized, there was no danger that "kulak nests" in cooperative societies would be a mass occurrence.

The Bukharin plan for reforming agriculture was not in principle hostile to the idea of collective farming, but it definitely excluded the possibility that mass collectivization of peasant farms would be the immediate basis for moving the countryside toward socialism, instead viewing mass collectivization as a thing of the future. In March 1925 at the All-Russia Conference of Kolkhozes, Bukharin said: "We cannot begin socialist structuring in the countryside by the mass organization of collective production enterprises. We should begin with something else. The main route lies rather along the cooperative line . . . . Kolkhozes are not the main route; they are one of the secondary, but also very essential and significant roads. When the cooperativization of the peasantry receives strong support from developing technology [such as] with electrification and an increasing number of tractors, then the pace of transformation to collective farming will quicken. One side of the movement will fertilize the other. One, as a stream, will join the other, becoming a gigantic river which shall carry us toward socialism."[39]

The speed of the transformation depended on how much time the peasant needed to convert to the new system of agriculture, based on his will and his ability. It seems likely, however, that Soviet agriculture, relying only on the practical means of mechanization and electrification, would have approached a statewide system of collective farming perhaps only in the 1980s or 1990s. In Bukharin's analysis of the cooperative process, the question of how much time was needed to carry out full cooperativization was not raised.

Still, the works of Chaianov and Bukharin suggest that the development of multiple forms of cooperative societies was a realistic alternative to Stalinist collectivization. Stalin's revolution from above, which began in 1928-1929, simultaneously scrapped both the NEP as a policy of transition toward socialism and the cooperative system as a democratic reform process carried out in the interests of the working masses.

The NEP set the stage for a surge in production in the countryside, and economic growth in the country as a whole. In doing so, it provided the needed backdrop for the cooperativization of peasant farming and the creation of a collectivized agricultural sector capable of independent development. While there would have been obstacles to continuing along this route, especially in connection with the goals of industrialization, they could have been surmounted without using force against the peasantry.

The resolution "On Work in the Village" ratified by the Fifteenth Congress of the Bolshevik Party in December 1927 seemed to support such a voluntary strategy. The resolution stated: "The experience of the preceding years . . . [has] confirmed the correctness of Lenin's Cooperative Plan, according to which socialist industry will—through cooperation—carry the small-scale peasant farm down the road to socialism while remaking fragmented production units into large-scale socialized farms capable of taking advantage of new technology [such as electrification]. . . . [This will occur] both through a process of conversion, but even more through the reorganization and collectivization of production."[40] The Congress spoke out against the use of compulsory measures against the peasantry, and did not set any deadlines or mandate any specific path to reform or model of cooperativization. The importance of all forms of cooperatives was underscored and their broadest development was envisioned.

Though both the spirit and the letter of the ratified resolutions were anti-kulak, the attack against the kulaks was limited to calls for more consistent limitation of kulak exploitative practices in the future, as well as their displacement through economic methods. The resolutions at the Congress on the attack against the kulaks were based on the arguments of Bukharin. The resolutions essentially proposed the continuation and development (but not the revision) of existing policies, including policies concerning the cooperativization of the countryside.

While evaluating the situation in the village, Bukharin had come to the conclusion that "kulaks [had] emerged," but at the same time the potential for "limiting the exploitative tendencies of the kulaks" had also increased. The following concrete proposals were put forward by the Congress: (1) "the refinement and improvement of progressive taxation with the goal of intercepting all kulak profits"; (2) "the struggle against violations of nationalized land, especially the buying and selling of land allotments"; (3) the reduction of rental periods "for those who do not work the land themselves" to no more than three to six years; (4) "the abolition of apportionment to kulak-style" farms; and finally (5) "the strict observance of laws concerning hired labor on kulak and peasant farms." Finally, Bukharin spoke out in support of a long-discussed proposal to deprive the kulaks of the right to vote in agricultural communes, where they had often been in charge of communal government.[41]

However one might evaluate some of the specifics of the Bukharin ideas for an on assault on the kulaks (it is not difficult to criticize them, especially the elimination of the right to vote), it is quite clear that none of the ideas was meant to intrude upon economic activity, let alone end accumulation, to immobilize production or to destroy the farmstead. Village policy on the whole was supposed to bear a "peaceful, economic" character. Resolutions of the Congress made it clear that the limitation in the growth of capitalist elements called for guaranteeing their relative curtailment with "absolute growth still possible."[42]

Nonetheless, other aspects of the declaration of the "assault on the kulaks" at the end of 1927 and the "Bukharin formulation of the question" have, until recently, remained thoroughly unclear. What is well known is Bukharin's decisive opposition in the spring of 1925 to "certain comrades" who spoke of the need "over the next two years" to conduct a "second revolution" that would be a "Bartholomew Night" for the village bourgeoisie.[43] Documents that have just been brought to light demonstrate that, in practice, the "second revolution" did actually begin two years later—in the spring of 1927. From March through May 1927, orders were circulated through the secret police or OGPU (Obedinionnoe Gosudarstvoe Politicheskoe Upravlenie) on the "utter unacceptability in print of any reports . . . on the difficulties or failures with regard to providing the nation with grain." This measure was to protect "steps for overcoming the current difficulties with regard to state grain procurement and supplying the nation."[44] The "steps" were, therefore, driven from the very beginning by state needs for grain procurement. The same holds true for the treatment of the peasantry that produced grain.

International relations were acutely aggravated in 1927, reaching their apogee in May, when Great Britain broke off diplomatic ties with the USSR. This break served as the grounds and cover for the implementation of the so-called steps. The stir of war in the press, the address of the Central Committee of the All-Union Communist Party (Bolsheviks) on the danger of war, warning of "attempts of Great Britain to break down our whole country," the July 10-17 "Defense Week," which was imbued with the character of "a great political campaign"[45] and other such measures allowed the Stalin government to implement repressive measures in the guise of national security. These measures were in fact the beginning of the second revolution, which was conducted from above and rained down mainly upon the village.

The mass repression was carried out, of course, by the OGPU. While this organization was formally part of the government, and reported to the USSR Council of People's Commissars, it was in fact totally subservient to Stalin and Stalin alone. From June through the beginning of July, twenty thousand searches were conducted and nine thousand people were arrested, of whom the official press reported twenty were shot.

In the city, the operation was directed against the "White Guard Monarchist circles" and "was relatively limited," according to OGPU Secretary V. P. Menzhinskii's report to the Central Committee of the All-Union Communist (Bolshevik) Party (CC AUCPB). The village was another matter: here, OGPU agents arrested "former landowners," "former White officers," "clergy," "kulaks," "the well-to-do, as hostages," and "merchants." These groups made up the majority of those arrested.[46]

An OGPU information summary from July 23, 1927, suggests that the villagers did not respond strongly to the incidents of arrest and shootings. These were explained by the peasants as a result of the international context: "there would be war any day now," "the war would start soon," "this is preparation for cleansing the whole country," and "they take hostages during war." Many testimonials suggest approval of these means on the part of "the poor and the majority of peasants of average means," and more rarely open dissatisfaction, as in the case of Alekseev village, Shakhtov-Donetskii Okrug: "This is for freedom, . . . it is impossible to say nothing . . . right now they are making arrests and . . . they are . . . silent about the fact."[47] Dissatisfaction and condemnation of the authorities was a fact in various places, but there was not one instance of active protest, demonstration in defense of those arrested, or appeal to higher authorities, let alone a call to arms, which had been typical during 1918-1920. The success cleared the road for future use of oppression by the Stalin government in the country-side—especially in the village.

After a short time, the OGPU appealed to the USSR Council of People's Commissars with proposals for "calling to account administratively" (i.e., nonjudicially) private merchants and especially the "bakers" who were interfering with the state grain procurement. At the same time, it was proposed that the Public Prosecutor and the Supreme Soviet call to account "officials guilty of nonfulfillment or ruining plans for grain procurement and delivery," as well as "negligence . . . in carrying out edicts in the area of regulating state procurement and daily markets."[48]

We still do not know who drafted this resolution and when. But from OGPU records, we know that by the beginning of April 1928, when "mass operations" were being carried out, organs of the OGPU arrested 6,542 private traders (including 3,971 bakers), as well as 252 white-collar workers.[49] This is without even considering those outside of the "mass operations" who were arrested by the police!

Against this backdrop in the villages, "the Bukharin formulation of the kulak question" raised at the Fifteenth Party Congress (December 2-29, 1927) was aimed at preserving the NEP, and its acceptance by the Congress is therefore understandable. At the same time, a directive was dispatched from the Central Committee to the party organizations for grain procurement in the rayons supporting the "Bukharin formulation of the question" and the corresponding Congress resolutions. The dispatch called for a "routine system" of "organizational measures from the top down, aimed at strengthening grain delivery on the part of the peasantry."[50] Bukharin explained difficulties in state procurement thus: "We have not eliminated the general problem of a shortage. If the peasants have nothing to buy, we face the danger of not being in a position to extract to any significant degree grain surpluses from the village. We now have a growth of natural grain reserves and their accumulation in the village."[51]

All subsequent attempts by Bukharin and A. I. Rykov and their supporters to successfully preserve NEP were rejected as a concession to the kulak and a display of opportunism. The conversion of agriculture toward the path of full collectivized production began to appear as the fastest means for solving the grain problem. The collectivization of peasant farms ceased to be an independent aim in the socialist reconstruction of society, one with its own internal logic and criteria for success, and became instead a means for achieving other aims. This was the principal perversion of the cooperative model and signified a renunciation of its realization.

Grain procurement problems were not new. In 1925-1926, the state grain procurement plan fell short by 200 million poods, which forced a decrease in the plans for industrial construction: capital investment did not reach 1.1 billion rubles, but totaled only 700-800 million. It did not occur to any one to resort to violence against the peasantry at that time. NEP was saved and the large harvest of 1926 covered the grain procurement shortfall of the previous year with interest. In 1927 grain procurement problems were the result of several reduced grain crops and the very positive situation with the production of industrial crops and animal husbandry. The peasant, especially the well-to-do peasant, easily "managed" routine, daily expenses without selling any grain and held grain in reserve until the higher prices in winter and spring. Of course the decrease in state grain procurement created a threat to the plan for industrial construction.

Under these conditions, the Stalinist group that had only just secured a majority in the political leadership displayed neither state wisdom nor an understanding of NEP's significance and possibilities. As we have seen, the group scrapped NEP and turned to the broad application of violence against the peasantry. Directives were sent to the provinces on January 6 and February 13, 1928, with threats aimed at party leaders and a call for "rousing party organizations, a decree that grain procurement is the entire party's concern" and that "in practical work in the village, henceforth, stress will be placed on the task of battling the kulak threat."[52]

The tone was set by Stalin's trip to *okrugs* in Siberia in January-February 1928. During his inspection tour, many dozens of local workers were discharged and penalized, beginning with party expulsion, for "spinelessness," "appeasement," and "grafting" with the kulaks. The administrative repression of provincial party, Soviet, and cooperative workers was widely applied in other regions of the country as well. During the two months that V. M. Molotov traveled to the Urals for grain procurement, 1,157 people were discharged from their jobs.[53] Fear of repression pushed many down the path of task fulfillment at any cost, with no line being drawn between arbitrariness and the use of force. The famous formula for party and Soviet workers' behavior in the countryside was born at this time, "Better to go too far, than not far enough."

Extreme measures were not limited to kulak farmers and fell even harder on the peasant of average means. Under the pressure of excessive grain procurement goals, provincial organizations set down the road of general searches and arrests, often expropriating not only grain stores but also seed grain, livestock, tools, and other property. From January to March of 1928, 3,424 people in the Northern Caucasus, 1,589 people in the Siberian territory, and 255 people in the Urals were convicted. Among those convicted in the Northern Caucasus were 759 owners of large farms and 641 speculators. In general, those convicted held grain reserves below 1,000 poods (roughly 16 tons), and few had grain stores of two thousand or more poods. Data for the Saratov *gubernia*, where the owners of 115 farms were charged under this act, gives us a sense of the impact on farms. Party workers confiscated a total of 75,000 poods of grain (an average of 650 *poods* per farm), in addition to five grist mills, two oil mills, three tractors, one threshing machine, one engine, and 179 assorted head of livestock.[54] As a result, these large-scale farms were reduced to the level of poor peasant farms or disappeared altogether.

The violent actions of the authorities finally provoked open protest from the peasants and even, in some places, armed revolt. By the spring of 1928, it was clear that estimates of grain reserves had been much too high. A wave of mass dissatisfaction had already swept through regions targeted for state grain procurement. In many provinces, there were demonstrations in the cities and instances where village delegations appealed directly to workers in industrial enterprises. Overall, around 150 mass demonstrations were recorded in Ukraine, the Northern Caucasus, Siberia, Kazakhstan, and other regions.

The April and July 1928 plenums of the CC AUCPB revealed a fundamental

Table 2.2 Mass Actions of the Peasantry in 1930
(In the Territory of Russia on the Whole)

Month	Total Number of Mass Actions	Actions Performed by women	Collectivization	Confiscation and Limitation of Anti-Soviet Elements	Church Closures and Bell Confiscations	Sowing and Harvest Campaigns	Grain and Oil Preparation	Tax Campaigns	Production Difficulties	Shortage of Industrial Goods	Other
Jan	402	229	158	68	159	7	2	—	4	—	4
Feb	1,048	379	723	178	103	19	2	1	9	—	13
March	6,528	1,172	5,010	749	514	160	2	5	65	—	23
April	1,991	550	789	457	391	147	—	2	172	—	34
May	1,375	486	284	338	126	154	3	1	433	—	36
June	886	301	175	214	69	37	4	1	348	3	35
July	618	167	170	177	38	9	29	2	141	5	47
Aug	256	105	50	61	25	7	73	1	17	3	19
Sept	159	82	12	40	10	2	65	3	9	7	11
Oct	270	141	6	33	23	1	173	11	9	2	12
Nov	129	56	3	17	12	1	67	3	10	6	10
Dec	91	44	2	7	17		36	11	3	1	14
Total 1930	13,754	3,712	7,382	2,339	1,487	544	456	41	1,220	27	257

Source: Secret-Political Committee of the OGPU, "Memorandum on the forms and dynamics of the class struggle in the village in 1930," Central Archive of the Federal Statistics Committee of the Russian Republic, 32. (Sekretno-politicheskii otdel OGPU, Dokladnaia zapiska o formakh dinamike klassovoi bor'by v derevne v 1930 godu, Tsentral'nyi arkhiv FSKRF, S. 32).

underscored the need for observing the principle of voluntary collectivization. Stalin blamed all "distortions," "official decreeism," and "unworthy threats against the peasants" on local party functionaries, who were accused of "bungling," "self-importance and conceit," and "adventuresome attempts . . . to [suddenly] solve all issues of building socialism." However, the article contained no concrete instructions for resolving the problems that had been created. Moreover, the fact that the process of collectivization was already half complete was hailed as proof that the "fundamental shift of the village toward socialism could already be regarded as guaranteed." Local party workers were called on "to fortify the successes that had already been achieved and to systematically use them for moving forward in the future."[87] Stalin's message was ambiguous: should the situation be corrected or reinforced?

Local party organizations were placed in an extremely difficult situation. Many suffered legal retribution, even severe repression. In addition, these punitive measures were carried out by the very same individuals and organs who themselves had ordered the campaign of violence against the peasantry in the drive to collectivization. From May through June 1930, when preparations were under way for the Sixteenth Party Congress, many communists delivered speeches at meetings of the local party organizations, sharply critical of the policy of full collectivization, dekulakification, and the absence of honesty in assigning blame for "exaggerations."

In most cases, however, the weight of the state was used to reinforce the "successes that had already been achieved." While crisscrossing the country, members of the supreme leadership left important testimonials on this score. On March 22, 1930, G. K. Ordzhonikidze reported from the Krivoi Rog *okrug*, Ukraine: "Everyone wants to explain things using the kulak as an excuse—they are not aware that they have overdone things, over-collectivized. . . . The great need for even more administrative pressure to rectify the situation is reflected in the order to shoot 25-30 people in the region in order to keep their percentages."[88] Around the same time, L. M. Kaganovich gave the following order to party workers in the Kozlovsk *okrug*, Central Chernozem *oblast*: "Before the end of the sowing period, we must fight for a collective turnout in the field, and for the exclusion of anti-kolkhozniks [by apportioning them land in remote areas, refusing them credit, etc]."[89] This was a typical reaction of party workers in the provinces. The obvious contradictions between words and deeds intensified the peasants' dissatisfaction. The number of protests in the countryside multiplied sixfold in March, reaching 6,528 (see table 2.2). The country again found itself faced with the threat of a universal peasant uprising, which would have disrupted spring sowing—and therefore the entire agricultural cycle. Only when faced with a general crisis did the Stalinist leadership take real steps to appease the peasantry. On April 2, 1930, a secret letter from the Central Committee was distributed to the provinces, announcing that the party's "greatest goal . . . is to ensure the successful implementation of the sowing campaign on the kolkhozes and individual peasant holdings." That same year it was suggested that "exaggerations" be corrected within three days, "not in word, but in deed," in the form of "practical measures." The goal that was brought to the fore was that of changing the "the treatment of the middle peasant . . . by first of all drawing him into the work of the kolkhozes," and second, by showing "real cooperation with the individual peasant farmer during the sowing campaign."[90]

The number of peasant demonstrations did not abate until the spring sowing season was in full force. There were 1,991 actions in April, of which 172 were explicitly related to "production difficulties." Of 1,375 demonstrations in May and 886 in January, 443 and 348 (respectively) were linked to "production difficulties." However, by July, only 141 demonstrations were attributed to these difficulties (see table 2.2). The forced collectivization of peasant farms and assets, especially of grain reserves, combined with state grain procurement and the mass slaughter of livestock, had left many peasants with no food reserves whatsoever. Even in normal years, April and May were difficult months for Russian peasants. In 1930, the hungry season extended from March through July, with many peasants simply starving.

One characteristic feature of the peasant protest movement was the great number of actions predominately or exclusively made up of women. The "women's revolts" account for over half of all actions in January 1930 (229 out of 402), and over a third of those in February (379 out of 1,048), before their percentage markedly decreased in March and April, when the conflict between the peasantry and the state became more open and violent. However, an OGPU memo noted that even "in the remaining actions, women comprised either the majority or an important number of participants."

The prominence of women in these mass actions, both as organizers and participants, was due in part to the fact that women were assumed to get more lenient punishment. The conventional wisdom was that "for a woman, all is possible," and that "nothing will happen to a woman." Women forbade their husbands to find a place in a crowd: This is women's business. There's no reason to go and stick your nose in our business. Typically, women's actions expressed opposition to grain confiscation during state grain procurements, to the arbitrary confiscation of livestock, seed, and equipment for the kolkhozes, and to church closures and dekulakification.[91] The women's revolts, as well as women's active participation in peasant movements in general, were not new to the Soviet period. Both had occurred in prerevolutionary Russia—in particular, during the Stolypin agricultural reforms—and for the very same reasons.[92]

Mass resistance was effective in forcing a state retreat. The rising tide flowing into the kolkhozes was replaced by an ebbing tide of peasants flowing out of them. (Even during the early 1920s, when goodwill reigned, there was always a large number of disaffected members leaving the kolkhozes.) "Paper" collectives (collectives in name only) disappeared, and the use of force to gain new members was also discontinued. In August 1930, 21.4 percent of peasant farms were joined in kolkhozes. It is difficult to say how many of these peasants would have remained in the kolkhozes after the distribution of the harvest if there had been another change in policy.

In the fall of 1930, after the spring had passed without a peasant war materializing, pressure on the peasantry increased again in connection with state grain procurements and the push for full collectivization. Intense agricultural labor had yielded good results. The harvest turned out to be very plentiful, especially for cereals. The harvest work was not yet concluded when a sealed letter went out in September from CC AUCPB to all regional committees. The letter, "On Collectivization," severely reprimanded party organizations for their passive attitude toward promoting a "new influx" of peasants into the kolkhozes and demanded that they "secure a new, powerful upsurge in the kolkhoz movement." In December 1930, the party ratified a resolution for completing collectivization in the coming year in the Northern Caucasus, the Lower and Middle Volga region, and in the Ukrainian steppes. The countrywide goal was set at 50 percent of peasant farms in kolkhozes.[93]

However, no notable increases in collectivization resulted. In June 1931, the CC AUCPB ratified a return to the policy of full collectivization in the country as a whole, citing "tremendous successes achieved in the practical implementation of the party slogan for full collectivization and the liquidation of the kulak as a class" in the Northern Caucasus. In the grain regions of the territory, they had "managed to unite two-thirds of peasant farms [in collectives]." The party claimed that the area under cultivation by the kolkhozes had grown "by one million hectares" in the fall of 1929-1930, and increased by an additional 10 percent in the winter of 1930. The party also boasted that the kolkhoznik enjoyed an "increase in income . . . in comparison to the individual peasant farmer," though this was simply a result of the preferential treatment given to the kolkhozes in state grain procurement and taxation. And in just two months, October and November of 1930, 100,000 new households joined kolkhozes.[94]

All this "permitted the full completion of collectivization by the December plenum of the Central Committee."[95] Notably absent from the document were concrete suggestions or new proposals regarding methods and forms of collectivization. Local party organizations once again embarked upon a path of pressuring the peasantry through increased taxation and the growing volume of the state grain procurements. In addition to increased agricultural tax rates for individual farmers, arbitrary taxes were also levied. Moreover, 1931 marked the start of a new and more widespread dekulakification campaign.

At the same time, the number of state machinery and tractor stations grew. The percent of draft power supplied by tractors (as opposed to animals) grew from less than 2 percent in 1928 to 19.6 percent in 1932, but this success must be viewed in light of the nearly 50 percent reduction in the number of horses during the same five years. Procedures for the collectivization of peasant assets were also established. In March, some limitations were set by the Central Committee, obliging local organizations to end forced collectivization of livestock and to assist the kolkhozniks in securing draft animals.[96]

As before, the response to the renewed collectivization campaign was "kulak" terrorism and its merciless (and successful) suppression. The state finally won the battle, and by the start of June 1931, the countrywide goal of 50 percent collectivization had been achieved: 52.7 percent of peasant farms now belonged to kolkhozes. However, in August 1931, the definition of "full collectivization" was increased to 68-70 percent of peasant farms. By the fall of 1932, 62.4 percent of peasant farms were united in kolkhozes, and it was claimed that full collectivization had been achieved.

Dekulakification

The campaign for dekulakification was one of the most tragic acts in the unfolding village drama. The term *dekulakification* was coined during the years of revolution and civil war, under conditions of exacerbated social conflict, when it referred to the full liquidation of farm and property of the kulaks and even their physical extermination. During the early years after the war, it most often referred to the partial expropriation, by other peasants, of lands owned by up to middle-level peasants—one of the most radical methods of implementing leveling ideals. In contrast, total expropriation of kulak farms was generally reserved as a punishment for counterrevolutionary acts.

In the early years, kulak farms not legally subject to expropriation were being drawn into the process of socialist reform and into the socialized sector of the economy. Kulak farms had the right to join agricultural cooperatives of all types, including kolkhozes, although they could not act as the founders of cooperatives or be chosen as members of the governing boards. This was based on the idea that exploitative relationships, not people, should be targeted, an argument most fully expressed by Bukharin in the mid-1920s.[97]

The formulation of the question on the fate of the kulaks changed in its fundamental shape at the end of the 1920s, however. The assault on the kulaks, begun in December 1927, grew over January-February 1928 into the extremity of Stalin's state grain procurements, at the epicenter of which ended up the most productive farms. This first phase of extreme measures included the confiscation not only of grain reserves but also of a portion of the farm assets, as well as the complete liquidation of independent peasant farms whose owners were found guilty of refusing to hand over grain to the state at fixed prices.

The excessive state grain procurements of 1928 became a prologue to the mass liquidation of kulak farms. Seventeen thousand owners of well-to-do farms in the Lower Volga were put on trial, and approximately half of them had their property expropriated. In the Northern Caucasus, 30-35,000 kulak farmers had their property fully or partially expropriated. In Ukraine, according to data from twenty-two of forty-one *okrugs*, 33,000 kulak farmers had property expropriated.[98]

After 1928, dekulakification included the levying of arbitrary state estimates of individual farm income. These taxes were levied in 1928-1929 against 1.6 percent, or some 400,000, peasant farms. For the 1929-1930 tax year, dekulakification was actually applied to 708,000 or 2.8 percent of farms.[99] As a result of the pressure, the number of kulak farms in the Russian Federation decreased from 3.9 percent in 1927 to 2.2 percent in 1929, and from 3.8 percent to 1.4 percent in Ukraine.[100] In practice, however, the kulaks as a class actually disappeared altogether, since all relationships and functions that had now became dangerous were terminated. The majority of kulaks fled to cities or other regions.

In the summer and fall of 1929, even more radical and severe steps were undertaken. In July, the CC AUCPB outlawed the participation of kulak families in kolkhozes.[101] This had the immediate effect of hardening kulak resistance, but also caused the peasantry to question the resolution: Why aren't kulaks—some of whom would work exclusively on the kolkhoz and would give up all their possessions—accepted into the kolkhoz? If a kulak will give over his entire farm for the benefit of the kolkhoz, should he be accepted or not? Will the kulak be accepted into the kolkhoz after liquidation—or several years later?[102]

Through August and September, directives were again issued stepping up the "hard tasks" (procurement quotas and taxes) for well-to-do farms. All party organizations were urged to "utilize any means for increasing the pace of state grain procurements" and to "show no weaknesses of character or spinelessness in carrying out the decisive steps of repression with regard to city residents and grain speculators connected to them, or in any other steps for grain procurements." Furthermore, the OGPU was ordered to "increase the threat of exile as a means of combating malicious speculative elements."[103] Thus the topic of exile—soon to become a key instrument of repression—first arose in a party document on the struggle against the kulaks. In October 1929, the judicial organs were instructed "to adopt decisive and rapid measures for repression—even executions—against the kulaks, who were organizing counter-revolutionary actions."[104]

Stalin announced the transition to a policy for "liquidation of the kulaks as a class" in a speech in 1929.[105] But the government's attempts to provoke a class struggle within the peasantry had not had not been very successful. The majority of peasants did not support dekulakification and even actively opposed it. The Stalinist leadership was thus forced to mount a top-down campaign for dekulakification. Local party organizations and soviets cooperated in the OGPU's activities by rounding up peasants to "show support" for dekulakification in choreographed demonstrations.

In late January 1930, the CC AUCPB ordered party and Soviet organizations to use harsh methods to carry out the confiscation of kulak land, livestock, buildings (including homes), agricultural processing enterprises, and seed reserves. The land and buildings, except that portion that went to settling kulak farm debts owed to the state and the cooperatives, were supposed to be given to the kolkhozes.

The targets of dekulakification were divided into three categories. The first consisted of those who had participated in anti-Soviet and anti-kolkhoz actions, or counterrevolutionary activists who were subject to arrest, trial, and long-term imprisonment in concentration camps or execution. Their families were subject to exile in remote regions of the country. The second group consisted of "large-scale kulaks and former smaller landowners who had actively worked against collectivization."[106] They and their families were exiled to remote regions. The third group consisted of the remaining kulaks, who were subject to relocation to special settlements within the borders of their administrative regions. Of course, the vague distinctions separating these groups resulted in much arbitrary treatment.

Though it was decreed that the number of those "dekulakified" per region (*raion*) was not to exceed 5 percent of the total number of peasant farms, this supposedly restrictive limit exceeded the number of kulak farms. For the regions targeted for full collectivization—the Northern Caucasus, the Lower and Upper Volga, the Central Black Earth (Chernozem) *oblast*, the Urals, Siberia, Ukraine, Belarus, and Kazakhstan—concrete "restrictive contingents" of those subject to exile to remote regions of the country were designated: 60,000 farms of the first category and 150,000 farms of the second.[107] In other territories, these numbers were probably higher.

In practice, poorer and average-means peasants who did not wish to join the kolkhozes were also targeted in the dekulakification campaign. At the beginning of March, the share of targeted farms rose to 10-15 percent in some regions. Simply expressing an opinion against the lawlessness being committed in the name of dekulakification was sufficient cause for being named a counterrevolutionary activist and arrested. On March 12, 1930, a Kursk school teacher, F. D. Pokrovskii, who was mobilized for dekulakification, described the human despair in a diary entry: "In two days I have had the occasion to witness a sea of human suffering. Just think: a family is torn from its familiar spot and, without even being allowed to take their belongings, is chased off to some unknown *krai*. . . . [Meanwhile] other recent targets of the dekulakification campaign keep coming and coming from other villages. Everywhere there is moaning and crying. They sob as for one deceased. The exiles are seen off by their kin who surround the house and also cry. It is terrible and painful!"[108] A well-known writer, Pavel Nilin, also recorded impressions of Ukraine dekulakification in his diary in 1931: "It was as though the land was burning up underfoot. It was terrifying, oppressive and torturous. I thought, I will never forget this, the foul language, the child's cry, the old woman's despair and the feathers flying from the feather-bed."[109]

The attitude of other villagers toward neighbors targeted as kulaks was not limited to the tears and farewells of relatives. In 1930, the OGPU recorded 2,339 mass actions carried out in defense of targeted families—17 percent of the total number of protests in that year (see table 2.2). Again, most participants in these actions were women. In some cases, women "appeared armed with pitchforks, sticks, stakes and knives." The actions sometimes lasted several days. Private property was defended, barricades were set up, and, in general, villagers showed stubborn opposition to the provincial authorities, even going so far as to assault government representatives and rout village soviets. Mass actions included demands for a return of confiscated property and dwellings, and for restoration of voting rights.[110]

The mass protests were successful in protecting some of the those targeted as kulaks from extermination and exile, especially those who had not already been liquidated by April. Targeted families were "rehabilitated" by special commissions (who reviewed complaints and generally overturned former decisions), and their farms were partially restored to them. Steps were also taken to return confiscated livestock and equipment according to norms set up for this purpose.

In January 1931, a resolution by theCC AUCPB nonetheless called for "the liquidation of the kulak as a class and of his every remnant, down to the roots, which interferes with the business of building socialism in agriculture."[111] While the resolution contained no concrete provisions, the fact that the phrase "remnants and roots" was added to the familiar slogan was significant. Since it had become impossible to find a real kulak farm after 1929-1930, it was proposed that the "remnants" now be eradicated.

There are varying estimates of the percentage of farms targeted by dekulak-ification, ranging from around 1 percent to 10 percent and higher. However, the former estimate is certainly understated, while the latter appears immeasurably overstated. Exact data are available only on the number of kulak families exiled to remote regions of the country. According to the computations of a special commission of the CC AUCPB, 115,231 families were exiled in 1930 and 265,795 in 1931. In two years, therefore, 381,000 families were deported to the North, the Urals, Siberia, and Kazakhstan. A certain number of kulak families (200,000-250,000) managed to liquidate or abandon their property and flee to the city before being apprehended. This group included roughly 400-450,000 families from the third category (who would normally have been relocated to special settlements within the borders of their administrative regions). From 1932 to 1936, the dekulakification campaign subsided somewhat, and the number of "kulak" farms liquidated during these years did not exceed 100,000.[112] Altogether, it appears that over a million farms were targeted.

Studies based on OGPU records can give only a rough indication of the number of victims. No in-depth study has been done on the number and fate of those classified under the first category—those arrested for counterrevolutionary activity. Their families were subject to exile along with the families from the second category, and are included in the data on exile given above. As for those who were arrested, there are OGPU testimonials only for January through September of 1930. These indicate that 283,717 individuals, including 124,889 kulaks (44.2 percent of the total) and 158,828 other "anti-Soviet elements" (clergymen, former landowners, mill owners, White Army officers, and others) were arrested. It is also known that of 140,724 people arrested before mid-April of that year, 50,632 were sent to concentration camps, 17,632 were exiled, 2,877 received suspended sentences, 9,333 were freed, and for 59,962, there were "similar decisions and no documents." An untold number in this last category may have simply been executed. Future studies will, of course, clarify this picture, but even the evidence amassed thus far is sufficient to demonstrate the arbitrariness and cruelty of Stalinist dekulakification, which was truly a national calamity.[113]

Organized Starvation

The use of force in the Stalinist collectivization drive was not limited to forced collectivization and dekulakification. Rather, it unavoidably spread to the internal regulation and operation of the kolkhozes, and to their relationships with the state. A universal command-and-control system was emerging. The preferential treatment in grain procurement and taxation granted to the kolkhozes in the spring of 1930 was never repeated. Now established as the basic form of organization for agricultural production, the kolkhozes were subjected to mandatory grain procurement and taxes and lost all their former privileges.

Stalin's "Great Leap Forward" along the path of industrialization created a limitless need for resources that needed to be extorted from agriculture. Hard currency was needed for importing manufacturing equipment, and grain exports were the chief means of obtaining it. The good harvest of 1930, which ostensibly yielded 835 million centners of grain, permitted an increase in state grain procurement to 221.4 million centners, of which 48.4 million centners were exported. (Of these three figures, the second and third are not in doubt, but the first should be used with caution.) In any case, the compulsory nature of grain procurement is indisputable.

The kolkhozes naturally strove to avoid the procurements, giving priority to their own consumption needs. The reaction of the Stalinist leadership was swift in coming. We again turn to the January 10, 1931, resolution "On Collectivization in the Northern Caucasus," which had become the plan of action for all regions of the country. The resolution declared a struggle against "self-serving elements and the emergence of a petit-bourgeois element within the kolkhozes."

It was proposed that party workers "secure exact and timely fulfillment by the kolkhozes of their duties before the state (grain payment, grain- sowing contracts, credit payment)." However, the matter was not limited to demands upon the kolkhoz's resources. The resolution also called for the creation of "a system of real planning for their operation. . . . Agricultural and other organs should present production goals to the kolkhozes [and] the kolkhozes should construct their production and financial plans on the basis of the planned tasks for agriculture which are established for a given region."[114]

As the state began giving the kolkhozes specific instructions, the kolkhozes lost their spontaneous cooperative nature and became the targets of state campaigns. The change was quick and brutal. The 1931 harvest was not as good as the previous year's—only 698 million centners, but state grain procurements nonetheless rose to 228.3 million centners, of which 51.8 million were exported. All grain, including seed grain, was confiscated from many kolkhozes. In Siberia, the Volga region, Kazakhstan, the Northern Caucasus, and Ukraine, serious food shortages arose and famine began. Both kolkhozniks and individual peasant farmers (and sometimes entire villages) packed up and left for the cities, seeking construction work. The kolkhozes began to disintegrate.[115]

Food and seed loans managed to avert mass starvation temporarily. However, a winter and spring of semistarvation left their mark: physically exhausted villagers could scarcely wait until the new harvest. As soon as an ear of grain began ripening on the kolkhoz fields, "trimmers" would appear—most often the mothers of starving children, who came out at night with scissors to cut some ears to make kasha. When the harvest work began, mass embezzlement of grain occurred. Grain left the kolkhoz threshing floor in people's pockets or hidden in women's bosoms. The state responded with a law written by Stalin's own hand and ratified on August 7, 1932, which established as punishment "for embezzlement [theft]" of kolkhoz property, regardless of the amount stolen, "the highest measure of social defense—execution and confiscation of all property, [or], under extenuating circumstances, the substitution of loss of freedom for a period of no less than 10 years accompanied by the confiscation of all property."[116]

The 1932 harvest of 699 million centners was again disappointing. Though grain procurement fell to 185 million centners, and grain exports fell to 18 million centners, this decrease did not reflect any consideration or wisdom on the part of the state. On the contrary, the figures reflected the mass resistance of the peasantry in the fall and winter of 1932, as well as unfavorable weather for the harvest in a number of regions. The single most important cause of falling procurement was that many kolkhozniks abandoned the harvest for other seasonal labor, including work on private farms. The kolkhozniks shied away from harvest work on the kolkhoz, which, to avoid theft, was organized like an assembly line—from the field to the threshing machine and then straight on to the state storage point. Due to a shortage of laborers, a portion of the crop remained in the fields.

In Ukraine, the Northern Caucasus, and the Lower and Middle Volga, the kolkhozes were unable to fulfill state grain procurement targets. In October and November, Stalin sent an extraordinary commission to these regions, which not only forcibly confiscated grain from the kolkhozes that had not fulfilled their quotas, but also carried out mass repression against local party organizations, soviets, and kolkhoz workers. The commission ordered the dismissal of local party leaders, mass exclusions from the party, widespread arrests, and the removal of all foodstuff from kolkhozes that were blacklisted as "malicious saboteurs."

A commission headed by Molotov was sent to Ukraine and another to the Northern Caucasus. In Kuban, populations were evicted from large Cossack settlements—Poltava, Medvedov, Uman, Urup, and a number of others—and banished to the northern regions. Reports began to appear from the Lower Volga in December 1932 that state grain procurements had been halted, and a telegram was immediately sent there bearing the signatures of Stalin and Molotov, ordering the guilty parties to be "arrested, . . . hastily condemned and given 5—better 10—years of imprisonment." In a letter dated April 16, 1933, Sholokhov again wrote to Stalin complaining about state grain procurement methods. Stalin responded with a letter accusing the kolkhoz peasantry of "sabotage" and even conducting "a war of starvation" against the workers and the Red Army.[117]

In the winter of 1932-1933, in the grain regions of the country (Ukraine, the Don and the Northern Caucasus, Lower and Middle Volga, the Southern Urals, and in Kazakhstan), mass famine broke out. In some areas, the entire population died of starvation. Emergency food loans from the state were negligible. Starving peasants attempting to flee to more prosperous regions or to the cities (as they had the previous winter) ran up against cordons, or were cruelly rounded up and returned to famine areas. In the spring of 1933, almost 220,000 starving people who had set off in search of grain in other provinces were detained and then returned. It is not clear whether the number of "returned" included those who had died in the place they had hoped to find salvation.[118]

It is very difficult to put a number on the victims of the famine of 1932-1933, especially since there is no clear way of distinguishing between those who starved and those who were simply malnourished. It has been estimated that some 10-15 million peasants suffered from starvation during the famine, of whom 5-7 million died. In the 1980s, these figures provoked sharp discussion in the scholarly literature and a new wave of historical-demographic studies.[119] Though it is too early to generalize from these more recent studies, it appears that a majority of investigators are revising their estimates downward—to 3-5 million people suffering from starvation during this period.[120]

The recent availability of archival materials convincingly demonstrates that the blame for the suffering and deaths of millions of people lies squarely with the Stalinist leadership. The fact that bread was taken from the kolkhozniks for industrialization needs can justify neither the violence used in creating the kolkhozes nor the famine that resulted from extortionate grain procurement. The famine of 1932-1933 is the most serious crime committed by the Stalinist leadership against the peasantry and against the people as a whole.[121]

The Completion of Agricultural Collectivization

Overcoming the crisis created by grain procurement and collectivization in the village required tremendous effort and time. In 1933-1934, the political branch of the Machinery and Tractor Stations (MTS) worked to restore the kolkhozes' production capacities in the grain regions of the country. Agricultural organization improved, but the success of the MTS was undermined by their repressive functions. These included cleansing the kolkhozes of kulaks who had "infiltrated" them "on the sly" (to use Stalin's words), taking over "the jobs of storeroom manager, bursar, bookkeeper and secretary," i.e., jobs where they would be in a position to hide grain and otherwise obstruct state procurement.[122]

Agricultural production continued to fall: grain production fell to 684 million centners in 1933 and to 676.5 million centners in 1934. Meanwhile, state procurement rose to 234 million and 268 million centners in 1933 and 1934, respectively, perpetuating hunger in the villages. Livestock procurement also continued apace. During the forced collectivization, the dekulakification campaigns, and the famine, meat procurement caused half the livestock in the country to be killed off. The cattle population fell from 60.1 million in 1928 to 33.5 million in 1933; the pig population fell from 22 million to 9.9 million in the same period; the sheep population fell from 97.3 million to 32.9 million (in 1934); and the horse population fell from 32.1 million to 14.9 million (in 1935). The livestock population regained and surpassed its 1928 level only in 1958.

Perhaps the most serious problems arose from the rapid remodeling of kolkhozes into large-scale enterprises, and the elimination of small-scale or individual productive activities such as tending private, supplementary kolkhoznik farms or plots. The elimination of private plots left no solution to the immediate problems of the collectivization of livestock and poultry.

Other problems were linked to compensation and incentive mechanisms. The search for suitable forms of work organization and payment for labor had of necessity been carried out during dislocations caused by mass collectivization. The years 1931-1932 marked the beginning of permanent brigades and piecework, with fixed labor expenditures and wages based on the workday. In 1933-1934, these ideas were widely disseminated by the political branch of the MTS. However, the search for suitable incentive mechanisms remained a real problem.

Agricultural yields continued to fall, forcing the Stalinist leadership to again restore elements of the NEP. At the November plenum of the Central Committee in 1934, a resolution was unexpectedly passed that liquidated the political branch of the MTS. Ration cards were abolisheded in January 1935, alongside an increase in the state grain procurement prices for the kolkhozes. "We wish," Stalin said at the plenum, "to strengthen the money economy . . . , to fully develop commodity circulation, having replaced . . . the current policy of mechanical distribution of food-stuffs. . . . This is the fundamental notion of the reform we have launched. . . . To establish trade between the city and the village without buying and selling is an unthinkable thing. . . . It is foolishness."[123] Of course, what Stalin deemed "foolishness" was his own economic policy as carried out since the winter of 1927-1928.

The years 1935-1936 are sometimes called the "kolkhoz NEP," despite the lack of significant economic reforms. The first commandment for the kolkhozes remained, Thou shalt supply agricultural produce to the state (with only symbolic payment). The subordination of the kolkhozes to state leadership and control also was preserved, though direct interference by officials in kolkhoz business was markedly reduced.

Agricultural yields revived in 1935-1937, though grain yields for the entire period of the second five-year plan (1933-1937) were lower than for the first five-year plan—729 million versus 735.6 million centners. The livestock population also began to grow, and wages for kolkhoz workers increased. The modernization of agriculture was also beginning to show results. By 1937 the MTS system was servicing nine out of ten kolkhozes.

Meanwhile, the individual peasant holdings that remained (about 9 million at the beginning of the second five-year plan) were being collectivized. From August to September, agricultural tax rates were raised for individual peasant holdings, and an additional one-time tax was levied that required private farms to sell 50 percent more produce to the state (for a token payment) than the kolkhozes. Particularly stubborn individual peasant farmers were also targets of continuing "dekulak-ification." Thus, even during the last stage of collectivization, the remaining smallholders remained under intense pressure from the state. In the end, large-scale socialized production became practically the sole form of agriculture in the USSR.

The kolkhozes' relationship with the state sharply limited their independence and initiative, and therefore also their economic growth. The kolkhozes were subjected to continuous mobilization for state needs, and were under orders from inefficient central planners (as was the economy as a whole). Practically all agricultural machinery, as well as qualified technical cadres, were concentrated in the MTS, which tilled the kolkhoz fields for barter wages, which were set from above. The centralization of technology and technological know-how may have hastened the modernization of agriculture, but it also created the basis for an unequal exchange between the kolkhozes and the state, and contributed to the centralization of decision making.

In January 1933, following another failed state grain procurement campaign, a system was introduced for the obligatory provision of agricultural foodstuffs to the state by the kolkhozes. Prices for grain and for most other products produced by kolkhozes were fixed at levels ten to twelve times below old market levels, while passports were issued to everyone in the country except for kolkhozniks, effectively tying them to their occupation. This added a compulsory element to kolkhoz labor, and the kolkhozes lost the last shred of their voluntary, cooperative nature.

Conclusion

As we have seen, the peasant revolution begun in Russia in the early 1900s was displaced by the Bolshevik workers' revolution, which put the Communist Party into power and set in motion socialist reform through revolutionary methods. Cooperative societies, which had been a means of strengthening and extending small-scale peasant farming, were transformed into instruments for state procure-ment and distribution of agricultural products, and stripped of their spontaneous, cooperative nature. Even the most diehard supporters of collective agriculture could not accept the wild outburst of violence that erupted during the winter of 1929-1930. The increasing development of top-down control of the economy and society had an extremely detrimental effect on the functioning of the cooperatives.

The forced collectivization of peasant agriculture and its destructive consequences could not help but have an impact on all subsequent development of kolkhozes and the village as a whole. The force used in the Stalinist collectivization drive unavoidably spread to the internal regulation and operation of the kolkhozes, and to their relationships with the state. The lack of independence and the situation of unequal exchange created problems with compensation and incentive mechanisms, which in turn had an impact on their economic growth.

Political repression continued through 1937-1938, after the completion of the collectivization campaign, falling now upon those kulaks who had one way or another so far avoided exile to prison camps or special resettlement camps and upon overly independent leaders of kolkhozes and other village organizations. The peasantry also had to live through abject poverty during World War II, when maximal labor was required from everyone—including teens and the elderly—and millions of lives were lost on the front and in the occupied territory. Despite the decades of attack on and exploitation of peasant labor, it remained the basis for rural existence and social development of society as a whole.

N. S. Khrushchev's reforms begun in the mid-1950s reduced the burden of state requisition and expanded kolkhoz independence, creating the opportunity for increasing agricultural development. The scale and tempo of mechanization of large-scale kolkhoz and sovkhoz production increased, agriculture and cattle farming improved, the volume of agricultural production grew, and public consumption finally improved. By the period 1986-1990, Russia produced 711 kg of grain, 245 kg of potatoes, 66 kg of meat, and 370 liters of milk per capita. These levels guaranteed population growth and independence for the country, but were not enough under conditions of "competition" with the developed countries in international markets and the cold war, with its unsustainable arms race.

The Gorbachev economic reforms, oriented toward market organization, guaranteed producer independence, beginning with liberation from state dictates and state requisition of production, and allowing peasants the right to leave the kolkhoz with their land and equipment. This would have opened the possibility of transforming the kolkhoz into a true cooperative alongside the simultaneous creation of individual farms, along the lines proposed by Chayanov and supported by Lenin decades earlier.

Unfortunately, the Gorbachev-Yeltsin agricultural reforms of the 1990s have not focused on the peasantry. Like Stolypin's reform and Stalin's collectivization, the post-Soviet reform plan was determined and even consumed from the very beginning by the swapping of one social form for organizing agriculture for another. Of course, it is not known to what extent the agricultural cooperatives could have grown under the NEP, since Stalin's "revolution from above" simultaneously scrapped both the NEP as a policy of transition toward socialism and the cooperative system as a democratic reform process in 1929. Still, the works of Chaianov and Bukharin suggest that the development of multiple forms of cooperative societies was a realistic alternative to Stalinist collectivization and may still be so today.

For now, the goals of increasing production, providing the population with food, and so forth have not generally been realized. They have been left up to the "lucky future" to resolve. Whatever the future path of reform, the defense of the interests of peasant farmers continues to be a primary goal. Achieving this goal requires an understanding that the role of cooperative agriculture in Russia cannot be understood through an exclusive focus on the forced nature of Soviet collectivization. Under market conditions, cooperation in all forms and every aspect, credit, market supply, and production, continue to offer a unique means for defending and developing peasant farming.[124]

Notes

1. Work on this chapter was completed in 1996.

2. Itogi desiatiltiia Sovetskoivlastiv tsifrakh. 1917-1927. M. 1927, S. 118-19 (ekz. istoricheskoi bibliotekii INION). *The Results of a Decade of the Soviet Regime in Numbers: 1917-1927* (Moscow: 1927), 118-19 (copy of the Historical Library INION).

3. See: "An Attempt at Numerical Calculations for the National Economy of 50 Gubernias in European Russia 1900 - 1913," ed. S. N. Prokopovich (Moscow: 1918), 80-83; A. M. Anfimov, "Large-Scale Landowner Farming in European Russia (The End of the 19th - Beginning of the 20th Centuries)" (Moscow: 1969), 236-37.

4. N. D. Kondrat'ev, Osoboe mnenie. Kn. 1. M. 1993. S. 303, 30; Tam zhe, 17, 19. Tam zhe, 17, 19. 4 (*A Special Opinion. Book 1*) (Moscow: 1993), 303-4.

5. See: V. P. Danilov, *The Soviet Pre-Kolkhoz Village: Social Structure, Social Attitudes* (Moscow: 1979), 169-71.

6. Dekrety Sovetskoi vlasti. T. 1. 25 oktiabria 1917-16 marta 1918 g. M. 1957. S. 18 (*Decrees of Soviet Government Volume One: October 25, 1917-March 16, 1918*) (Moscow: 1957), 18.

7. Dekrety Sovetskoi vlasti. T. 1. 25 oktiabria 1917-16 marta 1918 g. M. 1957. S. 18 (*Decrees of Soviet Government Volume One: October 25, 1917-March 16, 1918*), 17, 19.

8. Itogi desiatiletiia Sovetskoi vlasti v tsifrakh. S. 118-19 (*The Results of a Decade of the Soviet Regime in Numbers*), 118-19.

9. Sm: V. P. Danilov, Ukaz. soch. S. 297-332 (See: V.P. Danilov, [work indicated], 297-332).

10. Sm: Narodnoe khoziaistvo SSSR. 1922-1972 gg. Statisticheskii ezhegodnik. M. 1972. S. 52-53, 216 (See: *The National Economy of the USSR 1922-1972: A Statistical Annual Report*) (Moscow: 1972), 52-55, 216.

11. Vladimira Dalya, *Tolkovoe Slovare Zhivogo Velikoruskogo izoka Valadimira Dalya: vtoroe Izdanie, ispravlenoe I znachilyno imnozhenoe po ruskopisi avtora*, R2, (SP-M. 1881). A.N. Englehardt, *Iz derevni: 12 pisem 1872-1887* (M. 1987) S. 520-524. A.N. Englehardt, *From the Village: 12 Letters 1872-1877* (Moscow:1987), 520-524.

12. V.I. Lenin, *The Development of Capitalism in Russia* (Moscow: Progress Publishers, 1977).

13. Sm: V. P. Danilov, Ukaz. Soch. S. 49-80, 129-137 I dr (See: V. P. Danilov, [work indicated]), 49-80, 129-37, and others.

14. F. A. Shcherbina, Ocherki iuzhnorusskikh artelei I obshchinno-artel'nykh form. Odessa. 1881. S. 124-25 (*Outlines of the Southern Russian Artels and Commune-Artel Forms*) (Odessa: 1881), 124-25.

15. See: M. Popvskii, *Russian Peasants Speak: The Followers of L. N. Tolstoi in the Soviet Union, 1918-1977* (London: 1983); *Reminiscences of Tolstoyann Peasants, 1910-1930* (Moscow: 1989).

16. See: S. N. Prokopovich, *The Cooperative Movement in Russia: Its Theory and Practice* (Moscow: 1913); A.V. Merkulov, *An Historical Outline of the Consumer Cooperative Association in Russia* (Petersburg: 1915).

17. V. Danilov, " Alexander Chayanov as a Theoretician of the Cooperative Movement," introduction to *The Theory of Peasant Cooperatives*, by A. Chayanov (London, New York: 1991), xxii-xv.

18. Trudy 1-go Vserossiiskogo sel'skokhoziaistvennogo s"ezda v Kieve. 1-10 sentiabria 1913 q. Postanovleniia s"ezda. Kieve. 1913. Vyp. 1. S. 4-5 ("Works of the First All-Russia Agricultural Congress in Kiev: September 1-10, 1913," *Congress Resolutions*, Issue 1 [Kiev: 1913], 4-5).

19. A. V. Chaianov, Shto takoe agrarnyi vopros? M. 1917. S. 4 (*What is the Agrarian Question?*) (Moscow: 1917), 4.

20. Chaianov, Shto takoe agrarnyi vopros? M. 1917. S. 4 (*What is the Agrarian Question?*), 18-19, 23-25.

21. Chaianov, Shto takoe agrarnyi vopros? M. 1917. S. 4 (*What is the Agrarian Question?*), 18-19, 23-25.

22. Agrarnaia politika Sovetskoi vlasti (1917-1918 gg). Dokumenty I materialy. M. 1954. S. 512-13 (*The Agrarian Policy of the Soviet Government [1917-1919] Documents and Materials*) [Moscow: 1954], 512-13).

23. V. I. Lenin, Poln. sobr. soch. T. 37, S. 141 (*Collected Works* 37: 141).

24. V. I. Lenin, Poln. sobr. soch. T. (*Collected Works* 37): 356.

25. Agrarnaia politika Sovetskoi vlasti (1917-1918 qq). Dokumenty I materialy. S. 416-17 (*The Agrarian Policy of the Soviet Government [1917-1919] Documents and Materials*), 416-17.

26. V. I. Lenin, Poln. sobr. soch. T. (*Collected Works* 38): 200, 201.

27. KPSS v rezoliutsiiakh I resheniiakh s"ezdov, konferentsii I plenumov TSK. (Dalee - KPSS v rezoliutsiiakh) (*The Communist Party of the Soviet Union in the Resolutions and Decisions of the Congresses, Conferences and Plenums of the Central Committee* [Hereafter—KPSS in Resolutions] 2, 9th edition (Moscow: 1983): 110.

28. KPSS v rezoliutsiiakh, M. 1983. T.2 S. 109. (The KPSS in Resolutions 4 [Moscow: 1983]: 109).

29. A. V. Chaianov, Osnovnye idei I formy organizatsii krest'ianskoi kooperatsii. M. 1919. S. 42, 301, 303-5 (*The Basic Conceptions and Forms of Organizing Peasant Cooperatives*) [Moscow: 1919], 42, 301, 303-5.

30. Chaianov, *The Basic Conceptions and Forms of Organizing Peasant Cooperatives* (Moscow: 1919), 42, 301, 303-5.

31. V. I. Lenin, Poln. sobr. soch. T. 45, S. 372, 373 (*Collected Works* 45): 372-73.

32. Sm: Danilov, V. P. Ukaz. soch., S. 209-91 here and for the data on cooperatives in the 20s given below (See: [work cited]), 209-91.

33. Alexander Chayanov, *The Theory of Peasant Cooperatives*, with introduction by V. P. Danilov (London: 1991), 11.

34. Chayanov, *The Theory of Peasant Cooperatives*, 11.

35. Chayanov, *The Theory of Peasant Cooperatives*, 204-5.

36. N. I. Bukharin, "Put'k sotsializmu I raboche-krest'ianskii soiuz: Izbrannye proizvedeniia." M. 1988. S. 197 ("The Path to Socialism and the Peasant-Worker Alliance: Selected Works" [Moscow: 1988], 197).

37. Bukharin, "Put'k sotsializmu I raboche-krest'ianskii soiuz: Izbrannye proizvedeniia" ("The Path to Socialism and the Peasant-Worker Alliance: Selected Works"), 171, 173-75,

184.

38. Bukharin, "Put'k sotializmu I raboche-krest'ianskii soiuz: Izbrannye proizvedeniia" ("The Path to Socialism and the Peasant-Worker Alliance: Selected Works"), 181-85.

39. Pravda. 1925. 6 marta ("Pravada," March 6, 1925).

40. KPSS v rezoliutsiiakh. M. 1984. T. 4. S. 299 *(The KPSS in the Resolutions* 4) [Moscow: 1984]: 299.

41. N. I. Bukharin, Izbrannye proizvedeniia. S. 323-24, 339-40 *(Selected Works,* 323-24, 339-40).

42. KPSS v rezoliutsiiakh. T. 4. S. 278, 288, 305 *(The KPSS in the Resolutions* 4): 278, 288, 305.

43. Sm: N. I. Bukharin, "Iabrannye proizvedeniia" (See: *Selected Works,* 137-38).

44. Tsentral'nyi arkhiv (hereafter TS) FSB RF. F. 66. Op.1. D. 174. L. 162.

45. RTSKHIDNI (The Russian Center for the Preservation and Usage of Documentation of Recent History [Hereafter RTSKHIDNI]). F. 17. Op. 162. D. 5. LI. 52-53.

46. V. K. Vinogradov, "Zelenaia papka," "Nizavisimaia gazeta" (April 20, 1994).

47. TS FSB RF. F.2. Op.5. D.304. LI. 79-86.

48. TS FSB RF. F.2. Op.6. D.567. L. 5.

49. TS FSB RF. F.2. Op.6. D.53. L. 107.

50. RTSKHIDNI. F.17. Op.3. D.663. L. 4.

51. Sm: Osnovnye elementy I produktsiia sel'skogo khoziaistva SSSR za 1925/26 - 1928/29 qq. M. 1928. S. 32, 119-25 (See: *The Basic Elements and Produce of Agriculture in the USSR during the Years 1925/26 - 1928/29* [Moscow: 1928], 32, 119-25.

52. RTSKHIDNI. F.56. Op.2. D.52. L. 34.

53. Sm: V. P. Danilov, "Bukharinskaia al'ternativa."-Bukharin: chelovek, politik, uchenyi. Sb. statei. M. 1990. S. 106. (See: V. P. Danilov, The "Bukharin Alternative"–Bukharin: The Man, The Politician, The Scholar. Collected Articles [Moscow: 1990], 106.

54. V. P. Danilov, K kharakteristike obshchestvenno-politicheskoi obstanovki v sovetskoi derevne nakanune kollektivizatsii. -Istoricheskie zapiski. T. 79. M. 1966. S. 40-42 *(Toward a Description of the Social-Political Situation in the Soviet Village on the Eve of Collectivization: Historical Notes, 79* [Moscow: 1966]: 40-42).

55. Pravda, 18 aprelia 1928 g. ("Pravda," April 18, 1928).

56. Pravda, 19 aprelia 1928 g. ("Pravda," April 19, 1928).

57. N. I. Bukhain, Problemy teorii I praktiki sotsializma. Sb. statei. M. 1989. S. 299 *(Problem with the Theory and Practice of Socialism. A collection of Articles* [Moscow: 1989], 299).

58. Bukhain, Problemy teorii I praktiki sotsializma. Sb. statei. M. 1989. S. 264 *(Problem with the Theory and Practice,* 264).

59. KPSS v rezoliutsiiakh. T. 4. M., 1984. S. 328-54 *(The KPSS in the Resolutions* 4 [Moscow: 1984]: 348 - 54).

60. V. P. Danilov, "Bukharinskaia al'ternativa," S. 110-11 (The "Bukharin Alternative," 110-11.

61. Dokumenty svidetel'stvuiut. Iz istorii derevni nakanune I v xode kollektivizatsii. 1927-1932 gg. Sb. dokumentov I materialov. M. 1989. S. 232-34 *(The Documents Testify: From Village History on the Eve and during the Course of Collectivization 1927-1932 - A collection of Documents and Materials* [Moscow: 1989], 232-34).

62. RTSKHIDNI. F.17. Op.50. D.27. LI. 6-7.

63. Sobranie zakonov I rasporiazhenii Raboche-krest'ianskogo pravitel'stva USSR (dalee - SZ), 1928, N 12, st. 106; N 14, st. 119 *(Collection of Laws and Instructions of the*

Worker-Peasant Government of the USSR [hereafter SZ], no. 12, no. 14 [1928]: 106, 119). Sel'skokhoziaisttvennyi kredit (zhurnal). 1920. N20. S. 25, 53. (*Agricultural Credit* [a journal]), 1930 no. 20 S. 25, 53.

64. Kolkhoznoe stroitel'stvo. Tretii Vserossiiskii s"ezd kolkhozov (24-30 maia 1928 g). M. 1929. S. 128 (*The Kolkhoz Structure. The Third All-Russia Congress of Kolkhozes [May 24-30, 1928]* [Moscow: 1929], 128).

65. Rossiiskii gosudarstvennyi arkhiv ekonomiki (dalee RGAE). F. 3983. Op.1. D.69. L. 82 (*The Russian State Economics Archives* [hereafter: RGAE]).

66. RGAE. L. 82.

67. RGAE. L. 82.

68. RGAE. L. 82.

69. RGAE. L. 53-65.

70. Sm. V. P. Danilov, Sozdanie material'no-tekhnicheskikh predposylok kollektivizatsii sel'skogo khoziaistva v SSSR. M. 1957. S. 343-84. (See: V. P. Danilov, *Creating the Material and Technical Preconditions for Agricultural Collectivization in the USSSR* [Moscow: 1957], 343-84).

71. Sdvigi v sel'skom khoziaistve SSSR mezhdu XV I XVI partiinymi s"ezdami. M. -L. 1931. S. 22-3, 25 (Changes in Agriculture of the USSR between the XV and the XVI Party Congresses) [Moscow-Leningrad: 1931], 22-3, 25).

72. Gosudarstvennyi arkhiv Rossiiskoi Federatsii (dalee GARF). F. 5446. Op.1. D.571a, L1. 8, 25, 39 (State Archives of the Russian Federation [hereafter: GARF]).

73. V. P. Danilov, Kolkhoznoe dvizhenie nakanune sploshnoi kolletivizatsii (1927 g. - pervaia polovina 1929 g). - "istoricheskie zapiski". T. 80. M. 1967. S. 76 (*The Kolkhoz Movement on the Eve of Full Collectivization [1927 to the first half of 1929]: "Historical Notes"* 80 [Moscow: 1967], 76). GARF. F.5446. Op.1. D.49. L. 22; F.3316. Op.13. D.11. L. 178.

74. Danilov, *The Kolkhoz Movement on the Eve of Full Collectivization (1927 to the first half of 1929): "Historical Notes"* 80 (Moscow: 1967), 76. GARF. F.5446. Op.1. D.49. L. 22; F.3316. Op.13. D.11. L. 178.

75. RGAE. F.7446. Op.1. D.3. L1 65-67.

76. "Izvestnaia TSK VKP(b)". 1929. N 22. C. 23. "Proceedings of the Central Committee of the All-Union Communist (Bolshevik) Party, No. 22" (1929), 23.

77. I. V. Stalin, Soch T. 12. S. 124-25, 129-33 (*Works* 12: 124-25, 129-33).

78. KPSS v rezoliutsiiakh. M. 1983. T. 5. S. 29 (*The KPSS in the Resolutions* 5) [Moscow: 1984], 29).

79. Dokumenty svidetel'stvuiut. . . S. 264, 288-90 (The documents *Testify*. . . 264, 288-90).

80. V. M. Molotov, "O kolkhoznom dvizhenii." -Bol'shevik. 1929. N 22. S. 12 ("On the Kolkhoz Movement," no. 22 [Bolshevik: 1929], 12).

81. KPSS v resoliutsiiakh. T.5 S. 73-74 *(KPSS in resolutions* 5, 73-74).

82. Tsentral'nyi arkhiv FSK RF. Sekretno-politicheskii otdel OGPU. Dokladnaia zapiska o formakh I dinamike klassovoi bor'by v derevne v 1930 godu. S. 19, 23 ("Memorandum on the Forms and Dynamics of the Class Struggle in the Village in 1930," in *The Central Archives of the FSK of the Russian Federation. The Secret Political Department of the OGPU*, 19, 23).

83. Tsentral'nyi arkhiv FSK RF. Sekretno-politicheskii otdel OGPU. Dokladnaia zapiska o formakh I dinamike klassovoi bor'by v derevne v 1930 godu. S. 4, 6 ("Memorandum on the Forms and Dynamics of the Class Struggle in the Village in 1930", 4, 6).

84. Tsentral'nyi arkhiv FSK RF. Sekretno-politicheskii otdel OGPU. Dokladnaia zapiska o formakh I dinamike klassovoi bor'by v derevne v 1930 godu. S. ("Memorandum on the Forms and Dynamics of the Class Struggle in the Village in 1930").

85. Tsentral'nyi arkhiv FSK RF. Sekretno-politicheskii otdel OGPU. Dokladnaia zapiska o formakh I dinamike klassovoi bor'by v derevne v 1930 godu. S. ("Memorandum on the Forms and Dynamics of the Class Struggle in the Village in 1930", 4, 34).

86. I. V. Stalin, Soch T. 12. S. 192-194 (*Works,* 12, 192-94).

87. RTSKHIDNI. F. 85. Op. 27. D. 156. Ll. 1-2.

88. RGAE. F. 320. Op. 1. d. 121. L. 196.

89. Dokumenty svidetel'stvuiut. . . S. 393 (*The Documents Testify.* . ., 393).

90. "Dokladnaia zapiska o formakh I dinamike klassovoi bor'by v derevne v 1930." S. 12-15 ("Memorandum on the Forms and Dynamics of the Class Struggle in the Village in 1930", 12-15).

91. Sm: Dubrovskii, S. M. Stolypinskaia zemel'naia reforma. M. 1963. S. 556 (See: S. M. Dubrovskii, *The Stolypin Agricultural Reform* [Moscow: 1963], 556).

92. KPSS v rezoliutsiiakh. T. 5. S. 233-34 (*The KPSS in the Resolutions* 5, 233-34).

93. Spravochnik partiinogo rabotnika. Vyp. 8. M. 1934. S. 678-82 (*Handbook for the Party Worker,* Issue 8 [Moscow: 1934], 678-82).

94. Spravochnik partiinogo rabotnika, 679-80. (*Handbook for the Party Worker*, Issue 8 [Moscow: 1934], 679-80).

95. Dokumenty svidetel'stvuiut. S. 469-70 (*The Documents Testify.* . ., 469-70).

96. N. I. Bukharin, Izbrannye proizvedeniia. M. 1988. S. 133 (*Selected Works* [Moscow: 1988], 133).

97. V. P. Danilov, K kharakteristi,e obshchestvenno-politicheskoli obstanovki v sovetskoi derevne nakanune kollektivizatsii. -"istoricheskie zapiski." T. 79. 1966. S. 43 (*Toward a Description of the Social-Political Situation in the Soviet Village on the Eve of Collectivization: Historical Notes,* 79 [1966], 43).

98. Danilov, K kharakteristi,e obshchestvenno-politicheskoli obstanovki v sovetskoi derevne nakanune kollektivizatsii. -"istoricheskie zapiski." T. 79. 1966. S. 37 (*Toward a Description of the Social-Political Situation,* 37).

99. Sdvigi v sel'skom khoziaistve SSSR mezhdu XV I XVI partiinymi s"ezdami. M. -L. 1931. S. 66-67 (Changes in Agriculture of the USSR between the XV and XVI Party Congresses [Moscow-Leningrad: 1931], 66-67).

100. "Izvestnaia TSK VKP(b)". 1929. N22. C. 23. "Proceedings of the Central Committee of the All-Union Communist (Bolshevik) Party," No. 22 (1929), 23.

101. RTSKHIDNI. F. 17. Op. 3. D. 746. Ll. 2, 10.

102. RTSKHIDNI. F. 17. Op. 3. D. 753. L. 5; D. 756. L. 14; D. 758. Ll. 14-15; D. 759. Ll. 10-13.

103. RTSKHIDNI. F. 17. Op. 3. D. 761. L. 17.

104. Sm. Stalin, I. V. Soch. T. 12. S. 166-69 (See: *Works* 12, 166-69).

105. Dokumenty svidetel'stvuiut . . . (*The Documents Testify* . . .), 27-29.

106. Dokumenty svidetel'stvuiut . . . (*The Documents Testify* . . .), 27-29.

107. Dokumenty svidetel'stvuiut . . . (*The Documents Testify* . . .), 312.

108. "Dokladnaia zapiska o formakh I dinamike klassovoi bor'by v derevne v 1930" ("Memorandum on the Forms and Dynamics of the Class Struggle in the Village in 1930"), 49-50, 63.

109. Dokumenty svidetel'stvuiut . . . (*The Documents Testify* . . .), 46-7.

110. Spravochnik partiinogo rabotnika. Vyp. 8. (*Handbook for the Party Worker,* Issue

8), 682.

111. Dokumenty svidetel'stvuiut. . . (*The Documents Testify*. . .) , 46-7.

112. Spravochnik partiinogo rabotnika. Vyp. 8 *(Handbook for the Party Worker,* Issue 8), 679, 680.

113. Dokumenty svidetel'stvuiut. . . (*The Documents Testify*. . .) , 46-7.

114. I. E. Zelenin, "Kolkhoznoe stroitel'stvo v SSSR v 1931-1932 gg." -Istoriia SSSR. 1960. N 6 ("The Kolkhoz Structure in the USSR 1931-1932," in *History of the USSR, no. 6* [1960]).

115. Dokumenty svidetel'stvuiut. . . S (*The Documents Testify*. . .), 476-78.

116. Dokumenty svidetel'stvuiut. . . S (*The Documents Testify*. . .), 42-44.

117. V. P. Danilov, Kollektivizatsiia. . . - Perepiska na istoricheskie temy. M. 1989. S. 394-95 (See: *Collectivization*. . . - *Correspondence on Historical Themes* [Moscow: 1989], 394-95).

118. V. P. Danilov, Diskussia v zapdnoi presse o golode 1932-33 gg. I "demograficheski katastrofe" 30-40-kh godov v SSSR. -"Voprosy istorii." 1988. N. S. 116-21; Maksudov S. (Babenyshev, A. P.). Poteri naseleniia SSSR. Benson (USA). 1989. S. 191 ("Discussion in the Western Press about the 1932-33 Famine and the 'demographic catastrophe' of the 30s and 40s in the USSR," *Questions of History*, no. 3, [1988]: 116-21; (USSR Population Losses, Benson [USA]), [1989], 191).

119. Iz poslednikh rossiiskikh publikatsii sm.: Poliakov, Iu. A., Zhiromskaia, V. B., Kiselev, I. N. Poveka mochaniia. -Vsesoiuznaia perepis'naseleniia 1937 g. Osnovnye itogi. M. 1992. S. 21; Osokina, E. A. Ierarkhiia potrebleniia. O zhizni liudei v usloviiakh stalinskogo snabzheniig. 1928-1935 gg. M. 1993. S. 57-60 (Among the most recent Russian publications, see: Iu A. Poliakov, V. B. Ziromskaia, I. N. Kiselev, *A Half-Century of Silence: An All-Union Population Census for 1937. Basic Conclusions,* [Moscow: 1992], 21; E. Osokin, *A Hierarchical Consumption. On the Life of the Population under the Conditions of Stalin's Supply, 1928, 1935* [Moscow: 1993], 57-60).

120. Otmetim naibolee interesnye I vazhnye publikatsii o golode 1932-1933 gg. v Rossii, na Ukraine I v Kazakhstane: Kul'chitskii, S. V. 1933: tragediia goloda. Kiiv. 1989; 33-I: Golod. Narodna kniga-memorial. Kiiv. 1991; Kolektivizatsiia I golod na Ukraini 1929-1933: Zbirnik dokumentiv I materialiv. Kiiv. 1992; Abylkhozhin, Zh., Tatimov M. "Kazakhstanskaia tragediia." -Voprosy istorii. 1989. N 8; Oskolkov, E. N. Golod 1932-1933. Khlebozagotovki I golod 1932-1933 goda v Severo-Kavkazskom krae. Rostov-na-Donu, 1991; on zeh, Tragediia "chernodosochnykh"stanits: dokumenty I fakty. Izvestiia vysshikh uchebnykh zavedenii. Severo-Kavkazskii region. 1993. N 1-2; Alekssenko, I. I. Repressii na Kubani I Severnom Kavkaze v 30-e gg. XX veka. Krasnodar. 1993; Kondarshin, V. V. Golod v Povolzh'e. 1932-1933 gg - Voprosy istorii, 1991, N 6 (We shall mention only the most interesting and important publications on the famine of 1932-1933 in Russia, Ukraine, and Kazakhstan: S.V. Kul'chitskii, *1933: The Tragedy of Famine* [Kiev: 1989]; *1933: Famine. A National Written-Memorial,* [Kiiv: 1991]; *Collectivization and Famine in Ukraine 1929-1933: A Collection of Documents and Materials* [Kiiv: 1992]; Zh. Abylkhozhin and M. Tatimov, "The Tragedy of Kazakhstan," *Questions of History*, no. 8 [1989]; E. N. Oskolkov, "The Famine of 1932-1933: State Grain Procuerments and Famine 1932-1933" in *Northern Caucasus Territory, Rostov-on-th-Don* [1991]; "The Tragedy of the 'Blacklisted' Cossack Villages: Documents and Facts," in *Proceedings of Higher Educational Institutions, Northern Caucases Region,* no. 1-2 [1993]; I. I. Alekseenko, *Repression in the Kuban and the Northern Caucases during the 30s of the Twentieth Century, Krasnodar* [1993]; V. V. Kondrashin, "Famine in the Volga Region 1932-1933," *Questions of History,* no. 6 [1991]).

121. Sm. Zeflenin, I. E. "Politotdely MTS (1933-1934)" -Istoricheskie zapiski. T. 76. 1965; on zhe. "Politotdely MTS - prodolzhenie politiki 'chrezvychaishchiny' (1933-1934) - Otechestvennaia istoriia. 1992. N 6 (See: I. E. Zelenin, "Political Departments of the Machinery Tractor Stations (1933-1934)," *Historical Notes* 76 [1965]; "Political Departments of the Machinery Tractor Stations - The Continuation of 'Extremism' [1933-1934]," *History of the Fatherland,* no. 6 [1992]; I. V. Stalin, Soch. T. 13. S. 229; I. V. Stalin, [*Works* 13], 229).

122. RTSKHIDNI. F. 558. Op. 1. D. 3109. Ll. 32-34.

123. I. E. Zelenin, Kollektivizatsiia I edinolichnik (1933 - pervaia polovina 1935 gg.). 1993. N 3. S. 40-41 (Collectivization and the Individual Peasant Farmer [from 1933 to the First Half of 1935, no. 3] [1933]: 40-41).

124. Translated by James Boissonault.

3

Bulgaria: From Cooperative Village to Agro-Industrial Complex, The Rise and Fall of Collective Agriculture

*Mieke Meurs, Veska Kouzhouharova,
and Rositsa Stoyanova*

Between 1945 and 1957, the population of Bulgarian smallholders was almost completely collectivized into cooperative farms.[1] The process went relatively quickly. The share of agricultural land in collective farms grew from 7 percent in 1948 to 51 percent in 1950 and 87 percent by 1957.[2] Despite the hurried reorganization, the cooperatives contributed to early increases in agricultural productivity. Output grew at an average rate of 3 percent per year from 1948 until 1959, when collectivization was "completed," and even faster over the first half of the 1960s.[3]

As will be seen in detail below, a number of factors contributed to this relatively smooth transition. First, Bulgarian agriculture in the prewar period was characterized by fragmented holdings, limited mechanization, and rural poverty. Land was relatively equally distributed in the prewar period, so expropriation of large landlords was no solution to the problems of small-holding. Instead, Bulgarian activists had long advocated cooperatives as a means of modernization. Cooperatives seemed particularly appropriate in Bulgarian villages, with their long tradition of common property and cooperative labor.

Second, the Bulgarian state had been extensively involved in agriculture from the early 1900s onward, supporting agricultural credit cooperatives, setting agricultural prices, and periodically requisitioning agricultural products. Rural producers acquiesced to state guidance of agricultural production.

Finally, during the early years of collectivization, the Bulgarian state provided substantial amounts of machinery and support to the capital-starved agricultural sector, quickly making collective agriculture a viable alternative to traditional peasant agriculture. Mechanization provided relief from some of the heaviest burdens of agricultural work, while at the same time the collective farms increased food security and gradually also increased social benefits.

The early state-promoted cooperatives or TKZSs (Trudova Kooperativna Zemedelska Stopanstva) were organized according to cooperative principles widely practiced in late nineteenth century Europe, including payment of rent to landholding members, direct member election and control of management through a general assembly, and payment through the distribution of farm production and profits. In the earliest period, many households, both rich and poor, voluntarily formed cooperatives, believing these to offer a solution to agrarian backwardness and poverty.

This is not to say that collectivization was without problems. As this chapter will show, especially in the late 1940s and early 1950s, state plans for collectivization outstripped the willingness of the rural population to collectivize their land. The principles of voluntary cooperation were cast aside and various forms of social and physical pressure were used to ensure high collectivization rates. In addition, a single "correct" model of cooperative agriculture was imposed everywhere, including those areas where collectivization of land and mechanization could offer few productivity advantages. Nonetheless, substantial amounts of collectivization were possible without the use of force, and productivity gains in many sectors far outstripped prewar rates.[4]

In the early 1960s, however, the Communist Party leaders imposed two additional changes on collective farmers. Multiple agricultural collectives were consolidated into larger units and brought under increasing state control. At the same time, state investment priorities shifted increasingly to the development of industry and share of investments directed to agriculture was substantially reduced. Planners increasingly squeezed agriculture to support the industrial sector.

The increasing size and central administration fundamentally changed the nature of the farms. Whereas early TKZSs had been based on the village, a traditional base for peasant identity and cooperation, the consolidated farms were increasingly dependent on, and controlled by, "others"—those above and beyond the village. In addition, the new structures explicitly undermined the cooperative principles of membership control and rewards based on farm performance that had, to a greater extent, characterized the earliest TKZSs.

Thus, state policy reduced the possibility of and incentives for local initiative just at the moment that the state also reduced its commitment to raising productivity through capital investment. Over the following two decades, many of the TKZSs deteriorated into neglected cash cows, milked by alienated villagers to support personal subsistence agriculture and to provide social welfare benefits, and milked by central authorities for cheap food and export earns.

Agricultural performance eventually suffered accordingly. Domestic consumption continued to grow through the 1980s, and agricultural exports continued to outpace imports, but agriculture's contribution to foreign exchange earnings fell significantly (by almost half) from 1980 to 1989.[5] Further, the domestic resource cost of these earnings rose quickly, as efficiency declined.[6]

To tell this story in detail, the chapter draws on a diverse set of sources. In addition to a range of official documents and secondary sources in English and Bulgarian, we draw on a 1992 survey of 600 villagers in 100 randomly selected villages, and on life history interviews from 3 additional villages, selected to represent Bulgaria's diverse geography—mountains (Hirevo), plains (Okorsh), and semi-urban (Momino). This combination of sources allows us to supplement the institutional and statistical analysis with insights from the population directly affected by the process.

Background to Collectivization

Smallholding Bulgarian Agriculture Prior to 1944

When the Turkish occupation was driven out of Bulgaria in 1878, after 500 years of Ottoman rule, Bulgarian citizens received land in relatively equal small holdings. By 1926, the majority of agricultural households still farmed under 5 ha. Farms of this size made up 57 percent of farms, but accounted for only 24 percent of agricultural land. Middle-sized farms with 5-30 ha comprised 43 percent of farms and 71 percent of the land. Large-scale agricultural operations with over 30 ha were rare.[7] Landlessness was also fairly rare: about 15 percent of households had so little land that members worked full time as agricultural laborers.[8] Between 1926 and 1946, fragmentation increased considerably and smallholding spread, with farms with under 5 ha rising to 69 percent of all farms.[9]

Most households did not own a contiguous 5 ha, however. Instead, in 1934, the average household had seventeen parcels of 0.4 ha.[10] Average plot size varied greatly by region, with larger plots prevailing in the plains regions (map 3.1). Some plots were as small as 40 square meters.[11]

The majority (three-fourths) of agricultural land was planted in wheat and maize in 1934, but the landholding structure undermined agricultural modernization.[12] The small, scattered plots made mechanization impossible, both because most smallholdings could not provide a surplus with which to finance mechanization, and because machines could not be used on the small, scattered plots. Most machines in use at the time were owned by farms having more than 10 ha, while the majority of households continued to use either a

Table 3.1 Distribution of Land Holdings, Bulgaria 1926

Size, ha	% Total Holdings	% Arable Land
To 1	11.9	1.0
1-5	45.1	22.6
5-10	28.0	34.5
10-20	12.6	29.3
20-40	2.2	9.7
over 40	0.2	2.9

Source: Liuben Berov, *Ikonomicheskoto Razvitie na Bulgaria Prez Vekovete*, (Sofia: Profizdat 1974).

traditional wooden or steel plow.[13] Fragmentation also complicated crop rotation, increased transportation costs, and wasted an estimated 50,000 ha of land in the construction of boundaries.[14]

Smallholding agriculture was supplemented by a system of common land, which accounted for 9 percent of agricultural land in 1932.[15] Village assemblies controlled the use of this land, regulating its use in annual meetings. Collective pasturing of private livestock on village land was common. Hay often was harvested from this land collectively, by villagers organized by the elected village council. Harvesting of village-owned forest resources often was also done through a system of collective labor.[16]

During the years 1921-1944, the state passed several laws to promote consolidation of private land into larger plots.[17] Results were limited, however. In 1944, only 8 percent of arable land was consolidated.[18]

The state also tried to promote agricultural modernization through subsidized credit. In 1920, the state-run Bulgarian Agricultural Bank offered special credits for the import of agricultural equipment. While equipment imports grew, agricultural surveys carried out in 1926 and 1934 show continued low levels of modernization: one metal plow for every three holdings, fewer than one tractor-pulled plow for every 500 holdings.[19] Productivity remained low. Cereal output per capita from 1928 to 1932 remained below that of other East Central European countries, with the possible exception of Yugoslavia.[20]

Under these conditions, most households worked their land for subsistence. While land was bought, sold, and rented, and labor was hired, households mainly farmed their own land with their own labor. Richer households farmed their land and perhaps a bit more with the help of some hired labor, while poorer households farmed their own small plots, then hired out surplus family labor to supplement household income. In a 1992 survey, only 5 percent of households recalled that the family had hired labor in before the war, while another 13 percent recalled hiring labor out. Only 1 percent recalled hiring in

Map 3.1 Bulgarian Okrugs

land, while another 1 percent hired land out.[21] A small number of farmers practiced intensive farming for urban markets and Gerald Creed emphasizes that conditions for market production probably improved somewhat during the late 1930s. But most production for market was ancillary to subsistence.[22]

Despite the low level of mechanization and the resultant labor-intensive forms of cultivation, Bulgarian villages suffered from underemployment. Estimates for this period vary from 500,000 to 1 million underemployed workers (out of the same approximately 700,000 rural households).[23]

Cooperatives in Bulgarian Agricultural Development before 1944

This situation was fertile ground for the development of a rural cooperative movement, along the lines of those developing in Germany and Ireland in the late 1800s. Attempts to form agricultural cooperatives in Bulgaria actually dated from the turn of the century and built on the Bulgarian tradition of collective agricultural labor. Most of these early cooperatives lasted only a few years, however.[24]

After the turn of the century, politicians and state policy advisors moved to support credit cooperatives as a means of modernizing agriculture. The state-run Bulgarian Agricultural Bank, founded in 1903, and later the Bulgarian Central Cooperative Bank, founded in 1910, supported village-level credit cooperatives as a means of channeling funds into agriculture. Initially, excessively enthusiastic bank officials created problems by imposing cooperatives on unwilling villagers.[25] So great was the rush that half of all prewar cooperatives were formed in the two years between 1907 and 1908.[26]

Many political parties worked to broaden villagers' acceptance of cooperatives. One of the most important of these was the Bulgarian Agrarian National Union (BANU). Formed in 1890, BANU initially fought against taxation of the peasantry to cover growing state budget deficits. Led by agrarian populist Alexander Stamboliiski in the second decade of the nineteenth century, BANU supported a vision of smallholders joined in cooperatives based on the German Raiffeisen model.[27] BANU built such a strong following that the (peasants!) party governed the country from 1919 until Stamboliiski was tortured and assassinated in 1923. Under this government, agricultural credit cooperatives continued to expand.[28] The Bulgarian Workers' Party (BWP, precursor to the Bulgarian Communist Party) was also involved in promoting the early cooperative movement, especially after World War I. In the 1920s, the BWP formed its own cooperatives as alternatives to those supported by the state, eventually attracting 68,000 members.[29]

These various political forces often struggled for control of the cooperative movement. After the coup ended the BANU government in June 1923, the new government continued to support the expansion of credit cooperatives as a means of modernizing agriculture, but outlawed cooperative organizations supported by BANU. After the fascist coup of May 1934, Bulgarian

Agricultural Bank was mandated to impose strict control over cooperative activities, overruling decisions of cooperative general assemblies and excluding people viewed as dangerous from the executive bodies of the cooperatives. The communist cooperatives were liquidated.[30]

Despite the struggles for control of the movement, it continued to grow in the 1920s and 1930s. By 1939, the cooperative network consisted of 3,502 cooperatives with 955,805 members (both individual members and member cooperatives)—servicing about three-fifths of the families in Bulgaria.[31] The majority of individual cooperative members (over 90 percent) worked in agriculture, and cooperative banks were especially popular among smallholders. Some 36,262 cooperative members (26 percent) had 2 ha or less of land and another 42,209 (31 percent) had 2-4 ha, 57,032 (42 percent) held 4-10 ha, while only 1,612 (1 percent) had over 10 ha. Rural intellectuals, including teachers, priests, and clerks, were also significantly represented among the members, sometimes working as bookkeepers or agronomists in the cooperatives.[32]

While production cooperatives were becoming more popular in the 1930s, the vast majority of cooperatives remained credit cooperatives. These did little to consolidate landholdings. Still, as loans to these cooperatives by the Bulgarian Agricultural Bank grew from 102 million leva in 1921 to 1,390 million leva in 1930, these cooperatives provided capital for modernization that could not be accumulated within the sector itself.[33] This capital supported the introduction of the first 1,500 tractor-plow complexes and the first 4,000 motorized cultivators.[34]

In the 1930s, the state expanded its involvement in the cooperative movement, using the cooperatives as agents for a state purchasing monopoly over the majority of agricultural products.[35] The state claimed that this monopoly was to be used to provide price supports to agricultural producers hit by the world economic downturn. The monopoly also served, however, to centralize export earnings in the hands of the state.

Collectivization of Bulgarian Agriculture: 1944-1958

1944-1949: Beginnings

At the end of World War II, the coalition government inherited an agricultural sector that remained among the least developed in Europe and an economy leveled by the war.[36] The modernization of agriculture and the use of agricultural surplus to promote industrialization were important government priorities.

While the coalition government was heavily influenced by the pro-Soviet BWP, it also included important representation from BANU, on the basis of the party's prewar strength. G. M. Dimitrov, an ardent supporter of Stamboliiski, returned from exile to lead the agrarian party it a struggle to reestablish a peasant government. BANU continued to play an important role after the elections of 1946 (in this election, two BANU factions together received 22 percent of the vote).[37] Both the Soviet and Stamboliiski models of agricultural modernization probably figured in early support for collective forms of agriculture as a means of modernizing agriculture.

Clearly, agricultural modernization was not the only goal driving collectivization after 1944. Joan Sokolovsky argues that in Bulgaria, the need to pacify the activist peasantry was the most important motive for collectivization.[38] Certainly, as is seen below, the strength of BANU as a political alternative to the Communist Party was an important factor in agricultural policy after 1947. Sokolovsky's study of Bulgaria is not detailed, however, and our reading of both primary and secondary sources suggests that the goals of modernization and industrialization, combined with those of replicating the Soviet experience as closely as possible and the feasibility of collectivization, had greater direct impact on agricultural policy.[39] Creed also emphasizes the complex interaction of economic and political factors in driving collectivization.[40]

Whatever were the government goals, an immediate elimination of private ownership of land (following the Soviet model) would have been politically untenable. It would not have been supported by the majority of government parties, nor would it have found support among the pro-cooperative, peasant BANU members. Large landholders were few, and little animosity existed between the richer and poorer peasants. As Todorka, from the village of Okorsh recalled, "[The rich peasants] were rich in land . . . but I don't think they were living better than us."[41] Most of the peasants cultivated their own land, to which they were strongly attached. [42]

Given the food shortages caused by World War II, the government could ill afford a confrontation with agricultural producers. In the September 1944 Program of the Fatherland Front, the government instead sought to build on the legitimacy of the existing cooperative movement and BANU's long-standing vision of cooperative agriculture to encourage initial steps toward collective production on private holdings. The government promised credits, tax breaks, and increased supplies of tools and machinery to agricultural production cooperatives formed under the auspices of existing cooperative organizations.[43] In November, the Bulgarian Workers Party emphasized that cooperatives should be formed according to the cooperative principles of voluntary membership and independence for the cooperatives.[44]

In 1945, the state moved to further encourage collective agriculture. A model charter was written for a new, state-supported form of agricultural production cooperative—the labor collective farm or TKZS. The charter laid out some principles of organization: members would retain ownership of their land, including the right to sell it and to receive rent on pooled land from the TKZS, although rent was limited by the charter to 20-40 percent of distributed income.[45] The rest of net farm income was to be distributed according to labor contribution. For example, ten to fifteen labor units would be awarded for a single day of the more difficult activities, while two to three labor units per day would be awarded for work tending livestock, and one unit for basic field labor. All the TKZS work was to be done by the members themselves, with the exception of the provision of services by veterinarians, economists, accountants, and agronomists.[46] TKZS members would be permitted to keep small plots of 0.2-0.5 ha and a few animals for personal use (lichno pomoshtno stopanstvo—LPS).

Under the model charter, farm management was to be elected by, and responsive to, the general assembly of cooperative members. Because farms mainly collectivized the land of only one village, their organization paralleled traditional village institutions—commonly held land and (occasional) collective agricultural labor under the management of the village assembly and elected village leadership.

Benefits extended to the charter cooperatives included complete tax relief for cooperatives and their members for three years, extensive credit for mechanization, and a 50 percent reduction in land prices for land purchased from the state.[47] Relative to other sectors of the economy, however, the magnitude of state support was quite limited. Only 6 percent of investment planned for the period 1946-1948 was targeted to agriculture, which employed approximately 70 percent of the labor force.[48] State-controlled agricultural prices also remained low, preventing accumulation within agriculture itself.

In this initial period, cooperatives were not required to adhere to the model charter. Often, cooperatives were organized independently and without state support. Even for farms organizing under the official charter and applying for state support, the state's capacity for ensuring adherence to charter rules was very limited. In practice, the new cooperatives were under the control of local leaders and members. Organization and the distribution of income varied, and members often joined without knowing how things would be organized. Cooperatives formed and dissolved more or less freely, in response to local conditions.[49]

While promoting the formation of agricultural production cooperatives, the government also expanded private property in land through the Law on Work-Based Land Ownership—a land-reform law based on the principle of "land to the tiller."[50] This law limited privately owned land to 30 ha in the Dobrudja plains and 20 ha in the rest of the country. People who did not work the land were limited to 5 ha in the plains, 3 ha in other areas. Land above these limits was nationalized, and the owners reimbursed according to rates established by the state.[51]

Nationalized land was distributed among the land-poor peasants or given to the cooperatives free of charge.[52] Households with less than 8 ha in Dobrudja and less than 5 ha in the rest of the country could receive land, with priority given to households belonging to agricultural production cooperatives.

This law enjoyed broad popular support, in part because of the very small number of large landholders in Bulgaria. Even though the Bulgarian government's limit on private land ownership was lower than in other East European countries initiating similar reforms, nationalized land comprised only 7 percent of arable land in Bulgaria, compared to 35 percent in Hungary, 25 percent in Poland, 14 percent in Romania, and 38 percent in Czechoslovakia.[53]

The same reasons that made it popular also made the law ineffective in addressing the problem of smallholding. Land taken under this law amounted to 295,497 ha. Under other laws, the state acquired an additional 284,252 ha, for a total of 579,449 ha.[54] About 129,000 land-poor households received 127,604 ha., in plots averaging 1 ha.[55] More land was distributed in the relatively land-rich, grain-growing districts such as Silistra, Vratsa, and Yambol, than in land-poor mountainous and semimountainous areas such as Veliko Turnovo, Vidin, or Gabrovo.[56] In locales where expropriated land was insufficient to provide households with a minimum plot, TKZSs were formed and recipients received land in common.[57] TKZSs received 135,538 ha., while another 192,000 went to state farms and other state organizations. The remaining land was rented to producers by the state.[58] Of the over 450,000 households eligible to receive land based on 1934 landholding data, only 29 percent received individual plots.[59] Even if all nationalized land had been distributed directly to households, the reform could not have satisfied peasants' needs for land. There were nearly 120,000 households with under 1 ha of land. These would have required at least 4 ha to reach the legal minimum for a viable plot, and this would have more than exhausted the land fund, without providing anything to those with at least 1 ha but less than the established minimum of 5 ha.

The preference given to TKZS members in the distribution of land did encourage the expansion of collective farms. Additional pressure was exerted through a system of "exchange" used to consolidate the TKZS land. Under this system, nonjoiners with land close to the TKZS were forced to trade their land for lower fertility or distant land in order to consolidate TKZS holdings.[60] Compulsory deliveries of agricultural production, in place since the beginning of World War II, were raised for private farmers, and private farming households were given low priority in the receipt of rationed goods.

In this period, however, the government mainly relied on the mobilization of party members and the use of propaganda to support voluntary collectivization. In Zamfirovo, farm founders chastised the local party organization for failing to pressure its own members into joining.[61]

Collectivization proceeded slowly. By 1948, only 7 percent of agricultural land had been incorporated into TKZSs. Predictably, many early joiners were politically motivated: a 1945 survey found that 55 percent of cooperative members were members of the BWP, while another 12 percent were members of the BANU.[62] As had been the case in prewar cooperatives, village intellectuals were also among the first members. Life history informant Petko, in Momino, recalled that the TKZS was founded by the village teacher. In Hirevo, too, Vassil noted that the teacher played an important role, alongside members of the two political parties.[63]

Dwarfholders and landless households also joined in large numbers during this voluntary phase of collectivization. About half of those joining in 1947 contributed 0.2-0.5 ha.[64] Since households, as opposed to individuals, joined, women were incorporated at approximately equal rates to men.

Survey data and life histories indicate that some of the better-endowed households also joined in this period, however. Maria's household in Momino, which she describes as one of the wealthiest households in the village, was among the first to join the TKZS in 1945. Maria's father saw the cooperative as a rational response to the fragmentation of land and a means of promoting agricultural growth.[65] In the Mikhailovgrad village of Zamfirovo, the average contribution of founding members in 1947 was 3.2 ha, well above the average village holding.[66] Nationally, about 10 percent of households joining in 1947 contributed viable plots of 5-8 ha.[67] In addition, about 17 percent of households joining by 1948 contributed a tractor, well over the 1 percent of total households owning one.[68] This is related to the fact that collectivization started earlier in the grain-growing regions, where plot sizes were larger, households wealthier, and mechanization greater.

Still, the inclusion of large numbers of (usually landless) intellectuals and land-poor peasants reduced land available per cooperative household from 4.3 ha in 1945 to 2.3 ha in 1948 (see table 3.3), despite state contributions of land to the TKZSs.[69] Ivan Ganev, Director of State Property, noted that "the end result was that the viable private structures were destroyed to build new sovhozs and kolhozs based on membership with no land property whatsoever."[70] In these early postwar years, little capital was available for mechanization either. Collectivization initially produced "hundreds of over-extended estates worked by slow-moving buffalo."[71]

The poor conditions were exacerbated by the continuation of wartime price controls and delivery quotas. The work-point system did little to stimulate work effort of cooperative members when there was little or no surplus to distribute. Cooperatives instead had incentives to produce and hoard subsistence crops. The private sector faced the same situation and responded by slaughtering livestock.[72] Output fell, as did village incomes. At least 85 percent of one collectivizing village were reported to be "poor and needy," and peasants reverted to homespun products after enjoying mainly ready-to-wear clothing in the 1930s.[73]

By December 1947 the peace treaty had been signed. With this diplomatic task completed, the Bulgarian Communist Party (BCP—the renamed BWP) felt free enough from international pressure to push through a new national constitution, institutionalizing its leading role. Dimitrov, the Stamboliiski supporter and BANU leader, had already given up his efforts to form a peasant-led government. Nikolai Petkov, the new leader of BANU, was jailed and then executed on charges of conspiracy in a parallel of the anti-peasant political movements of the 1920s.

The efforts of the Communist Party to consolidate power both permitted a more forceful attack on the private sector and made it desirable, as a means of consolidating power. Private industry, banking, and mining were nationalized. Private trade, including trade of above-quota agricultural produce, was restricted. State organizations expanded to replace these, and state influence over purchasing cooperatives increased.

A year later, the Fifth Congress of the Communist Party turned its attention to agriculture. Performance in this sector was clearly a problem: collective farms were inadequately capitalized and private producers disgruntled. Further, BANU factions now outside the BCP government constituted a potentially significant political force. Collectivization of larger landholders might offer a solution to both problems. The party set itself two goals: to increase collective farms' holdings of arable land tenfold and, by raising productivity, to raise their share of agricultural production from 2.2 percent to 62.5 percent by 1953.[74] To support this goal, the government allocated 13 percent of planned national investment to agriculture in second five-year plan.

Pressure on larger landholders was increased. A 1948 law began the squeeze by mandating the sale of all large private agricultural machines to the state. The law was accompanied by a "campaign against the kulaks," intensifying demands on, and scrutiny of, those peasants holding more than 10 ha. Increasing quotas for sale to the state (at low, state-set prices) left little surplus for private sale and greatly reduced private agricultural incomes. Those not meeting their required sales to the state or found hiding goods on which the state had claims were jailed and their land was confiscated.[75]

As noted above, most of the larger farmers could not be considered "kulaks" in the Russian sense of moneylenders and exploiters of others' labor. Mainly, they were simply larger smallholders, who worked their own land with help. Nor could they provide the much-needed land to the new cooperatives: after the 1946 land reform, those holding over 10 ha constituted only about 6 percent of farming households and were concentrated in the Dobrudja.[76]

Further efforts were thus needed to provide land to the TKZSs, and the anti-kulak campaign was quickly extended to holders of 4-5 ha (below what had previously been considered a minimum viable plot). Households with between 3-5 ha made up 24 percent of total households and held 39 percent of agricultural land, and collectivization moved ahead. As another means of increasing cooperative holdings, TKZSs also annexed village common lands, reducing private farmers' access to grazing land. By 1949, there were 1,601 TKZSs, incorporating 13.6 percent of arable land. These were small, with an average of 346 ha and 97 members, but land per cooperative household rose slightly, to 3.6 ha.

During this period, "agitation" was intense. In the Mikhailovgrad region alone, 6,000 peasant households were personally visited two to three times. In the region of Vratsa, the number of party functionaires was doubled, to 2,300, to carry out the task.[77] Nedalka in Momino recalled: "[The communists] were not

Table 3.2 Investment in Collective Agriculture

Period	Share Total Investment (%)
1946-1948	6
First Five-Year Plan	13
Second Five-Year Plan	18
Third Five-Year Plan	27
Fourth Five-Year Plan	21
Fifth Five-Year Plan	16
Sixth Five-Year Plan	15
Seventh Five-Year Plan	13
Eighth Five-Year Plan	8

Source: Richard Crampton, *A Short Story of Modern Bulgaria* (Cambridge, Mass.: Cambridge University Press, 1987). TsSU (Tsentralno Statisticheski Upravlenie), *Statisticheski Godishnik na NR Bulgaria* (Sofia: 1988): 130.

so many, but . . . [t]hey were visiting day and night those who were reluctant about the TKZS."[78] Persuasion often shaded into pressure, raising resentment among the peasant population. The BCP, faced with growing hostility to the collective farms, made some attempts at appeasement. In July 1949, for example, the BCP formed eighty-nine regional committees to audit 1,264 (83 percent of all) TKZSs for illegal pressuring of peasants. They investigated 61,854 personal complaints, and decided over half (35,311) in favor of the plaintiffs. The committees criticized many cases of unjust treatment of private landowners, including extradition, property confiscation, and physical violence.[79] TKZS members who had joined under pressure were permitted to leave, and nonmembers who complained of unjust land "exchanges" received additional compensation. In 1949, with output falling to 85 percent of 1939 levels and political costs rising, the Ministry of Agriculture called a halt to the creation of additional cooperatives.[80]

1950-1954: Increasing State Pressure

The year 1950 marked a renewal of the collectivization campaign. The state again increased pressures on the private sector. The progressive requisitions were based on the amount of land privately owned, ranging from 5 percent of the harvest for 0.7-1 ha. of private land to 87 percent for over 20 ha.[81] Requisitions were also broadened to include a wide range of products, many of which were not produced in all regions. In the face of falling output, discriminatory rationing policies also began to weigh heavily on private producers.

Table 3.3 Process of Collectivization in Bulgaria

Year	Number of Cooperatives	Land in Cooperatives	% of Arable Land	Collectiv- ized House- holds per Cooperative	Land per Household
1945	382	1,466	3.1	34	4.3
1948	1,100	2,924	7.2	124	2.4
1949	1,601	5,543	13.6	156	3.6
1950	2,501	21,563	51.1	502	4.3
1951	2,739	25,704	56.4	582	4.4
1952	2,747	25,125	60.5	553	4.5
1953	2,744	25,562	61.1	569	4.5
1954	2,723	25,472	61.3	569	4.5
1955	2,735	25,622	62.5	591	4.3
1956	3,100	34,614	77.4	911	3.8
1957	3,202	36,765	86.5	1,017	3.6
1958	3,290	41,576	93.2	1,244	3.3
1959	972	44,894	98.0	1,290	3.5

Sources: *Bulgarskoto Selsko Stopanstvo po Putya na Sotsializma* (Sofia: 1957): 3; Tsentralno Statisticheski Upravlenie, *Statisticheski Godishnik na NR Bulgaria* (Sofia: 1960): 161, 168.

While similar to wartime requisitions, the impact of the increased requisitions became more severe as the BCP consolidated state power and began to enforce payment in a way that prewar governments had not. Local officials kept close track of who killed pigs or owned cows, appearing to search for products when expected requisitions were not forthcoming.[82]

The measures generated real pressure on private farmers. Many farms were only marginally viable in any case: one estimate suggests that in 1949 only one private farm in three was capable of producing enough for household subsistence, much less a surplus for government taxes and requisitions.[83] And many of the larger and more potentially viable farmers, having lost their machines and equipment, also could not pay the tax. Producing a surplus for more lucrative private sale was almost impossible.

Households interviewed in both the grain region of Dobrudja (Okorsh) and the vegetable region of Plovdiv (Momino) reported that the quotas were among the main forces propelling peasants into the TKZSs. In Okorsh, Todorka recalled, "The rich that had a lot of land couldn't pay the state. They had crops, but we didn't raise many animals here and where could they get milk and wool to meet the quotas? . . . and that made the rich join the TKZS."[84] Other interviews reflect similar dynamics: "From our twenty-five pails of wheat, they took ten to fifteen for the state. We had to keep five to ten pails for seeds for the following year, which left us with five pails for our own use. Nothing!"[85]

Propaganda and social pressure were also intensified. In early 1950, the villages of the Mikhailovgrad region, for example, reported holding 600 meetings and demonstrations involving over 50,000 people.[86] Unfair land "exchanges" also continued, and in Turgovishte, where only 419 of 1,800 households had joined the TKZS, all private farmers were forced to move to new locations.

Some peasants certainly felt that pressure and intimidation crossed the line into violence. The extremely repressive political climate of the early 1950s, in which opponents (imagined or real) of the government were routinely sent to concentration camps and government leader Traicho Kostov was executed as a Titoist, further complicates efforts to distinguish encouragement from force. Georgi in the village of Okorsh remembered that his father was detained at the Village Council building, in which it was rumored that a bull was also being kept. Ilia, from Hirevo, remembered that his father "did not want to join up. . . . That was the reason for me to be laid off for three days from the factory. . . . I spent three days in the village, begging my father to join. Finally he agreed." He adds: "But no one was imprisoned or beaten."[87] Both life history interviews and historians suggest that direct physical violence was rare.[88]

More positive incentives were also offered in response to falling production and peasant hostility. Delivery quotas for collective farmers were reduced and member households were permitted to keep significantly more livestock for household use. More production was left for distribution to members according to work points, improving incentives for cooperative work. Investment budgeted to agriculture in the 1949-1952 five-year plan began to flow into the collective sector, and was increased in the third five-year plan (1953-1958) to 18 percent of total investment (see table 3.2). State-run Machine Tractor Stations (MTSs) were developed to provide mechanized services to the new cooperatives, with the number of stations increasing from 81 in 1950 to 149 in 1954.[89] State support also promoted an increase in chemical inputs. In 1954, fertilizer applications reached over 10 times 1939 levels (in tons), while pesticides reached 12.5 times the 1939 level.[90] These improvements would also increase the payoff to members' work efforts.

While providing additional support, the state also increased its control over the previously independent cooperatives. A Council of Ministers directive from January 20, 1950, decreed that TKZSs formed as independent cooperatives would be transferred to the jurisdiction of the Ministry of Agriculture.[91] To increase state influence over local management, cooperative farms were required to send a villager to attend a state-run courses in farm management. Villagers in Zamfirovo recall that, upon his return, this young man assumed the presidency of the village farm, replacing the local founder.[92]

A new model statute was issued for TKZS, which lowered the permissible rent payments from 40 percent to 30 percent of cooperative income. Share was reduced again in 1953, to 25 percent.[93] The 1950 model statute also reduced members' rights to ownership of a share of TKZS land. This share could no longer be freely transferred, but could only be given, sold, or bequeathed to another TKZS member or to the TKZS itself. When leaving the TKZS, a member could receive their share of land back, but they no longer had a claim on a particular plot.[94] These standards were now strictly enforced.

Peasants responded to the increased pressure in this period with over 2,000 new requests for investigation in fifty-seven villages. The investigating commission ruled that in nineteen villages, land should be given back to the owners and in the other villages corrections should be made.[95] As a result of these investigations, a second exodus from the TKZSs occurred between 1952 and 1954, particularly in the mountainous region of Blagoevgrad, resulting in declines in cooperatives' membership and landholdings (see table 3.3).[96] A significant number of households remained in the cooperatives, however, having already become accustomed to the new organization of production and distribution.

The orderly complaint process finally erupted into outright violent resistance in a number of places in the early 1950s. In 1950-1951, women in several mountainous villages northeast of Sofia revolted, and bloody repression was used by the armed forces. Other cases of crop burning, livestock slaughtering, and sabotage were also reported in the unofficial press.[97] In Teteven, even members of the communist youth organization joined in the plundering of the collective farm.[98] The violence was limited to isolated instances, however, and did not characterize the process generally, even in this period.[99] Peasant resistance more often took the age-old form of reducing production and slaughtering livestock that it had become uneconomical to keep.

In 1951, resistance died down. Many members of the Social Democratic Party and splits of BANU, who had been active in opposing collectivization, had been arrested, and the peasant holdouts had perhaps tired of resistance. As Vassil, from Hirevo, put it: "When they realized there was no other possibility, they just joined up."[100] Increasing levels of mechanization of TKZS production may also have helped convince reluctant peasants (see below), and those who could not be convinced could take advantage of new industrial jobs in the cities.

The number of TKZSs rose rapidly, from 1,601 in 1949 (14 percent of arable land) to 2,739 in 1951 (56 percent of arable land) and 2,723 in 1954 (61 percent of arable land). About 12 percent was in "private" plots (see table 3.3).[101] Landholdings per member recovered significantly during this period, to 4.5 ha in 1954 (see table 3.3).

Collectivization proceeded fastest in the grain regions, where mechanization offered real productivity advantages. In 1950, the grain-growing regions of the northern plains and Burgas had substantially higher levels of collectivization than the mountainous regions of Blagoevgrad, Sofia, and Haskovo, where potential for mechanization was limited. The fertile, peri-urban district of Plovdiv, where private production was particularly lucrative, also lagged (see map 1). By 1954, collectivization levels in grain districts ranged from 61 percent to 80 percent of arable land. In the mountainous regions, however, TKZSs controlled 16 percent to 40 percent of arable land (see table 3.3). On average in 1954, mountain zones had only 30 percent of arable land in TKZSs, about half the national level.[102] Collectivization of livestock production, which was concentrated in mountainous areas, was also difficult. About 22 percent of cattle and 28 percent of sheep were collectivized in 1953.[103]

1955-1958: The Final Push

Over the period 1955-1958, the Bulgarian government "completed" the collectivization process, bringing the remaining reluctant households, or at least their land, into the collective farms. To achieve this, both incentives and pressure were again used. The lagging mountainous regions were particularly targeted by incentive programs, receiving special incentives including the right to keep more livestock and take more land for individual self-sufficiency production.[104] Additional credits and tax breaks were also extended to these farms, and higher prices were offered for their products.[105]

Overall corrections in agricultural policy were also introduced at this time. Through the period 1950-1954, continuously falling agricultural prices had led to a withdrawal of land from production and a fall in the incomes of cooperative members. In 1955-1956, the prices of many agricultural products were increased, and the prices of chemicals, veterinary assistance, and services from the MTSs were reduced. New tax breaks were also given.[106]

In 1956, the government received a 300-million-leva credit from the Soviet Union (slightly more than the value of total Bulgarian exports that year) to help the TKZSs in the modernization process.[107] This contributed to a substantial increase in mechanization by 1957, with the number of MTSs rising to 200 and the ratio of tractors per 1,000 ha doubling between 1953-1957 to 3.6, ten times the 1939 level.[108] Other agricultural inputs also rose rapidly. By 1958, fertilizer applications more than doubled from 1954 levels, while pesticide applications increased 2.5 times.[109]

This mechanization substantially improved working conditions for peasants. In Momino, Guina described premechanization conditions as "this monster, threshing by hand . . . sun from above and you had to keep bent over and harvest these big fields, burning inside for a drop of water." She remembered the combine harvesters that arrived after 1956 as "a great achievement. We threw away the hand threshers!" Vassil in Hirevo echoed this sentiment: "It was a pleasure! The machine was harvesting while we watched."[110]

With the intensification of agriculture, the earnings of TKZS members began to rise relative to industrial wages. From 35 percent of industrial wages in 1956, average TKZS member earnings rose to 48 percent in 1957.[111] In 1957, the government also extended pensions to TKZS members, who previously had been excluded on the ground that their work was not "social" (the returns from it did not benefit society as a whole, but only members of the individual cooperative). Bulgaria was the first state in Eastern Europe to include peasants in state pensions.[112] At the same time, however, local control was further reduced, and the remaining rent payments to members were eliminated.[113]

For those not convinced by improving material conditions in the TKZS, however, political and economic pressure were again increased throughout the country. Every peasant who wished to join the BCP had to join the TKZS. Many people were excluded from the BCP for refusing to comply with this ruling—441 in the Plovdiv region alone. The only remaining (nominal) political alternative, a split of BANU, followed a similar policy, and by early 1957, 66 percent of all BANU members were TKZS members.[114]

A 1955 law once more increased the delivery quotas for private farmers. Many producers responded by refusing to cultivate their land, and it was promptly confiscated by the state. The violent outbreaks of the early 1950s were apparently not repeated, however. The remaining landholders either quietly joined the cooperatives or migrated to urban areas to take new, industrial jobs. This process became known as the "self-extinguishing of the kulaks."[115]

Between 1955 and 1956, the share of collectivized land rose to 77 percent. Collectivization rates in mountainous districts (except Blagoevgrad) increased significantly, although they still lagged far behind grain regions. Pressure on the lagging regions continued, however, and the process was nearly completed by 1958; 93 percent of arable land was collectivized.[116] Average landholdings per member fell with this incorporation of mountainous regions, however, to 3.3 ha (see table 3.3).

Initial Results of Collectivization

Despite the massive dislocations of this period, the agricultural sector recovered quite rapidly. The consolidation of landholdings and intensification of production, which the prewar government had been unable to achieve, paid off with rapid productivity increases.

Initially, as the private sector responded to low government prices and requisitions in the late 1940s, crop production fell and livestock were slaughtered, creating food shortages and even hunger (see table 3.5).[117] By 1953, however, increases in both mechanical and chemical inputs had raised crop and livestock output well above 1939 levels.

Table 3.4 Level of Cooperativization by *Okrug*

Okrug	1953		1954		1955		1956	
	# of TKZSs	% of Arable land	# of TKZSs	% of Arable land	# of TKZSs	% of Arable land	# of TKZSs	% of Arable land
Bulgaria	2,744	61.1	2,723	61.3	2,735	62.5	3,100	77.4
Blagoevgrad	53	15.9	53	16.6	56	16.6	76	19.9
Burgas	214	64.3	212	64.1	206	65.4	210	76.0
Varna	358	68.5	354	69.0	353	71.5	371	86.9
Vratsa	372	73.5	361	73.5	360	73.9	378	89.7
Shumen	240	61.9	238	60.6	239	60.9	275	81.4
Pleven	184	80.5	183	80.1	182	79.9	193	84.8
Plovdiv	235	56.6	235	57.7	233	61.3	266	77.7
Ruse	259	64.7	258	65.4	273	66.1	287	87.5
Sofia	257	31.1	256	31.1	256	31.1	415	52.3
Starazagora	320	61.1	321	61.0	320	63.9	332	91.3
Turnovo	121	52.3	121	52.1	123	53.6	136	56.8
Haskovo	131	40.1	131	40.4	134	39.7	161	50.6

Source: Bulgarskoto Selsko *Stopanstvo po Putya na Sotsializma* (Sofia: 1956): 54.

Total production grew at an average annual rate of 3 percent from 1948 to 1958, to reach 132 percent of its 1939 level by 1958 (see table 3.5). Labor productivity rose to 165 percent of its 1939, as the agricultural labor force fell by 467,000 people (16 percent). This resulted in an increase in *net* output of 2.5 percent per year from 1948 to 1958, so that net output reached 128 percent of 1939 levels.[118]

Yields rose more quickly in the easily mechanized grains than in the more labor-intensive crops, however. TKZS wheat yields rose from 13.8 tons per ha in 1939 to an average of 15.6 tons per ha (13 percent) from 1955 to 1958, corn yields rose from 13.7 tons to 16.4 tons (20 percent), and sunflower yields rose 20 percent. These crops accounted for over 90 percent of TKZS land. As grain production rose, so did livestock productivity: milk per cow and meat per head of livestock rose about 40 percent each. Some vegetable yields, for example in tomatoes, also rose by over 30 percent. But egg production remained constant, while yields in labor-intensive tobacco and fruit production fell, 96 percent for tobacco and 76 percent for plums.[119]

Productivity increases in the major crops translated into improved living standards for many rural producers. While agricultural wages remained relatively low, they rose with respect to industrial wages, reaching 60 percent by the mid-1950s.[120] More important from the perspective of the interviewees in our life history project, TKZS members received substantial in-kind payments. Oil and sugar, likely from central state sources, were distributed in all three villages examined. In addition, farms distributed a share of their own production: rice and flour in Momino, squash, peppers, tomatoes, and corn in Okorsh, beans, honey, cheese, and wool in the mountain village of Hirevo. Combined with the LPS plots, these allowed peasant households to do "well," in the words of Ilia in Hirevo, and to live "like kings," in the words of Marin from Okorsh.[121]

Unlike the cash earnings of cooperative members, which were highly dependent on state price policies, the in-kind payments were closely tied to the work of the relatively small group of villagers collectivized in the cooperative. As a result, they provided strong incentives for cooperative work.

The productivity increases in agriculture also led to improvements in the standard of living for the general population. By 1956, per capita consumption of sugar and meat had risen above the levels of the interwar period, doubling in the case of sugar, and rising 23 percent for meat. Bread consumption was nearly twice the level recommended by the United Nations.[122] At the same time, exports of foodstuffs made up 28 percent of exports for the period 1955-1957, generating the revenues needed for the import of machinery for industrialization.[123]

Second Stage of Collectivization Process: 1959-1967

Consolidation

With the collectivization completed in 1958, the number of TKZSs reached its peak of 3,290. These farms had an average of 1,264 ha of arable land and 378 member households. In 1959, the BCP began a consolidation of the TKZSs. In this process, multiple TKZSs were unified into one unit, the OTKZS (unified TKZS), with its center in one of the villages of the municipality. Farms were, in principle, to consolidate on a voluntary basis, but the process was pushed along quickly by local party functionaries. By 1960, the nearly 3,200 TKZSs were reduced to 932 units, averaging 4,266 ha of land and 1,736 permanent workers.[124]

The party offered economic arguments to justify the policy of consolidation. First, policymakers argued that they could achieve economies of scale through consolidation.[125] Second, they argued that the OTKZS would permit better use of scarce agricultural specialists, such as agronomists, veterinarians, and economists.[126] Some officials pointed to the locally initiated unification of small TKZSs in the grain regions of Varna, Vratsa, Pleven, and Tolbuhin in 1952 as evidence of the rationality of such a measure.[127] For central planners, the smaller number of agricultural units would also be easier to supervise.

Political and ideological considerations were also important in the decision to consolidate the collective farms. In the 1950s and 1960s, victory of the cooperative mode of production in the Bulgarian village was declared. While cooperatives were seen as a form of "socialism in a village setting," state ownership (ownership by the "whole people") continued to be regarded as a higher stage of socialism than ownership by a group of villagers. According to this analysis, the move from group to social ownership was a natural evolution. Consolidation into OTKZS was a first step in this direction, bringing ownership and control from the village to the municipal level.

Intensification of Production

Investment in agriculture continued to increase with the consolidation, peaking at 27 percent of national investment for the 1958-1960 plan, then falling back slightly to 21 percent for the period 1961-1965 (see table 3.2). As a result, the number of available tractors more than doubled from 1957 to 1965, reaching 61,723, while the number of available combines nearly tripled, to 11,984. By the mid-1960s, plowing, seeding, and harvesting were almost entirely mechanized.[128] Even so, the level of mechanization in Bulgaria remained two times lower than in the GDR and Czechoslovakia, and lower than in the less mechanized USSR, Poland, Hungary, and Romania.[129]

The consolidation of production was accompanied by an increased allocation of machinery directly to the OTKZSs (rather than to MTSs). The share of machines held directly by farms rose from under 1 percent to 60 percent, giving farms closer control of mechanized processes. These machines were also used to service the LPS plots of collective farm members, creating a symbiotic relationship between the two forms of production: farms provided mechanization to individual plots, while some production from the plots was used to fulfill the OTKZS's plan.[130]

Chemical intensification also continued to rise. Whereas annual applications of nitrogen and phosphorus climbed steadily from 3,400 and 10,000 tons, respectively, in 1948 to 53,000 and 24,000 tons in 1958, over the period 1960-1965 applications averaged 117,665 and 86,000 tons.[131]

Control and Incentives

On the new farms, the village-level TKZSs were brought under a common plan and leadership, but village-level organization did not disappear completely.

The old units retained independent accounting and governance structures, and their general assembly continued to make decisions about plan implementation and the organization of work at the village level. In principle, each TKZS continued to control its own assets and liabilities.

In practice, however, uniting the formerly independent TKZSs fundamentally changed the relationship between villagers and the production units. Whereas the TKZS had been coterminous with villages, the traditional bases of collective identity, organization, and labor, integration into the OTKZS meant being subsumed by a foreign organ, run by outsiders. The local farms had little choice about unification, and many found themselves suddenly forced to cooperate with groups with whom they had few traditional ties (and sometimes traditions of antagonism).

Some interviewees in the life history project believed that, as the planners had hoped, unification did have economic benefits—rationalizing the use of equipment and skilled labor. In the mountainous village of Hirevo, Ilia argued that "Sennick [the central village of the OTKZS] helped us a lot—with machines, with tractors." In Okorsh, the center of the local OTKZS, Maria noted that they were united with poorer TKZSs: "If we had not united with them, they would have failed totally."

The reactions of others, however, illustrate the level of distrust between residents of different villages. Many perceived unification as a means of redistributing resources to the central village of the OTKZS. Nikola in Hirevo recalled: "We went to work in the village of Sennick. They rarely came here to work." In Momino (not the center of the OTKZS), Guina felt that "the people of the neighboring village, like wolves, wanted to grab everything," and Nedyalka recalled: "We worked; they only sucked."[132] Production units were no longer populated only by fellow villagers against whom social pressures and networks might be used to limit shirking, and in far-flung and uneven agricultural labor, professional supervision was a poor substitute. Without a means to ensure just treatment by the "outsiders," many villagers felt themselves to be victims of free riding, and reduced their work effort in response.

To improve overall incentives for agricultural production, the state raised agricultural prices in 1958. Wheat prices, for example, rose from 5.5 to 12 leva per kilogram, corn prices doubled to 10 leva and beef prices increased from 38 to 50 leva.[133] In 1961 and 1962, substantial premiums were paid for animal products from mountain and semimountain areas.

These price increases, in turn, permitted greater accumulation at the farm level and allowed farms to offer additional benefits to worker-members. Retained earnings ("funds") available per member approximately tripled from 1958 to 1965, and these provided a number of collective benefits to the local population, including the extension of electrification and water supplies and the paving of roads.[134] Funds for compensation for job-related injuries or death were also formed from TKZS earnings, as was a "cultural" fund.

As members of a more social form of production, OTKZS members also became eligible for a greater share of state-funded benefits than TKZS members had been. A fund to cover minimum wage payments to members in case of poor farm performance was supported by the state, with the OTKZS contributing only 2 percent of total funds.[135] After 1962, the system of work points was replaced with a wage system, in which the state directly contributed a share of the wage fund, and monetary payments largely replaced payments in kind.[136]

These changes provided important improvements in economic security for the rural population. In addition, where state planning or pricing resulted in structurally unprofitable farms or in mountainous areas where productivity gains from collectivization were limited, this system allowed farm workers to be more fairly compensated. These changes brought a movement away from cooperative principles, however, and reduced labor incentives by further weakening the link between labor effort and rewards.

To address the growing incentive problems, the state supported the organization of the 2,000 worker farms into permanent production brigades. These sub-farm units were designed to recreate the smaller work groups of the TKZS, in which individuals might identify with production results and social pressures could be used to promote quality work. In the brigades, wage payments were to be linked to the brigades' final production. Members would receive 80-90 percent of expected earnings as a wage, with the rest to be paid at year end if production targets were fulfilled.[137]

The brigades proved a poor substitute for village organization, however. The measurement of production of a single agricultural brigade proved difficult (the quality of work of a single fertilizer-spreading brigade, for example, is hard to measure in final output), so that pay could not be readily tied to a brigade's share of plan fulfillment. If production did not cover even advances, which was not unusual given the state policy of low agricultural prices, state contributions covered the difference. In this case, no link between work effort and rewards was attempted. Even if pay were accurately linked to group work, brigade members were but a small part of a person's social base, reducing their ability to discipline a shirker.

Performance of the OTKZS

In the first half of the 1960s, agriculture grew rapidly, at 5 percent per year.[138] In part, this was due to continued intensification of agriculture. The combination of mechanization, the availability of industrial jobs, and dissatisfaction with collective farming resulted in the out-migration of another 790,000 workers (30 percent) between 1958 and 1965.[139] As labor was replaced by capital, labor productivity grew at an average annual rate of 8.3 percent and land productivity grew at 3.8 percent.[140] Despite the rapid increases in input intensity, net output also increased rapidly, at about 4 percent per year.[141]

During the early 1960s, agricultural growth was accompanied by continued improvements in the economic conditions of TKZS members. By 1965, member earnings had risen to 78 percent of industrial wages and, as noted above, TKZS benefits also increased significantly.[142] In addition, households benefited from LPS production. By 1965, LPS production had increased from 12 percent of total agricultural output in 1955 to 19 percent of production, and the production consumed and sold by households accounted for approximately 18 percent of rural household budgets.[143]

Food supplies to the general population continued to improve. Meat consumption per capita rose 48 percent from 1956 to 1965, consumption of milk and milk products rose 21 percent, and vegetable consumption rose 26 percent. The share of foodstuffs in exports rose from 28 percent in 1955-1957 to 38 percent in 1960 and 32 percent in 1965.[144]

By the late 1960s, however, agricultural growth began to slow. Additional freeing of labor from agriculture was limited by the uneven mechanization of agriculture and the seasonality of demand for agricultural labor. Grain production was completely mechanized, but in other crops plowing was mechanized while weeding and sometimes harvesting were done by hand, requiring a substantial amount of manual labor. Students and other volunteer labor brigades helped somewhat, but many permanent workers were also retained to provide seasonal labor. To reduce the underemployment of this labor, farms developed sideline enterprises, but these were developed with employment, and not productivity considerations, in mind, and did little to improve farm performance.

With continued high investment rates (22 percent of total investment 1963-1967) (see table 3.2), labor productivity continued to grow at an average of 4.5 percent per year from 1966 to 1970. Agricultural wages continued to rise relative to industrial wages, reaching 82 percent by 1969.[145] Average annual growth rates of gross output fell off dramatically, however, to 1.2 percent for 1966-1970.[146]

With slowing output growth and continuing growth in food exports to finance industrialization, overall living standards fell slightly as well: per capita consumption of bread, fruit, and vegetables fell between 5-10 percent, while consumption of rice and sugar products fell to a lesser extent. The share of foodstuffs in exports also fell, to 29 percent, although exports continued to grow in absolute terms.[147]

While investment rates remained high through the late 1960s, it appears that slowing growth rates resulted from the exhaustion of easy gains from technological "catching up." New growth would have to come through improved use of existing technology or from innovation. This shift from extensive to intensive growth came, however, just as the increasing state control reduced both labor incentives and the possibility of using local information to improve organizational efficiency.

From Collectives to State Farms: 1968-1989

Further Reorganization, Growing Distance

In response to slowing agricultural growth at the end of the 1960s, the state moved to further "industrialize" and "socialize" collective agriculture. All remaining pretenses of local control and independence were eliminated, as the collective farms were integrated into state-run Agro-Industrial Complexes (APKs). The completion of this process effectively ended the experiment with collective agriculture, replacing it with state agriculture. This period thus plays a much less important role in our analysis of collective agriculture. This section will mainly outline the nature of the changes involved in "statization" and their implication for agricultural performance.

The idea of merging the OTKZSs into larger farms controlled by the state was first floated in preparation for the 1967 Congress of TKZSs. Party officials argued that the mergers were a means of increasing agricultural productivity through the further realization of economies of scale. Closer state control would also justify increased state investment in the sector, since the investment would be made in property belonging to and controlled by the "whole people." The strategy was also in line with Communist Party attempts to eliminate the peasantry as a class, bringing agricultural producers into the (ideologically preferred) working class.

The idea met with opposition from within the BCP, however, and languished until the 1970 April plenary session of the Central Committee. At this meeting it was finally resolved that the 744 OTKZSs would be consolidated and merged with the 156 state farms to form state-run Agro-Industrial Complexes (APKs).[148] The process of horizontal integration would be accompanied by vertical integration, as specialization was intensified, processing units were established on certain farms, and farms were grouped under regional and then national agro-industrial unions.

Officially, mergers were to occur on the principle of voluntary participation. As had happened before, the principle of voluntary participation was quickly discarded in the interests of meeting party targets. From 1970 to 1971, the number of independent farms fell from 900 to 161. The fall continued to a low of 146 units in 1976, each managing an average of 24,300 ha and 5,836 workers. The last farms to be included in the APK system were those from mountainous and semimountainous areas, where the unified direction of scattered production units was particularly difficult. Over the following decade, the level of concentration was reduced somewhat, with the number of independent APKs rising back to 298 by 1985, each managing an average of 17,921 ha and 2,949 workers.[149]

As the agricultural units were brought under direct control by the state, the farms were permitted to retain additional shares of profit for farm use. As state workers, agricultural producers became eligible for state social security, and the old flat-rate pension of 60 leva for TKZS members (compared to an average TKZS income of 797 leva in 1965) was replaced by pensions based on years of employment (these averaged 288 leva per year in 1970, compared to an average agricultural income of 1,295 leva).[150] Maternity leave, child payments, and sick pay were also finally extended to female TKZS members.

While these changes further improved the living standards and economic security of the agricultural producers, they completed the transformation from cooperative to state farm that was begun in the 1950s. Farms were controlled by distant state planners and workers' incomes and benefits depended on state policies. Any remaining sense of local ownership of and responsibility for the farm was further eroded.

The wage and benefit reforms and partial enterprise self-financing were meant to motivate workers and managers. But the funds for cultural activities and other worker benefits that were based on APK profit depended on the combined earnings of the many individual TKZSs and other APK subunits (such as processing plants). With 3,000 workers, many of whose work was interdependent, poor performance was nearly impossible to trace to any particular group.

Even if responsibility could be established, performance-based pay was hard to justify. Planning and management problems led to input shortages and work disruptions, which often had a much greater impact on production results than did work effort. Specialization imposed by planners in the distant agro-industrial unions resulted in decreasing consideration of the specific geographical conditions and production capacities of individual production units. In some cases, profitable production branches were eliminated in the name of specialization, and productive traditions based on the practical knowledge of the TKZS members were ignored. In one famous case, a massive sugar complex was erected on swamp land. Production capacity far exceeded locally available input supplies, and the great Soviet trucks that were to bring in additional supplies sank in the swamp. The lack of inputs prevented the complex from ever running at capacity. Workers could not be held responsible for this.

Organizational problems were exacerbated by state investment policy. In 1974, Bulgarian economist Liuben Berov noted that, with investment in agriculture falling after 1960, "most of the machines in use at the beginning of the 6th 5-year plan (1971-1975) are already physically old, past their amortization dates." In 1970, 16 percent of the tractors had already been in use for ten to twelve years. Only 50 percent of the machines were in optimal condition (in the first five years of use).[151]

But the BCP controlled investment, and the party's priority remained industrial modernization. Agriculture's share of investment continued to fall—to 15.3 percent of planned investment for the sixth five-year plan, 13.3 percent in the seventh five-year plan, and 8 percent in the eighth (see table 3.2). By 1980, the share of tractors in use for over ten years reached 27 percent, rising to 35 percent by 1984.[152]

These problems were, of course, not new. The incentive problems had been developing since the 1950s, and state investment policy had been squeezing agriculture since the late 1960s. But as the management grew more distant, the investment squeeze intensified. And the distant management combined with exploding farm size to further limit the potential for using local information and initiative to coax more output out of given inputs.

Agricultural Performance under the APK

As might be expected, the further centralization of agricultural production and management failed to restore growth rates. Instead, average annual growth of gross output fell to 0.3 percent over the period 1971-1975. Growth rates then recovered slightly (to 2 percent) in the period 1976-1980. Labor productivity continued to grow by an average annual rate of 3.6% from 1971 to 1975 and 3.8 percent from 1976 to 1980, but this was well below the rate of 6.4 percent per year realized for the period 1960-1969.[153]

National consumption standards continued to improve, but this was largely due to continued increases in APK-aided LPS production. Per capita consumption of meat and meat products (of which over 40 percent came from LPS) nearly doubled from 1960 to 1979, while consumption of milk and milk products (about 25 percent from LPS) rose 82 percent. Animal products increased from 14 percent to 20 percent of total calorie intake.[154] But agriculture's contribution to exports stagnated and then fell in the mid-1980s, falling from an annual average of 2,390 million foreign exchange leva for 1979-1984 to 2,214 million for 1988-1989.

In his careful econometric study of Bulgarian agricultural growth, Michael Boyd found that the rapid technical change that had driven output and productivity improvements through the 1960s had ceased by the 1970s. The lack of technical change could not explain all of the growth slowdown, however. Boyd found that organizational (and perhaps motivational) problems associated with the large farms were also a significant factor in declining productivity and growth. Under the prevailing conditions, farms could not effectively use the inputs that were provided.[155]

Despite the declining growth rates of labor productivity, relative agricultural wages continued to rise. Agricultural wages rose to 112 percent of industrial wages by 1975, fell to 91 percent by 1980, and hovered around 90 percent through the 1980s.[156] Cooperative markets for private agricultural production were liberalized in this period, permitting additional sideline incomes for agricultural workers (about 6 percent of rural households reported selling on this market in 1986). LPS production accounted for over a third of total income for some 12 percent of rural households, and these were among the highest income households.[157] Combined with increased social benefits, this resulted in continued rapid increases in the standards of living among farm workers.

Despite the fact that under the APK agricultural workers were better off materially than previously, the APKs failed to win much support from old TKZS members. Todorka from Okorsh believed that "if they hadn't made the APK it would have been better. The more bosses there were, the more they stole." In Momino, Guina found that under the APK "things were not so good. There were many villages, many people. It was difficult to manage them." Vassil, from the mountain village of Hirevo, noted simply, "When the APK was formed, we totally failed."

Many people recalled the early cooperatives more favorably. Georgi in Okorsh and Petko in Momino reflected these sentiments. "It was best in the beginning when we were an independent TKZS, before the consolidation" and "We got rich after we joined the TKZS. We were helping each other." In Hirevo, Tota recalled the period of consolidated OTKZSs as "good times. After that we were too many," and her neighbor Vassil emphasized that higher wages were not everything. "Why did they unify us? The APK did not make things better! We were getting more money, I think, but not much more."[158]

Part of the reason that the cooperatives are remembered so favorably is that they coincided with the "easy" stage of economic growth, which resulted from mobilizing resources underutilized in Bulgarian smallholding agriculture and from providing the credit needed for agriculture to "catch up" technologically with industrialized countries. But the cooperatives also offered real advantages to producers compared to the APK, or even the OTKZS. In the small production units in which producers depended heavily on their own production for livelihood, the cooperatives linked rewards to work effort to a certain extent. Clearly, the link was never perfect, because the state influenced farm management, controlled prices, extracted significant taxes, and provided investment capital. But compared to the later situation, the cooperatives provided relatively strong incentives for hard work. Perhaps equally important, cooperative members knew that when a new barn was built or animal mortality was low, these achievements reflected on them. "Their farm" (that of their village) was a source of pride in a way that "the peoples' farm" never was.

Apparently, the central government came to the same conclusion as the producers. In the mid-1980s, the BCP again granted legal independence to the former TKZS. In practice, however, the established and powerful APK managers were not easily dislodged from their role in controlling local agricultural resources. At the time of collapse of BCP state in 1989, the return to cooperative agriculture in Bulgaria had made little progress.

Conclusion

As this chapter has shown, the nature of collectivized agriculture in Bulgarian changed significantly over the nearly five decades of communist power. As a result, no simple description or evaluation of this experience is possible.

Certainly, a number of characteristics of prewar Bulgarian agriculture contributed to a relatively smooth collectivization of producers and land into cooperatives. These included the small and decreasing size of most plots, the resulting difficulties in modernization of private farming, the tradition of collective village labor, and the existence of a strong, long-lived peasant movement that supported cooperatives as a strategy of rural development. When state support for agricultural production cooperatives was increased after 1945, a significant number of rural households voluntarily collectivized their land, especially in the flat, grain-growing regions where mechanization offered real productive advantages.

As pro-Soviet factions of the Communist Party gained strength in the mid-1950s, and as the party enforced a political monopoly, support for a range of forms of cooperative production was replaced by the imposition of a single "correct" form of collective agriculture, based on the Soviet model. The imposition of this model on all producers resulted in its use in regions where collectivization could offer few productivity advantages. Populations in these areas resisted especially strongly, and political, and in some places, physical, repression resulted.

Dissatisfaction with the model was far from universal among the peasant population, however, and collective agriculture produced some substantial successes in this first period. State-supported investment in the mechanization and intensification of agriculture paid off with very rapid increases in output and productivity. At the same time, the cooperatives facilitated mechanization and risk sharing, and greatly improved the working and living conditions of rural households.

Beginning in the 1950s, however, the cooperative nature of the TKZS began to be eroded. Agricultural prices were kept low by the state, to provide cheap food to workers and promote industrialization. As in the prewar period, this prevented accumulation of resources at the farm level. While the socialist state was willing to provide capital for agricultural modernization, the use of state resources justified increasing state guidance of production through the system of central planning. Local control of production was reduced. In addition, with central planning dictating product mix and prices to farms, it became increasingly difficult to justify a tight link between members' incomes and farm "profit."

Still, in the 1950s, state intervention into farm management was relatively limited, and farm management remained centered in the village, accessible to villagers by location and by tradition. Where the link between pay and work was reduced by state intervention, shirking might be mitigated by strong traditional institutions for monitoring collective labor and by mutual dependence on farm production to supplement households' food supplies.

From the 1960s onward, however, these mechanisms were also eroded. As the state followed ideological preferences for central control of production and the homogenization of the village population into a class of nationally identified workers, farm management was increasingly distanced from villagers, first to the municipal level and then beyond, to the APK. Production results came to depend on decisions made far from the village and on the work of others, over whom the villagers could exercise little influence. Pay was increasingly determined by state policy and payment in kind from farm produce was reduced. While villagers did not resist the measures overtly, the changes clearly reduced local initiative and concern for farm performance.

At the same time, the growth potential offered by technological "catching up" was exhausted, and state investments shifted increasingly to modernizing the industrial sector. Further growth would have to come from better use of existing resources. Long-standing attempts at reform in socialist agriculture suggest that this would be impossible, however, without the use of locally available information and flexible adjustment to rapidly changing conditions in agriculture—both of which were precluded by the complete integration of the farms into the system of central planning. Unable to influence farm performance, frustrated local populations, including local farm managers, increasingly diverted collective farm resources to LPS production.

It is this phase of decline, along with the disturbing phase of forced collectivization, which has come to characterize the experience of collective agriculture in the minds of most observers. However, a more comprehensive evaluation suggests that the experience of collective agriculture can also yield some positive lessons.

The Bulgarian experience suggests that, at least under certain circumstances, rural households will see in the collectivization of agricultural production a rational strategy for overcoming impediments to rural development. Collectivization can facilitate combining resources and spreading risk when markets fail to play these roles. Where collectivization can facilitate the mechanization and intensification of agriculture, the collectivizing rural producers will be proved right—collectivization can yield important improvements in productivity and working conditions. Massive transfers from the state are not a precondition for this success. Bulgarian data show that the growth in productivity rapidly offsets the rising input costs.

While agricultural production cooperatives may be a successful development strategy in some instances, the Bulgarian case highlights a number of ways in which this strategy can be undermined—dangers not limited to the context of central planning under the control of a one-party state. In particular, the experience highlights the importance of maintaining cooperative principles of democratic control of management and dependence of member income on production results in maintaining the incentives producers. In addition, the experience highlights the importance of overall agricultural policy for cooperative viability. Excessive extraction of resources from the agricultural sector seriously undermined the viability of the Bulgarian collectives, even when the state offset the impact of this policy on agricultural incomes.

Clearly, the system of central planning and the one-party state contributed to both the extraction of resources from agriculture and the difficulties in creating effective incentive schemes in the farms. Central planners preferences for industry are well known, as is their preference for large enterprises, their inability to impose hard budget constraints on firms, and their fear of democratic control. These were part of the problem.

But other contexts can produce the same effects. Low, state-set agricultural prices and purchasing monopolies have also been common in developing economies that do not practice central planning, and the incentive impact is the same. When farm incomes must be supported through other means, incentives for cooperative work are weakened. Appeals to the scarcity of technically skilled management and to economies of scale are also not limited to central planners, and the Bulgarian case suggests that these appeals must be carefully examined.

Collectivization was not a simple solution to all the complex problems of agricultural development in Bulgaria. But neither was it a road to unqualified disaster. Rather, the policy offered poor producers a means of modernization and initially promoted rapid growth. In the face of increasing state control and extraction of resources from agriculture, however, collectivization went hand in hand with the decline of incentives, alienation of producers, and eventual severe agricultural stagnation.

Notes

1. State farms were also developed in Bulgaria, but these were never a significant part of socialist agriculture. In 1957, they numbered under 100 and accounted for only 3.5 percent of arable land. (See Tsentralno Statisticheski Upravlenie, 1961: 224).

2. Rositsa Stoyanova, "A Periodization of Bulgarian Collectivization: Prewar Background and Early Collectivization," Institute of History, Bulgarian Academy of Sciences (1992), 35.

3. Gregor Lazarcik, "Bulgarian Agricultural Production, Output, Expenses, Gross and Net Product and Productivity at 1968 Prices, 1939 and 1948 - 1970," Occasional Paper of the Research Project on National Income in East Central Europe, Economic Studies Riverside Research Institute (1973), 15, 53. Michael Boyd, *Organization, Performance and System Choice* (Boulder, Colo.: Westview, 1991), 86.

4. Whereas grain yields for the period 1926-1930 reached only 104 percent of the 1909-1912 average, crop production for the period 1954-1958 reached 120 percent of 1939 levels. By the period 1964-1968, they had reached 184 percent of 1939 levels. See B. Mateev, *Dvizhenieto za Kooperativno Zemedelie v Bulgaria pri Ysloviata na Kapitalizma* (Sofia: 1967), 18.

5. Mieke Meurs and Simeon Djankov, "The Alchemy of Reform: Bulgarian Agriculture in the 1980s," in *Privatizing the Land*, ed. Ivan Szelenyi (London: Routledge, 1998, forthcoming).

6. Boyd, *Organization, Performance.*

7. Note that the literature includes many different ways of categorizing middle and large producers. For estimates relying on other categorizations, see Liuben Berov, "Sotsialnata Struktura ha Seloto v Balkanskite Strani Pres Perioda Mezhdu Dvete

Svetovni Voiini," in *Trudove na Vishiya Ikonomicheski Institut Karl Marx* 4, (1977): 62–65 and A. Totev, "Suotoyanieto na Prenacelenost v Nasheto Zemedelsko Stopanstvo," in *Spisanieto na Bulgarskoto Ikonomichesko Dryzhestvo* 6 (1940): 370.

8. Richard Crampton, *A Short History of Modern Bulgaria* (Cambridge, Mass.: Cambridge University Press, 1987), 136. Statisticheskii Godishnik na Tsarstvo Bulgaria (Sofia: 1939), 181.

9. Berov, "Sotsialnata Struktura ha Seloto v Balkanskite Strani Pres Perioda Mezhdu Dvete Svetovni Voiini," 62-65.

10. Tsentralen Durzhaven Istorichieski Arhive (165/1/82): 4. Y. Mollov, *Problemi na Bulgarskoto Zemedelie* (Sofia: 1935), 514.

11. D. Toshev, *Razpredelenie i Komassatsiya na Zemite v Bulgaria* (Sofia: 1937), 22.

12. Statisticheskii Godishnik na Tsarstvo Bulgaria, 270.

13. On the basis of official statistical data, Mateev estimates that 165,000 producers, mainly those with less than 5 ha., have no machinery or plow. Most producers with less than 2 ha. had not even a good wooden plow; only 5 percent had a metal plow. Even those with 5-10 ha. lacked adequate equipment. See Mateev *Dvizhenieto za Kooperativno Zemedelie*, 18. Stopanska Istoria na Bulgaria 681 - 1981 (Sofia: 1981), 375.

14. Toshev, Razpredelenie i Komassatsiya, 19.

15. Rositsa Stoyanova, "Municipal Land in Bulgaria: Laws and Use from the End of the Nineteenth Century to 1944," typescript, Institute of History, Bulgarian Academy of Sciences (Sofia: 1993a). Statisticheskii Godishnik na Tsarstvo Bulgaria, 181.

16. Interviews, Life History Interviews on Municipal Land Use before 1944 (Institute of Sociology, Bulgarian Academy of Sciences, 1994).

17. Toshev, Razpredelenie i Komassatsiya.

18. Istoria na Bulgaria 1 (Sofia: 1969): 571-72.

19. Stopanska Istoria na Bulgaria 681 - 1981, 323. Statisticheskii Godishnik na Tsarstvo Bulgaria, 226-29.

20. Doreen Warriner, *Economics of Peasant Farming* (London: Frank Cass, 1964), 84.

21. Survey Data, International Comparative Study of Households in the Decollectivization, Institute of Sociology, Bulgarian Academy of Sciences (1992).

22. John Lampe, *The Bulgarian Economy in the Twentieth Century* (London: Croom Helm 1986), 56. Gerald Creed, *Domesticating Revolution: From Socialist Reform to Ambivalent Transition in a Bulgarian Village* (University Park, Pa.: Pennsylvania State University Press, 1997).

23. *Statisticheskii Godishnik na Tsarstvo Bulgaria*, 181.

24. Mateev, *Dvizhenieto za Kooperativno Zemedelie*, 18, 63-76.

25. A. Yanchulev, "Postizheniya i Buzmozhnosti na Kooperatsiite v Bulgaria," *Spisanie na Soyuza na Populyarnite Banki* 5 (1931): 11.

26. Stoyanova, (Sofia: 1993c), 8.

27. Lampe, *The Bulgarian Economy*, 29-30.

28. Rositsa Stoyanova (Sofia: 1993c), 16.

29. Rositsa Stoyanova (Sofia: 1993c), fn44.

30. Rositsa Stoyanova (Sofia: 1993c), 19ff.

31. Richard Crampton, *A Short History of Modern Bulgaria* (Cambridge, Mass.: Cambridge University Press, 1987), 138.

32. Tsentralen Durzhaven Istorichieski Arhive (165/1/82): 20. Tsentralen Durzhaven Istorichieski Arhive (288/4/7580): 36.

33. D. Nachev, "Nasochvane i Kontrol na Kooperativno Dvizhenie," *Kooperativno Delo* 1 (1937): 1-5.

34. A. Yanchulev, "Postizheniya i Buzmozhnosti na Kooperatsiite v Bulgaria," *Spisanie na Soyuza na Populyarnite Banki* 5 (1931): 225.

35. Lampe, *The Bulgarian Economy*, 82.

36. *100 Godini na Bulgarska Istoria* (Sofia: 1978), 119. *Istoria na Bulgaria* 1, 572. *Stopanska Istoria na Bulgaria* 681 - 1981, 374-75.

37. After Stamboliiski was murdered in the coup of 1923, the various factions of the party split, presenting at least two candidates in each subsequent election. Election Statistics, Election Statistics for Peoples' Representatives to the Great National Assembly (Sofia: 1946).

38. Joan Sokolovsky, *Peasants and Power: State Autonomy and the Collectivization of Agriculture in Eastern Europe* (Boulder, Colo.: Westview Press, 1990).

39. Teodor Shanin, *Peasants and Peasant Societies: Selected Readings* (Harmonsworth, U.K.: Penguin, 1971)

40. Creed, *Domesticating Revolution.*

41. Interviews, Life History Interviews on Collectivization (Institute of Sociology, Bulgarian Academy of Sciences, 1992).

42. B. Mateev, "Osnovni Cherti v Razvitieto na Sotsialicheskoto Selko Stopanstvo v Bulgaria" in *V Chest na Akademik Hristo Hristov* (Sofia: 1976), 465. *100 Godini na Bulgarska Istoria*, 134.

43. Ustanoviyavane i Ukrepvane ha Narodnodemokratichnata Vlast (Septembri 1944-Mai 1945), *Subronik Dokumenti* (Sofia: 1969).

44. Zl. Zlatev, "Stopanska politika na Narodnodemokratichnata Vlast," in *V Chest na Akademik Hristo Hristov* (Sofia: 1976), 442.

45. Durzhaven Vesnik (Sofia: 1945), 95.

46. B. D. Jones and A. Jankoff, "Agriculture" in *Bulgaria*, ed. L. A. D. Dellin (New York: Praeger, 1957), 293. Interviews, Life History Interviews on Collectivization.

47. M. Trifanova, "Sotsialichesko Preystroiistvo i Razvitie na Selskoto Stopanstvo v Bulgaria," in *Sotsialicheskata Revoliutsiya v Bulgaria* (Sofia: 1965), 419. Durzhaven Vesnik (Sofia: 1945), 95. Ustanoviyavane i Ukrepvane ha Narodnodemokratichnata Vlast (Septembri 1944-Mai 1945), *Subronik Dokumenti* (Sofia: 1969), 300.

48. Crampton, *A Short History.*

49. Interviews, Life History Interviews on Collectivization.

50. Durzhaven Vesnik (Sofia: 1946), 81.

51. Land owners were compensated at 10-50 percent below the market value of the land, depending on its quantity. Only 1 ha was paid for in cash. The rest was paid with bonds at 3 percent interest for fifteen years. After 1949, land payments were discontinued. See Istoria na Bulgaria II (Sofia: 1969): 249.

52. Durzhaven Vesnik (Sofia: 1952), 29.

53. *Istoria na Bulgaria II*, 252. *100 Godini na Bulgarska Istoria*, 135, 249.

54. *Istoria na Bulgaria* II, 250, 252.

55. Lampe, *The Bulgarian Economy*, 125.

56. Survey Data, International Comparative Study of Households in the Decollectivization, Institute of Sociology, Bulgarian Academy of Sciences (1992).

57. Jones and Jankoff, "Agriculture," 292.

58. *Istoria na Bulgaria* II, 248.

59. There was no new national census before 1946. However, this figure is more likely to underestimate the number of households needing land, as fragmentation was proceeding rapidly over this period. *Statisticheskii Godishnik na Tsarstvo Bulgaria*, 181.

60. Ivan Ganev, *Agrarnata Reforma v Chyzhbina i u Nas* (Sofia: 1946), 208-09.

61. Creed, *Domesticating Revolution*, 87.

62. *Istoria na Bulgaria* II, 314.

63. Interviews, Life History Interviews on Collectivization.

64. Jones and Jankoff, "Agriculture," 295.

65. Interviews, Life History Interviews on Collectivization.

66. Creed, *Domesticating Revolution*, 89.

67. Jones and Jankoff, "Agriculture," 295.

68. Tsentralno Statisticheski Upravlenie, *Statisticheski Godishnik na NR Bulgaria* (Sofia: 1968). Edmund Stillman, "The Collectivization of Bulgarian Agriculture" in *The Collectivization of Agriculture in Eastern Europe*, ed. Irwin Sanders (Lexington, Ky.: University of Kentucky Press, 1958). Survey Data, International Comparative Study of Households in the Decollectivization.

69. Note, however, that this is still more land per worker than the 0.86 ha estimated to have been available in household production in the prewar period. See Totev "Suotoyanieto na Prenacelenost v Nasheto Zemedelsko Stopanstvo," PN.

70. Ganev, *Agrarnata Reforma,* preface.

71. Stillman, "The Collectivization of Bulgarian Agriculture," 85.

72. Lampe, *The Bulgarian Economy*, 125-26.

73. Creed, *Domesticating Revolution*, 81.

74. Bulgarska Komunicheski Partii, BKP v Resoliutsii i Reshenie IV (Sofia: 1957): 152.

75. Interviews, Life History Interviews on Collectivization.

76. Berov, "Sotsialnata Struktura ha Seloto v Balkanskite Strani Pres Perioda Mezhdu Dvete Svetovni Voiini."

77. *Istoria na Bulgaria II*, 343-44.

78. Interviews, Life History Interviews on Collectivization.

79. *Istoria na Bulgaria II*, 340-41.

80. Vl. Migev, "Borbata Sreshto Kulachestvoto i Negovoto Likvidirane v Bulgaria (1944-1958)," Isvestiya na Insituta po Istoria 27 (1984): 53. Lazarcik, "Bulgarian Agricultural Production, Output, Expenses, Gross and Net Product and Productivity at 1968 Prices, 1939 and 1948-1970," 53.

81. Durzhaven Vesnik (Sofia: 1950), 89.

82. Creed, *Domesticating Revolution.*

83. Lampe, *The Bulgarian Economy*, 125.

84. Interviews, Life History Interviews on Collectivization.

85. Creed, *Domesticating Revolution*, 77.

86. *Istoria na Bulgaria* II, 343 - 44.

87. Interviews, Life History Interviews on Collectivization.

88. Not surprisingly, this issue is subject to conflicting interpretations. See Dellin, "Introduction" (1957) and Sokolovsky, *Peasants and Power*. Dellin reported that the Bulgarian case was exceptionally violent. But evidence to support this position is not offered. While there was real violence against the organized political opposition, it

appears that most of the peasantry, in the words of one life history participant, "realized they had no alternative" in the face of high taxes and restrictions on credit and machinery use, "and joined up." See Interviews (1992). Lampe (1986) also notes, as I emphasize here, that Bulgarian private farmers had not had an easy time in the market economy, and that after the Russians liberated Bulgaria from the Turks in 1878, there was a substantial degree of readiness to follow the Russian lead in exchange for aid. Lampe, *The Bulgarian Economy*. Creed, *Domesticating Revolution.*

89. Jones and Jankoff, "Agriculture," 303.

90. Lazarcik, "Bulgarian Agricultural Production, Output, Expenses, Gross and Net Product and Productivity at 1968 Prices, 1939 and 1948-1970," 47.

91. Durzhaven Vesnik (Sofia: 1950), 31.

92. Creed, *Domesticating Revolution*, 95.

93. D. Sapundiev, *Bitovi Kooperativni Sdruzheniya* (Sofia: 1946), 310.

94. Stillman, "The Collectivization of Bulgarian Agriculture," 78.

95. M. Trifanova, "BKP i Materialno-Teknicheskata Baza na TKZS sled Preloma v Kooperatiraneto (1951-1955)," Isvestiya na Instituta po Istoria na BKP 32 (Sofia: 1975): 162-65. Interviews, Life History Interviews on Collectivization.

96. I. Smilyanov, *Suzdavane i Ykrepvane na TKZS v Blagoevgradski Okrug (1944-1958)* (Sofia: 1983), 42-43.

97. Jones and Jankoff, "Agriculture," 304. Migev, "Borbata Sreshto Kulachestvoto i Negovoto Likvidirane v Bulgaria (1944-1958)," 74.

98. Creed, *Domesticating Revolution*, 99.

99. Interviews, Life History Interviews on Collectivization. Crampton, *A Short History,* 136.

100. Interviews, Life History Interviews on Collectivization. Creed (*Domesticating Revolution*, 105) offers a nice example of this aspect of joining up once everyone else had done so. Describing the use of traditional village ritual practices to convince villages to join, he quotes a woman in Zamifirovo remembering: "It did not seem so bad when you saw all the people celebrating, singing and the band playing. It seemed like the thing to do and we wanted to join the festivities."

101. Tsentralno Statisticheski Upravlenie, *Statisticheski Godishnik na NR Bulgaria* (Sofia: various years).

102. Trifanova, "BKP i Posledniyat Etap na Sotsialicheskoto Preystroiistvo na Selsko Stopanstvo," 285.

103. Jones and Jankoff, "Agriculture," 308.

104. *Istoria na Bulgaria* II, 277.

105. N. Popov, "A Niyakoi Osobenosti pri Koito se isvershi Sotsialistichesko Preustroistvo na Selskoto Stopanstvo v NR Bulgaria," in *Godishnik na Sofiiskiya Universitet*, ed. Ioridicheski Fakultet (Sofia: 1969).

106. Bulgarska Komunicheski Partii, *BKP v Resoliutsii i Reshenie* V (Sofia: 1957): 40-45, 50-51. Trifanova, "Sotsialicheskoto Preystroiistvo i Razvitie na Selskoto Stopanstvo v Bulgaria," 434.

107. Trifanova, "BKP i Materialno-Teknicheskata Baza na TKZS sled Preloma v Kooperatiraneto (1951-1955)," 299-300.

108. Lampe, *The Bulgarian Economy*, 148.

109. Lazarcik, "Bulgarian Agricultural Production, Output, Expenses, Gross and Net Product and Productivity at 1968 Prices, 1939 and 1948-1970," 47.

110. Interviews, Life History Interviews on Collectivization.

111. Tsentralno Statisticheski Upravlenie, *Statisticheski Godishnik na NR Bulgaria* (Sofia: 1958).

112. Crampton, *A Short History*, 178.

113. Creed, *Domesticating Revolution*, 108.

114. Trifanova, "BKP i Materialno-Teknicheskata Baza na TKZS sled Preloma v Kooperatiraneto (1951-1955)," 305-09.

115. Interviews, Life History Interviews on Collectivization.

116. Trifanova, "BKP i Materialno-Teknicheskata Baza na TKZS sled Preloma v Kooperatiraneto (1951-1955)," 289-293, 305-310.

117. Jones and Jankoff, "Agriculture," 296.

118. Lazarcik, "Bulgarian Agricultural Production, Output, Expenses, Gross and Net Product and Productivity at 1968 Prices, 1939 and 1948-1970," 5, 20, 22.

119. Tsentralno Statisticheski Upravlenie, *Statisticheski Godishnik na NR Bulgaria* (Sofia: 1962).

120. Eugene Keefe, *Area Handbook for Bulgaria* (Washington, D.C.: American University, 1974), 84.

121. Interviews, Life History Interviews on Collectivization.

122. Jones and Jankoff, "Agriculture," 292. Lampe, *The Bulgarian Economy*, 194.

123. Lampe, *The Bulgarian Economy*, 180.

124. Tsentralno Statisticheski Upravlenie, *Statisticheski Godishnik na NR Bulgaria* (Sofia: 1966), 210.

125. Poyva i Razvitie na TKZC v Bulgaria (Sofia: Zemizdat, 1979), 110. Georgi Dimitrov, *Collected Works* (Sofia: Sofia Press, 1971).

126. Poyva i Razvitie na TKZC v Bulgaria, 112.

127. Poyva i Razvitie na TKZC v Bulgaria, 111.

128. Tsentralno Statisticheski Upravlenie, *Statisticheski Godishnik na NR Bulgaria* (Sofia: 1966), 210.

129. Liuben Berov, *Ikonomicheskoto Razvitie na Bulgaria Prez Vekovete* (Sofia: Profizdat, 1974), 266.

130. Berov, *Ikonomicheskoto Razvitie na Bulgaria Prez Vekovete.*

131. Lazarcik, "Bulgarian Agricultural Production, Output, Expenses, Gross and Net Product and Productivity at 1968 Prices, 1939 and 1948-1970," 47.

132. Interviews, Life History Interviews on Collectivization.

133. Poyva i Razvitie na TKZC v Bulgaria, 124.

134. Poyva i Razvitie na TKZC v Bulgaria, 115.

135. Ivan Lutsov, "Trudovo-Kooperativnite Zemedlski StopanstvaBGlaven Put za Radikalno Reshenie na Agrarno-Selskiya Vupros v NR Bulgaria," in *Kooperastiyata i Agrarnite Preobrazovaniya v Bulgaria* (Sofia: 1967): 147-48.

136. James Brown, *Bulgaria Under Communist Rule* (New York: Praeger, 1970), 210.

137. Poyva i Razvitie na TKZC v Bulgaria, 129.

138. For the period after 1965, I rely for growth rates on Boyd's data (1991). For comparison, Lazarcik's data show a growth rate of 3.5 percent (Lazarcik, "Bulgarian Agricultural Production, Output, Expenses, Gross and Net Product and Productivity at 1968 Prices, 1939 and 1948-1970," 54). Boyd, *Organization, Performance*, 86.

139. Lazarcik, "Bulgarian Agricultural Production, Output, Expenses, Gross and Net Product and Productivity at 1968 Prices, 1939 and 1948-1970," 20.

140. Boyd, *Organization, Performance*, 86.

141. Lazarcik, "Bulgarian Agricultural Production, Output, Expenses, Gross and Net Product and Productivity at 1968 Prices, 1939 and 1948-1970," 54.

142. Tsentralno Statisticheski Upravlenie, *Statisticheski Godishnik na NR Bulgaria* (Sofia: 1971), 280.

143. Tsentralno Statisticheski Upravlenie, *Biudjet na Domankinstvata v Bulgaria* (Sofia: 1970).

144. Tsentralno Statisticheski Upravlenie, *Statisticheski Godishnik na NR Bulgaria* (Sofia: various years).

145. George Fiewel, *Growth and Reform in Centrally Planned Economies: The Lessons of the Bulgarian Experience* (New York: Praeger Press, 1977), 321.

146. Boyd, *Organization, Performance*, 86.

147. Tsentralno Statisticheski Upravlenie, *Statisticheski Godishnik na NR Bulgaria* (Sofia: various years).

148. Paul Wiedeman, "The Origins and Development of Agro-Industrial Complexes in Bulgaria," in *Agricultural Policies in the USSR and Eastern Europe,* ed. Ronald A. Francisco, Betty and Roy D. Laird, (Boulder, Colo.: Westview Press, 1980), 101.

149. Tsentralno Statisticheski Upravlenie, *Statisticheski Godishnik na NR Bulgaria* (Sofia: various years).

150. Tsentralno Statisticheski Upravlenie, *Statisticheski Godishnik na NR Bulgaria* (Sofia: various years). Veska 2:162.

151. Berov, *Ikonomicheskoto Razvitie na Bulgaria Prez Vekovete*, 270.

152. Tsentralno Statisticheski Upravlenie, *Statisticheski Godishnik na NR Bulgaria* (Sofia: 1986), 35.

153. Boyd, *Organization, Performance*, 87, 101.

154. Karl-Eugen Wadekin, *Current Trends in the Soviet and East European Food Economy* (Berlin: Dunker and Humbolt, 1982), 38-39. Mieke Meurs and Stanka Dobreva, "Clients, Prols, and Entrepreneurs: State Policy and Private Agricultural Producers Under Central Planning," (Washington, D.C.: American University Working Paper, 1993).

155. Boyd, *Organization, Performance*, ch. 5.

156. Meurs and Djankov, "The Alchemy of Reform: Bulgarian Agriculture in the 1980s."

157. Survey Data, Town and Village (Institute of Sociology, Bulgarian Academy of Sciences: 1986).

158. Interviews, Life History Interviews on Collectivization.

4

Hungary: Cooperative Farms and Household Plots

Imre Kovach

After the end of World War II, the need for radical agricultural reform was clear to most politicians. The semifeudal structures that persisted in rural areas undermined modernization and economic growth and contributed to massive landlessness and rural unrest. A first phase of agricultural reform was the land reform and distribution legislation, passed just after World War II with multiparty support. A second phase of agricultural reform, collectivization, began after the Hungarian Communist Party (Magyar Kommunista Partja, after 1948 Magyar Dolgozok Partja) gained control of the government in 1948.

Early collectivization met with substantial peasant resistance. In responding to this resistance, and to the revolution in 1956, the Hungarian communist leaders adopted a new way of collectivization and a new cooperative model. The reformulation of the Soviet kolkhoz took partially into consideration the fragmented nature of Hungarian rural society and long-standing peasant aspirations of family farming. The new policy, and renewed pressure, resulted in the rapid incorporation of the majority of Hungarian peasants into cooperatives between 1958 and 1963.

Over the following decades, the Hungarian cooperatives developed a two-tiered structure. Small household plots were worked as "part-time farms" by cooperative farm members, as well as employees of other organizations. These farms existed alongside large, collective agricultural enterprises. This structure was similar in some elements to the semifeudal arrangements that had persisted in Hungary up to World War II, but benefited from extensive government investment.

After 1968, both types of farms also benefited from new economic relations and increasing international and domestic demand. Collective farms aided individual producers in responding to demand, by offering them historically unprecedented access to resources. From the 1960s through the early 1980s, this model produced respectable agricultural growth rates of 2-3 percent per year, generated one-third of hard currency income, and helped to meet Hungary's obligations for exports to CMEA (Council for Mutual Economic Assistance) markets.[1] The model also allowed Hungarian rural households to supplement cooperative farm incomes with steady earning in the second economy.[2]

After the late 1970s, as international markets became more competitive, agricultural production in many countries took on flexible, "postfordist" character-istics. The Hungarian two-tiered model of collective farming, which was built on a somewhat rigid division of labor between large, mechanized cooperative farms and relatively limited, labor-intensive household plots, proved incapable of effective adjustment. Agricultural output stagnated after 1982 and meaningful reform had to wait.

Agriculture in Hungary before Collectivization

Agriculture's Role in the European System

The history of Hungarian agriculture, like the medieval and modern history of Central Europe, reflects a peculiar feature: as Hungary was increasingly connected with the central regions of Europe through market relations, it could not keep pace with the development of the center. The modernization of agriculture became a crucial problem for the Hungarian economy, especially toward the end of the 1800s, as the points of connection with western Europe multiplied and strength-ened.

The relative backwardness of the peripheries of Europe changed in waves. As a result, the position of Hungarian agricultural production as compared with the centers and peripheries changed over time. From the fifteenth century onward, Hungarian agriculture was connected more and more closely with the central markets of Europe. As early as the fifteenth century, the level of agricultural development on feudal estates made it possible to produce a significant quantity and quality of surplus goods for the markets of the Hungarian towns, for the regular or provisional army organized to counter the Muslim threat, and, to an increasing degree, for the European (mainly German and Italian) markets. But Hungarian agriculture could not keep pace with the development of the center in terms of quantity and quality of production. Located in the middle of Europe and having favorable geographical and climatic conditions, the territories of the Hungarian state were never ranked among the most backward regions of Europe, but in no period could they achieve the level of development of the center.

The general upswing of commodity production was disrupted by the Muslim invasion in 1526. The occupation of central parts of historic Hungary, including

Buda until the end of the seventeenth century, caused constant warfare in most regions of the country. This impeded commodity production in the earlier centers of agriculture—those areas of the northwestern Transdanubia closest to western markets, and the regions of the Great Hungarian Plain that offered the best conditions for agriculture. On the other hand, the wars helped producers in those regions that were less affected by the wars, which found stable markets in the armies. The religious wars in Europe also contributed to this growth of market opportunities for agriculture.

Many Hungarian historians now argue, however, that already in the seventeenth century the region as a whole began to fall behind the European centers, due to the persistence of the system of feudal estates.[3] After the wars with the Turks, the Hungarian economy became integrated in the Habsburg Empire, providing the more industrialized provinces (especially the Austrian provinces and Silezia) with foodstuffs. Hungarian agriculture rested on feudal structures until the middle of the nineteenth century, however. Alongside the Prussian-type large estates, with their system of enforced labor, masses of serfs lived on subsistence farming and engaged only marginally in commodity production. This system proved an unsuitable basis for economic modernization.

When the feudal framework was abolished by the revolution of 1848-1849, and capitalist relations began to expand in agriculture, this transformed the organization of agricultural production. Still, the new capitalist relations were grounded in the same dual structures of large estates and peasant units.

The period between 1887 and 1898 represents the most dynamic period of Hungarian capitalist development: between 1863 and 1989-1900, output grew from 175 million gold crowns to 1,400.[4] This was followed, however, by a general economic crisis in 1900-1901 and a depression lasting until World War I. The devastation of World War I further aggravated the economic situation, as did the new, unfavorably drawn state boundaries. The Hungarian state regarded the problem of modernization as crucial to its economic relations with the center and recovery from the economic downturn, especially as the points of international connection multiplied and strengthened over time. The backwardness of agriculture, and its continued predominance within the economy, was a key impediment to this modernization.

Changing Structure within Agriculture

The nineteenth century brought the emancipation of serfs, the distribution of about half of agricultural land to former serfs, and the partial commodification of land. Table 4.1 demonstrates that the forty years after the emancipation of the serfs did not modify essentially the pattern of landholding, however. The structure of tiny plots alongside large estates remained largely unchallenged, as did the predominance of payment in kind. The inalienability of parts of the large estates was decreed by law, thereby preventing the decline of the economic and political power of the landholding aristocracy.

Within the overall pattern of landed property, however, there were some changes in the composition of the owners. One of them consists of the emergence of a relatively rich stratum of peasant-owners, possessing 50-100 holds (1 hold equals 0.57 ha). This social group, while very thin, represented a possible path or capitalist transformation of the peasantry. At the same time, the percentage of holders having more than 5 holds fell greatly, as masses of peasant families lost so much land as to endanger even their everyday subsistence.[5] A third social process, the shift of the medium-sized landowner gentry into state administration or other intellectual jobs, is not reflected by the data.

At the beginning of the twentieth century, the large estates began to be transformed into capitalist enterprises. The separation of ownership from control of much of the land continued, as did the dual structure of small and large production, but these took new forms. Many landless and smallholding former serfs now rented or received land as payment in kind from the big latifundia. As will be seen below, this two-tiered system survived the land reform in the middle of the twentieth century and the subsequent collectivization.

As land that had been previously allotted to the serfs was gradually taken back by the landlords, and peasants concentrated family labor capacity on self-provisioning, statute labor and tithes were replaced by wage relations. The large-scale enterprise lost both the manpower reserves and the produce received previously in the form of tithe, significantly increasing the costs of production on large estates.

Still, stable markets and high prices in the emerging Austro-Hungarian state allowed production to continue, even as it came to be guided increasingly by the considerations of profitability. The composition of products, especially on the large

Table 4.1 Changes in Hungarian Landed Property 1895-1935

Size in Holds*	Percent Units		Percent Land	
	1895	1935	1895	1935
0-5	53.7	72.5	6.0	10.1
5-20	35.3	21.3	24.2	21.8
20-100	10.0	5.4	23.4	20.0
100-1,000	0.8	0.6	13.4	18.2
1,000+	0.2	0.2	33.0	29.9

* 1 hold=0.57 ha
Source: Gyorgy Ranki, ed. *Magyarorszag tortenete 1918-1945* (Budapest: Akademiai Kiado, 1976); Ferenc Hanak, ed. *Magyarorszag tortenete 1890-1918* (Budapest: Akademiai Kiado, 1978).

estates, changed. The most spectacular consequence was the development of animal husbandry, especially cattle breeding, which, in turn, led to the cultivation of new plants. Much of the new production, including livestock breeding and the related plant cultivation, required large tracts of land. More intensive production also flourished, however, producing the famous centers of fruit and vegetable growing, primarily in the vicinity of the cities (for example, peach production near Budapest). Some smaller regions also achieved fame through their fine market gardening without direct links with cities (such as onion production in Mako).

The degree of capitalist development should not be overestimated, however. First, even the large-scale production was not commercialized fully. The preservation of fee-tails prevented full commodification of land, and workers of the large-scale enterprises continued to receive a high proportion of their income in kind. The relations of the workers to the large-scale enterprise were also regulated by very severe government decrees, which guaranteed the owners of the large enterprises protection from workers' demands. In addition, in the first half of the twentieth century both large-scale enterprises and smallholders were obliged to deliver their products to the state at fixed prices during the long periods of war, and the state took an active role in guiding the agricultural development overall, through customs and tax and credit policies, especially after 1938.

Second, a very narrow stratum of the rural population was in a position to orient its production to the market. The number of farms that specialized in producing primarily vegetables or fruits or whose main purpose consisted in selling their products on the market was estimated to be in the thousands, and the share of land oriented to vegetables or wine production did not change significantly. The majority of households continued to produce mainly corn. Thus, even in the 1930s and 1940s, an estimated 70 percent of all agricultural production was for self-provisioning, and agriculture continued to serve as a means of absorbing family labor capacity.[6]

While some technical modernization of production accompanied the increasing land pressures and rising labor costs during this period, its impact was quite limited. Steam threshers in use in agriculture rose from 2,500 in 1871 to 30,000 in 1914, while fertilizer use rose from 1.7 kg per ha in 1898 to 7.6 in 1911.[7] Still, at the beginning of the 1940s, the value of all the industrial machines and tools used in agricultural enterprises constituted no more than 3 percent of the inventory value of the enterprises. The equipment was concentrated in the large enterprises—for one hold, these employed 230 percent more machines than the small-scale farmers. Important productivity differences between the sectors resulted.

This combination of increasingly extensive commercial production, peasant households' need for land for survival, and expanding population growth in the late nineteenth century resulted in an acute struggle for land. As can be seen from table 4.2, arable land available per person (without taking into account distribution) fell

Table 4.2 Population and Arable Land in Hungary, 1850-1910

Year	Population (thousands)	Arable Land (thousands ha)	Land per Capita (ha)
1850s	13,800	22,662	1.6
1870s	15,739	26,430	1.7
1880s	17,464	26,508	1.5
1910	20,866	26,546	1.3

Source: Ferenc Hanak, ed. *Magyarország története 1890-1918* (Budapest: Akademiai Kiado, 1978); Istvan Orosz, "A differencialodas es kisajatitas" in *A parasztság Magyarországon a kapitalizmus koraban,* ed. Istvan Szabo (Budapest: Akademiai Kiado, 1965). (Years used in calculations: 1850s (1850, 1855); 1870s (1869,1880); 1880s (1885, 1890); 1910 (1910, 1913)

from approximately 2.9 holds in the late 1850s to approximately 2.2 holds around 1910.

At the same time, the two-tiered structure of semicapitalist estates and widespread subsistence production resulted in agricultural stagnation. The proportion of the population working in agriculture remained stable at around 50 percent between 1920 and 1941, while the contribution of agriculture to national income fell from 42 percent to 37 percent. Taking the level of agricultural production in 1911-1915 (in constant 1925-1927 prices) as a base of 100, output grew to an average level of 103 by 1925-1927 and 107 by 1937-1938. The total number of cattle, horses, pigs, and sheep, measured in standard animals on the territory of Hungarian state in 1920, fell from 2,987 in 1911, to 2,593 in 1929, and rose only slightly to 2,622 in 1938.[8] Given the growth rate of the population, this stagnation resulted in a decrease in the volume of agricultural production per person.

Partly in response to this problem, the state took on an increasingly important role in Hungarian economic development from the middle of the nineteenth century until the communist consolidation in 1948. In particular, the investments and enterprises of the state assumed strategic importance in belatedly developing Hungarian industry. In this period of capitalist development, the redistributive function of the state also increased in significance.

In the development of industry, in addition to the upswing of food-processing and light industry spurred by the growing market, a central part was played by the rapid building of a comprehensive railway system, completed for the most part in the two last decades of the nineteenth century. Railway and road building, the drainage of marshlands, and river control were all financed primarily by state funds or by the local governments, which were also subjected to a certain degree of state control. State guidance proved decisive also in building the Hungarian banking system.

State guidance and support also extended to agriculture. Export opportunities for agricultural products were determined primarily by the customs, tax, and credit policies of the state, especially after American corn had appeared in Europe and European countries responded with protectionist tariffs. In these policies, one of the most powerful political blocks in Hungary and representative of the upper and middle strata of the landed aristocracy exerted a strong influence.

The economic role of the state was enhanced by the fact that the growing need for capital, resulting from the general capitalization of the Hungarian economy, was met—besides direct state intervention—partly by foreign loans. The most common forms of the latter—state bonds and communal bonds—required guarantees on the part of the state as well as the participation of foreign capital in building the railway system. State direction and participation, quite intensive even in the periods of economic prosperity, became much more marked in the years when the state prepared for the two world wars and took part in them and also in the periods of reconstruction.

This phenomenon is not unknown to most economies, but if we include those years that were characterized by an especially high level of state intervention owing to the two world wars, then we find that from 1900 until 1948 there were few years in which agriculture could develop without a significant degree of state control. A new generation of historians are of the opinion that the redistributive function of the state had become stable from 1938 on, some ten years before the communists took power. Nineteen thirty-nine was the first year of state price regulation. From 1940 to 1942, agricultural producers were obliged to sell their products to the state. By 1942, a new intensive delivery system had been inaugurated and the production of industrial crops was fixed by statute.

The Fragmentation of Rural Society

The social structure underlying this stagnation was even more fragmented than table 4.1 suggests. In 1940, approximately 4.5 million people made their living in agriculture. From among them, the number of those who owned or rented land over 100 holds was an estimated 32,000-33,000, about 3 percent of all agricultural holdings. The overwhelming majority of those who made their living by farming owned plots smaller than 10 holds.

Nearly half the holdings under 10 holds were extremely small—under 5 holds. As a result of this landholding structure, only some 30 percent of all peasants could support their families by cultivating their own land. Members of most of these smallholding families regularly had to work as agricultural or industrial laborers; some commuted to towns to part-time jobs. In addition to the small-scale farmers, small holders also included large masses of servants, totaling almost 2 million people. The exceptional smallholder was a gardener producing intensively for the market, but the number of these did not exceed 22,000-23,000, barely 2 percent of all peasant enterprises. Among the 32,000-33,000 owners of large estates, the landed aristocracy and the church owned most of the land. These two social groups commanded the greatest social and political power, not only in rural society, but also in national politics. The gentry, owning medium-sized estates and still enjoying considerable political influence in the second half of the nineteenth century, was gradually losing its economic assets. Though some managed to convert their medium-sized estates into capitalist enterprises, more and more members of this stratum lost their inherited lands and turned to jobs provided by the state.

In the last third of the nineteenth century, a new stratum of agrarian capitalists emerged, renting the large estates. Much of the rented land was connected with processing factories. For example, the famous sugar refinery of Hatvan owned large tracts of land for growing sugar beet, but the better part of the utilized land was rented to individual farmers. It bears eloquent testimony to the spirit and prestige of the landed aristocracy that even those whose capital had originally been accumulated not in agriculture, but in industry, wished to acquire land. Thus, the land question became crucial not solely for rural society, but also in the political and social life of the whole country, especially after the 1930s.

In fact, two kinds of class conflicts coexisted in this period. One centered around the struggle for land between the small-scale and large-scale enterprises. The outcome of this struggle favored unambiguously the owners of the large estates. The limited land reform carried out at the beginning of the 1920s distributed only 927,000 holds (about 10 percent of large estates) to 400,000 families. No radical land reform, along the lines of the neighboring countries of Yugoslavia, Romania, and Czechoslovakia, was implemented before 1945, and Hungary remained a country of latifundia and small peasant units.

The other class conflict was within the ranks of the peasantry itself. Because land could not be acquired from the large estates, land conflicts were concentrated in the ranks of the peasants, especially between those peasant owners who could employ wage laborers and those forced to sell their labor to make ends meet.

The peasantry was further divided by feudal principles and regional settlement patterns. The rural population included many strata of peasants, as well as craftsmen, merchants, and part-time industrial workers. Feudal principles included a strategic order of economic behavior among these groups that were at least as influential in regulating social and economic relations among rural landholders (and also their chances of social mobility) as the class structure. Settlement patterns, including the peculiar Hungarian system of detached ranches (*tanyas*), villages, and country towns existing side by side, also divided the population.

Political Relations in the Countryside

As noted above, political relations of the countryside were dominated by the large estates. Owners of these estates secured their economic position by commanding all possible weapons of the state machinery, including the local administration and local police. As the owners of the largest economic assets and as the greatest taxpayers of the community, landlords automatically became members of local governing bodies. In the country towns of the Great Hungarian Plain (composed of 20,000-30,000 people, many of whom worked in agriculture), not every social group had the right to vote, or, if they could take part in elections, they did not have the same political weight as the richer strata.

In the last third of the 1800s, an initial response to the problems of land shortage, low agricultural wages, and power inequalities was found in the emerging agrarian socialist movements. In the 1880s and 1890s, violent conflicts often erupted, with police firing on the population in an effort to suppress the movements. Despite their local power, the agrarian socialist movements remained outside the framework of institutionalized political life throughout the prewar period and, as a result, could enforce practically none of their major demands. For example, with no agrarian socialist MPs (Members of Parliament) in parliament, the Employment Law of 1907 reinforced severe measures against domestic servants and agricultural laborers.

The only real political alternative, the Social Democratic Party, focused almost exclusively on the problems of the industrial workers and had very little to say on the land question up to World War I. After World War I, this situation was formalized in a pact between the governing elite and the social democrats, giving the Social Democratic Party the right to field candidates in the general elections in exchange for not extending its activities to the countryside. As an additional consequence of this political compromise the system of suffrage was changed: in towns and cities citizens could vote secretly, but in the countryside voting had to take place openly.

At the beginning of the 1920s, however, a new, peasant- and village-based political movement began to change the political balance in Hungary. The Smallholder Party emerged as a powerful representative of the interests of the richer stratum of peasants, capable of challenging the aristocracy. The party successfully implemented the limited land reform of the early 1920s and otherwise promoted the conditions for the expansion of large peasant landholders. With the passage of time, however, the traditional governing elite recaptured power from the Smallholder Party, though some representatives of the party remained key figures in political life. Only after World War II did the Smallholder Party briefly reemerge as the governing party. At this point, it had lost its identity as a peasant party

The Communist Party, which gained power for a few months in the revolution of 1919, held little appeal for the peasantry. The party did not recognize that Hungarian peasants wanted nothing more fervently than land, and focused on collectivization of small plots rather than the distribution of land. During the few months of communist rule in 1919, the countryside was either neutral or openly hostile to the regime. While the communists modified their agrarian policy as a result of this experience, this change made little impact on political relations in the countryside in the interwar period or during World War II, since the communist movement was confined to illegality.

A final political response to agrarian problems prior in 1945 was the movement of the so-called folk writers. This movement drew on diverse groups, all of which saw the roots of Hungary's economic and social problems primarily in the countryside. These analysts believed the peasantry to be the only social force capable of leading the country out of its economic stagnation. Most of these writers had peasant origins, and they had produced a great number of village descriptions and sociographies by the beginning of the 1930s. These more accurately described the society and peasantry of Hungary than anything previously, emphasizing the need for a thorough land reform and convincingly documenting the poverty of the agricultural laborers and poor peasants. The movement tried to influence the political leadership of the country primarily by the means of literature. As some of the traditionalist ideological assumptions of the movement were accepted by the ruling regime, the movement was not outlawed, although some of its representatives were brought to court and their works banned. Nonetheless, the folk-writers' movement only gained political influence after World War II, when its members formed the Peasant Party and played a decisive part in preparing and implementing the 1945 land reform. The group continued its activities until the communist consolidation in 1947-1948.

None of these political movements could gain significant political power prior to World War II. Thus, neither the road to agricultural development favored by the Smallholder Party, nor the more populist solution favored by the folk-writers' movement was attempted. Agriculture remained in a state of semifeudal stagnation, accompanied by extensive social fragmentation and poverty.

The 1945 Land Reform and Its Consequences

At the end of World War II, the need for land reform was so clear that it was included in the program of every political party in the first postwar government. Land reform was also urged by the Soviet Red Army, which hoped that reform would encourage the anti-fascist struggle in those areas of the country still occupied by German troops. Hardly had the military operations of World War II stopped, therefore, when the land reform law was passed. Under the law, land of former fascist leaders and other war criminals was confiscated, as were estates over 100 holds. In addition, all large estates exceeding 100 holds held by the gentry or the church were to be nationalized without compensation. In the case of peasant holdings, the limit was set in 200 holds (114 ha); the rest of their land was taken away and compensation was promised but never fully paid. Altogether 5.6 million holds, accounting for 35 percent of arable land, were nationalized.[9]

Sixty percent of the nationalized land was allotted to individual peasants, while the rest remained in the hands of the state or became the property of state-supported cooperatives. Of the 730,000 people who wanted to receive land, some

660,000 did. Land went to the most needy—90 percent of recipients were agricultural laborers, domestic servants, or dwarfholders. Together, these groups received 93 percent of the allotted land. Still, 52 percent of agricultural laborers, 47 percent of domestic servants, 44 percent of dwarfholders, and 75 percent of smallholders received nothing.

On average, recipients received 5.7 holds.[10] As the large-scale farms were dismantled, the number and proportion of agricultural small-scale producers grew rose from 21 percent of producers in 1941 to 43 percent after the land reform. Many of the smallholdings consisted of several scattered strips. Although approximately 400,000 agricultural machines were redistributed along with the land, more often than not the new owners could not even till their new land for lack of machines, equipment, and animals. Agricultural productivity fell 15 percent from 1938 to 1948; the value of agriculture production fell from 1,745 million pengo in 1938 to 928 million pengo in 1947.[11] Commodity production fell even further as consumption rose in the countryside.[12]

While peasant commodity production was declining, the economic leaders of the country needed urgently to secure the food supply for the population and to pay war reparations. They introduced a system of tight control on the already-weakened agricultural sector, including a system of required deliveries from every agricultural household to the state (resembling wartime requisitions), taxes, and physical force to punish kulak resisters. Market relations, limited in the prewar period, were of course not strengthened under these conditions.

While the land reform was being implemented from 1945 to 1949, the Hungarian Communist Party was involved a cutthroat political struggle for capturing the government of the country. The land reform contributed to this struggle on two fronts. It built peasant support for the party, while destroying the class of large estate owners, who were the staunchest enemies of the communists.

The organization of cooperatives began in the years after the 1949 land reform, especially among those smallholders who had neither the draft animals nor the equipment to till their newly won land. While this cooperative movement did not result from political pressure, neither did it strike broad roots in the Hungarian countryside. About 20 percent of agricultural land was incorporated into the cooperatives by 1953, but many of these early cooperatives operated for only a very short time.[13]

The appeal of the new cooperatives was limited by their poor economic performance. The new farmers, paupers in the previous period, joined precisely because they lacked the draft animals, tools, and knowledge needed for production. But the new Hungarian state could offer little direct aid, and the cooperatives of poor peasants could not qualify through the (still commercial) banking sector for the credit necessary for planting or mechanization. Government restrictions on sales only exacerbated the financial problems. Unable to form viable farms, many people gave their plots back to the state. By 1949, approximately as many households had returned their land to the state as had been given land.[14] The populist land reform, though it responded to century-old peasant demands, had failed to resolve the problems of Hungarian smallholders or provide the basis for agricultural modernization. Government measures that stifled commodity production contributed to this failure.

The Collectivization

Uncertain Beginnings

When the Communist Party finally took control of Hungarian politics, society, and economy between 1947 and 1949, this proved a historic turning point for agricultural organization. To address the growing agricultural crisis, the party followed Stalinist agricultural policy. Right from the start Communist politicians looked to the development of Soviet-type kolkhozes to improve conditions in agriculture, leaving no place for small-scale individual enterprises.

Three types of cooperatives were officially sanctioned. These ranged from cooperatives that consolidated land, plowed and sowed collectively, but harvested individually, to cooperatives that completely collectivized production under the kolkhoz model. The government began by expanding the cooperatives of poor peasants, which numbered almost 300 by 1948. State aid was provided to the kolkhoz-type cooperatives, including tax and delivery concessions, credit, and subsidized services from the state-run machine tractor stations.

Actual investment in these farms was limited, however. Total investment in agriculture fell from 18 percent of national investment in 1949 to under 10 percent in 1950-1951.[15] As a result, the number of grain combines available in Hungarian agriculture as a whole grew slowly, from 21 in the prewar period to 25 in 1950, then jumped to 764 by 1952, as agriculture's share in investment rose back above 13 percent. Fertilizer available per ha of arable land remained at the 1938 level until 1952, when it increased from 6 kilograms to 8.[16] Further, only about one-third of total agricultural investment was targeted to the collective farms, with the rest going to state farms, which increased in importance from 25 percent of agricultural land in 1949 to 37 percent in 1953.[17]

To accommodate peasants' desires for land, cooperative farm members were permitted to retain up to 0.43 ha of land for household use. In addition, after 1954 some cooperatives began to permit households to work collective land on a sharecropping basis: families farmed cooperative land individually, paying a share of production to the farm.

To further promote the cooperatives, the government also increased by all possible means the burdens on medium-income and better off peasants.[18] The system of required deliveries to the state, which accounted for only 9 percent of total marketed crops in 1949, was expanded considerably and weighted against the larger holdings.[19]

Land taxes and other financial pressures were also increased, especially against family units with commodity production, which were declared "kulaks." Taxes on the peasantry rose from 285 forints per capita in 1949 to 500 forints in 1955 (in constant 1954 value).[20] Brutality also figured importantly in this period: over 21,000 "kulaks" were imprisoned by August 1950 for alleged antigovernment activities or acts of "sabotage," such as sleeping in their own fields.[21]

As a result of these policies, from 1949 to 1953 the share of agricultural land in collective farms rose from 0.6 percent to 18.3 percent, while the farms' share of agricultural employment rose from 0.5 percent to 19.1 percent. The 3,307 collective farms in 1953 had an average of 58 members and 427 ha (tables 4.3 and 4.4). At this point, about 32 percent of the land was in cooperatives or state farms.[22]

The majority of the early members, like those before 1948, came from the poorest peasants. From 1949 to 1951, 57 percent of members joined without land, while another 38 percent had only received their land in the 1945 land reform. As pressure to collectivize was increased, however, the situation changed. As a result of increasing pressure on the middle-income and rich peasants, by 1952, 77 percent of members had joined with some land.[23]

With the limited investment and predominance of poor peasants among members, productivity in the cooperative sector remained below that in either the state or private sector. In 1952-1953, private households produced about 30 percent more per ha than the collective farms.[24] The majority of land was still in private hands, however, and agricultural productivity recovered somewhat after 1948. Nonetheless, for the important grain crops of wheat and corn it remained below 1938 levels. [25]

The poor cooperative performance forced a reconsideration of collectivization policies beginning in 1953. Imre Nagy, an activist in the 1945 land reform, became prime minister and adopted a more peasant-friendly policy, allowing peasants to leave cooperatives. The number of cooperative farm members fell back quickly, to 193,000 in 1953 and 175,000 in 1954. The majority of those leaving were ex-land owners who had joined under extreme pressure.[26]

Investment was also increased slightly in this period of reconsideration, rising from an average of 13 percent of national investment for the period 1950-1953, to 24 percent in 1954.[27] Total available combines jumped from 764 in 1952 to 2,227 in 1955, while tractors increased from 12,700 in 1950 to 23,700 in 1955.[28] Some of this investment must have made its way onto the collective farms, because from 1954 to 1955 these registered higher productivity than private farms for the first time.[29]

The improved performance opened political space for those favoring faster collectivization, and a renewal of government pressure produced a slight recovery in collectivization levels in 1955. This quickly resulted in increased rural resistance, however, in the form of both public calls for de-collectivization and massive outflow of population to urban areas. When the government fell in Budapest in the uprising of 1956, the majority of the collective farms collapsed.

The number of farms fell from 3,759 in 1955 to 1,617 in 1956, while membership fell from 253,000 to 96,000 (table 4.4). This proved a turning point for the Hungarian approach to collectivization.

The Second Phase of Collectivization

The agricultural policy of the government that came to power in November 1956 was focused on two related problems: improving political relations with the agricultural population, which constituted half of the inhabitants of the country, and improving agricultural performance and the food supply in order to support modernization. The stand of the political leadership on these dual objectives changed repeatedly between 1956 and 1958, in keeping with the internal struggle for authority and with foreign political conditions.[30] The political struggle did not challenge the basic goal of collectivization, however, but focused on revising the method used in view of the failure of the first attempt at collectivization.

In early 1958, a decision was taken to proceed slowly with a second collectivization, this time in only one form of cooperative—that of completely collectivized production. The government expected the transfer of half of arable land to large-scale state or collective farms by 1965, and the completion of collectivization about ten to fifteen years later.

The renewed collectivization effort brought about unexpected results, however. From 1959 to 1960, the share of agricultural land held by collective farms jumped from 22 percent to 45 percent, while the share of agricultural earners in those farms jumped from 9 percent to 37 percent.[31] The approximately 4,500 collective farms that existed in 1960 were twice as large as those in 1953 (averaging 747 ha) and had nearly four times as many members (212). Not all members were active in the cooperative, however.[32]

The rapid success of the second wave of collectivization, unexpected even by the political leadership, may be explained by two causes.[33] First, the peasantry saw in the campaign-like renewal of collectivization, two years after the suppression of the revolution and the execution of its leaders, the inevitability of the "socialist" system and collectivization. Second, the political leadership, having learned a lesson from the failure of the first attempt at collectivization, introduced new methods. While a massive collectivization campaign was launched, attempts were also made to make entry easier for the peasants.

The campaign was organized with the greatest circumspection. Committees for the development of cooperatives, consisting of twenty to forty members, were set up in the individual settlements. Collectivization was announced as voluntary and nonviolent in principle, but some 4,000 civil servants, mostly teachers, were organized to visit peasants until they could be convinced to join. At the same time, it became increasingly difficult to sell land. Physical violence and imprisonment were also used in places, however, and one deterrent example in a village was sufficient to invoke the methods of the early 1950s.

Significant changes in the government's organizing strategy were also designed to increase the viability and appeal of the cooperatives. In the second wave of collectivization, it was not primarily the poor and landless peasants who were targeted, but the middle-income peasants who knew more about cultivation and had greater prestige in the villages. Middle-income peasants were even encouraged to assume the leadership of the new cooperatives. In recognition of the social fragmentation of the Hungarian countryside, villagers were permitted to form cooperatives on the basis of categories of peasant holdings (medium-income peasants, poor, and smallholders) or among groups of relatives and acquaintances.

The political leadership was forced to make other compromises as well. Forced deliveries were stopped, as the government turned to other incentives to increase production and sales. Resources were further redirected from industry into agriculture under a strategy of balanced growth, and agriculture's share of national investment rose toward 18 percent. By 1963, available grain combines exceeded 4,000, tractors available reached 48,000 by 1964, and fertilizer applications per ha of arable land rose to almost 30 kilograms.[34] While fertilizer use still lagged behind most other East Central European countries, tractor power per 100 ha had surpassed that in most other countries, except the GDR and Czechoslovakia.[35]

Controls over the organization of labor on the collective farms were loosened, a change that fundamentally influenced the structure of Hungarian agricultural production later on. Individual, family production retained a significant role, and the permissible size of household plots was raised to 0.86 ha in 1959. The use of sharecropping arrangements on collective farms was extended after 1957 in areas difficult to collectivize.[36]   The accumulating investment and new organization of the farms paid off in improved productive results. After stagnating around the level of 1950 for the first half the decade, gross output improved significantly after 1956. The index of gross production increased from a base of 100 in 1950 to 120 in 1960.[37] This resulted partly from improved grain yields, which rose from an average of 15.8 quintals per ha for the period 1950-1956 to an average of 18.8 for the period 1957-1960.[38] Despite the improved performance, the incomes of collective farm members dropped, from 11,956 forints in 1958 to 7,572 in 1960, about 88 percent of the average industrial wage.[39]

Social Responses to Collectivization

With the completion of collectivization and the consolidation of the redistributive economic system, opportunities for collective peasant resistance appeared closed. Responses of rural residents could be only individual, and these included a number of strategies.

Many peasants responded to the collectivization of by leaving agriculture—after 1945, there was a constant migration from the sphere of agricultural production. At the beginning of the 1950s, when state policy channeled investment into industry, approximately 400,000 people left the countryside and settled in towns, where the building of heavy industry had created jobs. This migration continued into the later 1950s and early 1960s, when the redistributive character of economic and social policy had been consolidated and more peasants realized there was no escape from collectivization within agriculture. Between 1959 and 1963 another almost half a million more active earners left agriculture, accounting for almost one-third of the labor force.[40] However, the pace of industrialization and urbanization slowed in this later period, and this began to close the opportunities that had attracted the rural population into the towns.

Instead of going directly to towns, some people moved between agrarian settlements. The system of tanyas was virtually eliminated in the 1960s and the beginning of the 1970s. Very often the elimination of these detached ranches, which were difficult to incorporate into the large-scale production cooperatives, was carried through under the pressure of the cooperative leaders. Smaller agrarian settlements were also depopulated, leaving mainly the old, the unskilled, and new gypsy arrivals in the village.

Reliance on the household plots was also a significant part of peasant response to collectivization. Small-scale production did decline temporarily in the 1960s, as the consolidation of central planning reduced local market opportunities. The framework of the cooperative in many ways strengthened small-scale production, however, and contributed to its transformation into a viable form of commodity production. The cooperatives provided stable base incomes to households, as well as increasingly providing mechanized services and fodder for household agricultural production.

Government acceptance and even encouragement of the household plots resulted from economic considerations, including the inability of the central government to supply local markets, the unsatisfactory character of large-scale production for certain crops, low agricultural incomes, and the desire to more fully employ the labor force and slow the pace of migration into industry.

In many places, households could also take advantage of opportunities for sharecropping, which made it possible for the peasant families to take as much land as they could till. In the first half of 1960s, sharecropping provided an estimated one-third of the agricultural work on the collectives, an estimated one-third of crop production, and about half of the income of cooperative households.[41]

The statues of the cooperatives allowed individual farming on household plots up to the level of self-provisioning, but small-scale production exceeded this level right from the start. Households and sharecroppers were free to dispose of part of their produce, selling it if they wished to do so. Market production could not be called a typical form of household farming in the 1960s, however. Peasant families produced primarily for self-provisioning. While about 50 percent of the income of collective farm workers came from their household plots during the 1960s, but much of this was consumed in kind.[42] Still, in the 1960s a significant part of agricultural production was produced by small-scale production—an estimated one-third to one-half of all agricultural products.[43]

Adjustments after the Mid-1960s

This basic structure in agriculture underwent some adjustments after the 1960s, but the fundamental organizational structure remained unchanged. Collective farms continued to grow in size and intensify production, increasingly resembling state farms. Economic reforms after 1968 allowed the cooperatives greater autonomy, however, and encouraged their increased support for and integration of household production.

From 1960 to 1970, the cooperatives increased their share of agricultural land from 49 percent to 68 percent, mainly through the incorporation of the remaining private farms by 1963.[44] The collective farms were consolidated, reducing their number from a peak of 4,507 in 1960 to 2,840 in 1968. Farm size nearly doubled as a result, to an average of 1,391 ha and 360 members in 1968.[45]

The share of investment going into agriculture fell back slightly, to about 16 percent through the late 1960s and the 1970s.[46] This level of continued investment allowed mechanization to reach levels comparable to those in other East and Central European countries, however, as available grain combines and tractors more than doubled. Fertilizer use per ha of arable land also rose, from 29 kilograms in 1960 to 112 kilograms in 1968, although applications still lagged behind Poland, Bulgaria, and Czechoslovakia.[47]

Gross output grew relatively slowly in the 1960s despite the intensification, averaging 2 percent per year from 1960 to 1968. The incomes of collective farmers increased more quickly, rising to 109 percent of industrial wage levels by 1966 (although agricultural workers continued to work longer hours), and collective farm output grew with respect to that on household plots.[48]

Slow growth rates in the economy as a whole led to the implementation, in 1968, of the most unique aspect of Hungary's socialist experiment—the New Economic Mechanism (NEM). This set of reforms significantly reduced the role of central planning in firm decision making (by abolishing the annual plan) and freed many prices (80 percent of them) from government control. To improve incentives, firms were given some latitude in using retained earnings to finance investment, and wages were linked to enterprise profits. While similar reforms were tried in almost every other centrally planned economy, the reforms in Hungary were broader, deeper, and more completely implemented than anywhere else.

The reforms had somewhat less impact in agriculture than elsewhere, as the government had already abandoned centrally determined delivery targets in agriculture in 1957. Still, for the collective farms, the NEM resulted in three significant changes. First, the farms, like other production units, gained increased autonomy. In addition to having more control over their input plans, they also gained the right to make contracts independently with other collective farms and with state farms, including contracts for the marketing of their output. Agricultural price limits were adjusted upward in two price reforms, one in 1966 and one in 1968, and many farm debts were canceled, thereby creating the conditions for

Table 4.3 Members of Hungarian Cooperatives 1948-1959

Year	Number Coops	Total Members (thousands)	Members/Coop	Land/Coop
1948	279	2	8	34
1949	1,290	34	26	111
1950	2,149	118	55	282
1952	2,626	202	77	427
1953	3,632	291	78	
1954	3,307	193	58	
1955	3,239	175	54	
1956	3,759	253	67	
1957	1,617	96	59	
1958	2,557	120	47	198
1959	2,755	140	51	
1960		703		
1970	2,441	773	317	1,391 [a]
1980	1,338			3,097 [b]
1989	1,253	450	360	

[a] 1968
[b] 1978

Sources: KSH, *Magyar statztikai evkonyv*, (Budapest: KSH, 1993 and various years); Ivan Peto and Sandor Szakacs, *A hazai gazdaság négy évtizedének története 1945-1985*, (Budapest: Kozgazdasagi es Jogi Konyvkido, 1985); Nigel Swain, *Collective Farms Which Work?* (Cambridge, Mass.: Cambridge University Press, 1985); Karl-Eugen Wadekin, *Agrarian Policies in Communist Europe*, (London: Allanheld, Osmun, 1982).

farms to independently finance their own investment and certain worker benefits. Investments remained under close central scrutiny, however.[49]

Second, labor relations on collective farms were substantially transformed. After 1968, collective farm members received a wage like any state worker and were eligible for similar social security benefits, including maternity leave. Wages in state farms and cooperatives alike were increasingly linked to farm performance, however, so that in the 1970s an estimated 50 percent of cooperative members' earnings were linked to performance.[50] In the second half of the 1970s, the central government mandated further amalgamation of the cooperatives. Two or three village farms were combined in one cooperative, resulting in an increase in size to 3,097 ha in 1978.[51] By the late 1970s, production relations in cooperatives closely resembled those on the large state farms.

At the same time, however, household production began a period of transformation. After 1968, household plots (which had been issued to households) began to be issued to individual collective farm members, creating the possibility of member households expanding production onto several plots. After 1970, limitations on the number of animals a household could keep were also eased.

As household production was permitted to expand, it was increasingly integrated with production of the collective farms. The farms were encouraged to subcontract the raising of young livestock to households, to provide households with increased fodder and technical assistance, and to purchase and market their production.

The division of labor in cooperatives thus became more specialized. Production of grain crops came almost completely under control of the highly mechanized collective farm, while the more labor-intensive vegetable and certain livestock tasks were increasingly transferred to the control of households.

These changes accompanied a continued evolution of living patterns. During the late 1960s and 1970s, the young labor force continued to leave the village and settle in the towns. Commuting also took on increasing importance in the Hungarian countryside, as people traveled monthly, weekly, or daily to work in a city or town. In the 1970s, some 1 million people were regular commuters.[52] While the towns were still able to provide jobs, they were no longer able to offer homes for the newcomers, and commuters continued to produce on their small-scale household enterprises in the village. A large stratum of peasant-worker households was formed, in which primarily men worked in regional centers and towns, while women remained in the village and took care of the household plot.

This strategy was facilitated by a further loosening of regulation of small-plot farming in the middle of the 1970s. Access to land for small-scale agriculture became more and more independent of membership in a cooperative, and at the beginning of the 1980s some two-thirds of the small-scale producers did not work in agriculture. This allowed households that had no history in agricultural production to enter the field. Altogether, some 60-65 percent of all households took part in small-scale agricultural production—20-25 percent more than the proportion of rural dwellers in the population.

The growth of small-plot farming was linked to the changing aspirations of the rural population. Those who commuted between town and village became acquainted with the urban way of life, taking home some of its elements and contributing to a new structure of consumption in the villages. New types of economic behavior, not typical in the traditional economy, began to emerge among the peasantry. Families sought to expand commodity production into the so-called second economy to finance the new consumption habits.

Table 4.4 Distribution of Land By Organizational Form 1949-1958 (ha)

Year	State Farms	Cooperatives	Peasant Farms
1949	64	43	5,347
1950	264	239	4,769
1951	391	714	4,481
1952	599	623	3,733
1953	741	1,413	3,144
1958	905	546	3,846

Source: Peto and Szakacs, *A hazai gazdaság négy évtizedének története.*

At the end of the 1960s and the beginning of the 1970s, markets for household production were also expanding. The export orientation of agriculture increased and, simultaneously, the domestic demand for agricultural products grew. While the possibility of selling goods on local and regional markets had decreased with the strict state organization of commercial activities in the 1960s, it had not vanished by the 1980s. Further, the partial decrease in local sales was offset by increasing possibilities to take part in national commerce through sales to the state or the cooperatives.

As a result of these dynamics, commodity production of the small-scale enterprises increased considerably at the expense of self-provisioning. By the middle of the 1970s, the number of households engaging in commodity production exceeded those producing only for self-provisioning. Small-scale commodity production became more marked than in any earlier period, including before 1945. While at the beginning of the century the proportion of agricultural products sold on the market was estimated to have been 20-30 percent, the proportion rose by the 1980s to 70 percent.[53]

The households' potential for expansion was limited, however, by the legislated state monopoly on the ownership of most land and means of production. The scarcity of the means of production began to be remedied in the beginning of the 1980s, when individuals were allowed to buy lorries and tractors, but this limited access did not affect significantly the ability of the small-scale enterprises to expand.

Success and Failure (1963-1994)

The Hungarian Agricultural "Miracle" between 1968 and 1982

While the period following initial attempts at collectivization was character-ized by agricultural stagnation, agricultural performance began to improve after 1956. From 1956 to 1968, gross output grew by an average of almost 3 percent per year. Gross output grew slightly faster after 1968, reaching 3 percent per year from 1968 to 1982 and achieving 226 percent of 1950 levels by 1982.[54] This growth was, in part, driven by a jump in yields. Wheat yields, for example, rose from 2,470 kilograms per ha in 1968 to 4,380 in 1982, while corn yields rose from 3,140 to 7,230.[55] Livestock yields rose similarly, with milk production per 100 ha, for instance, rising from 123 hecto-liters in 1965 to 309 in 1982.[56] In per capita value of agricultural production, Hungary rated sixth in the world by the early 1980s.[57]

The exceptional performance of Hungarian agriculture can be explained by the particular way in which Hungary managed the agricultural collectivization, compared to other countries following the Stalinist model. By allowing coopera-tives to be formed along the lines of existing social groups, the Hungarian regime built a reasonably broad social base for collectivization, winning at least some of the middle-income peasants to the cause of collectivization. When the cooperatives were consolidated into larger farms in the 1970s, the government drew on, and strengthened, traditions and aspirations of family farming to promote growth of labor-intensive products. In doing so, the government mobilized part-time labor available in emerging worker-peasant households and replicated the traditional Hungarian farming structure of small plots alongside latifundia. The organizational structures of the cooperatives were thus adapted both to local conditions and history and to the changing needs of the rural population.

After 1956, the commitment to balanced growth ensured adequate investment in the cooperatives, thereby overcoming some of the limitations of Hungary's traditional agricultural structure. When investment further increased, reaching a peak of 19 percent of national investment in 1970, this promoted a "green revolution" in agriculture, especially in animal husbandry, corn production, and market gardening.[58] Fertilizer use rose from 118 kg per ha on collective farms in 1968 to 322 kg per ha in 1982, and standardized tractor capacity rose from 349 units per 1,000 ha in 1968 to 552 in 1982. The effect was the rapid productivity increase seen above.[59]

Legal changes after 1968 ensured basic economic security for member households, while maintaining strong links between earnings and farm perfor-mance. Cooperative members' earnings were supported, in part, by legal changes allowing the cooperatives to diversify into industrial and commercial production. The creation of these supplementary branches of cooperative production offered employment to those who could not be employed year-round in agricultural production on the cooperatives, but the side branches soon became an important source of rural revenue investment funds as well. By the late 1970s and early 1980s, about half of all income of the cooperative came from nonagricultural activities.[60]

Stagnation in the 1980s

After 1982, agricultural output in constant prices began to stagnate and then decline. From 1982 to 1989, output fell by an average of 0.3 percent per year.[61] In part, this was driven by declining yields. Wheat yields, for example, fell from a peak of 54 quintals per ha in 1984 to 44 quintals in 1987. Yields of other grains fell as well, although not so dramatically.[62]

This declining performance can be attributed to both the changing international context and the limits of Hungary's reform model of collective agriculture. As global food markets were increasingly saturated, and the socialist-bloc economies began to decay in the 1980s, profit margins for Hungarian agricultural producers were squeezed. Small producers, producing mainly to support increased consumption levels, kept producing even though stagnating output prices did not keep up with rising input prices. This resulted in further deterioration in domestic market conditions.

Potential for adjustment to the new conditions was limited. Whereas the two-tiered agricultural structure had supported the intensification and commercialization of individual farming by providing land and services to the previously land-hungry Hungarian peasants, the structure could not provide the basis for further growth under the new conditions.

In particular, the inflexibilities caused by the absence of a market in land and other capital assets began to cause serious problems by the 1980s. The more prosperous individual peasants could not expand production, and the income of family farmers, even in the commercially oriented small family farms, was not invested for further productive use, but was channeled into ever higher levels of consumption.

On the large collective farms, innovation and adaptation to changing conditions were slow. The green technologies began to backfire: the extensive use of fertilizers was expensive and had negative effects on the quality of the soil. Without direct access to foreign markets and their hard currency earnings, however, managers' ability to change technologies in line with the demands of international competitiveness was limited, and they were unable to complete with vertically integrated capitalist agribusinesses. Adjustment on sharecropped land was little better. As the majority of sharecroppers had no security of tenure, they had little interest in making investments or even in protecting the fertility of land.

Simultaneously, the industrial organization of agriculture resulted in the deskilling of the majority of labor. While management on the collective farms was highly trained, most workers had only very specialized skills or no special skills at all. The family plot did not help much in this respect. Most of the tasks on the family plot were simple or could be learned fast. The average agricultural proletariat on the cooperatives thus lost some of the traditional skills but did not gain many modern skills.

Under these conditions, lacking middle-sized farms and entrepreneurial potential, Hungarian agriculture was unable to enter a postfordist state. As agriculture in the 1980s faced stronger international competition, and cooperatives were challenged to find new, flexible organizational forms and technologies, it turned out that they lacked both the legal context and the human capital necessary to do so. By the late 1980s, those cooperatives that avoided losses did so by developing successful commercial or industrial sidelines. To reinvigorate agricultural production itself, more flexible forms of organization and division of labor between the private and cooperative sectors were needed. Experiments of this type, however, would have to wait until after 1989.

Notes

1. Nigel Swain, *Collective Farms Which Work?* (Cambridge, Mass.: Cambridge University Press, 1985), 197. Istvan Harcsa, Imre Kovach, and Ivan Szelenyi, "The Price of Privatization," *Sociological Review* (Budapest, 1995).

2. Ivan Szelenyi, *Socialist Entrepreneurs: Embourgeoisment in Rural Hungary* (Madison, Wis.: University of Wisconsin Press, 1988). Imre Kovach, "Rediscovering Small-Scale Enterprise in Rural Hungary in: Rural Entreprise," in *Critical Perspectives on Rural Change,* ed. S. Whatmore, P. Lowe, T. Marsden (London: David Fulton Publishers, 1991). Imre Kovach, *Termelok es vallalkozok* (Budapest: Tarsadalomtudomanyi Intezet, 1988).

3. This is a hotly debated thesis. See Berend T., Ivan and Gyorgy Ranki. *Közép-Kelet-Európa gazdasági fejlődése a 19-20.* Budapest: Közgazdasági és Jogi Könyvkiadó, 1976, Orosz, István, "A differenciálódás és kisajátítás," in *A parasztság Magyarországon a kapitalizmus korában,* Szabo, Istvan, ed., Budapest: Akadémiai Kiadó, 1965, and Gunst, Peter, *A paraszti társadalom Magyarországon a két világháború között.* Budapest: MTA Történettudomnyi Intézet, 1987.

4. Ivan T. Berend and Gyorgy Ranki, *A magyar gazdaság száz éve* (Budapest: Közgazdasági és Jogi Könyvkiadó, 1972).

5. Istvan Orosz, "A differenciálódás és kisajátítás," in *A parasztság Magyarországon a kapitalizmus korában,* ed. Szabó, István (Budapest: Akadémiai Kiadó, 1965).

6. Peter Gunst, *A paraszti társadalom Magyarországon a két világháború között* (Budapest: MTA Történettudomnyi Intézet, 1987).

7. Berend and Ranki, *A magyar gazdaság száz éve.*

8. The territory of the Hungarian state was reduced by approximately two-thirds by the peace treaty of World War I. Ivan T. Berend and Gyorgy Ranki, *A magyar gazdaság száz éve* (Budapest: Közgazdasági és Jogi Könyvkiadó, 1972). Ivan T. Berend and Gyorgy Ranki, *Kozep-Kelet-Europa gazdasagi fejlodese a 19 - 20* (Budapest: Kozgadasagi es Jogi Konyvkiado, 1976).

9. Ferenc Donath, *Reform és forrdalom. A magyar mezögazdaság turktúrális átalkulása 1945-1975* (Budapest: Akadémiai Kiadó, 1977).

10. Ferenc Donath, *Demokratikus földreform Magyarországon 1945 -1947* (Budapest: Akadémiai Kiadó, 1969).

11. Ivan Peto, and Sandor Szakacs, *A hazai gazdaság négy évtizedének története 1945 - 1985* (Budapest: Közgazdasági és Jogi Könyvkidó, 1985).

12. Joan Sokolovsky, *Peasants and Power: State Autonomy and the Collectivization of Agriculture in Eastern Europe* (Boulder, Colo.: Westview Press, 1990), 94.

13. Peto and Szakacs, *A hazai gazdasag.*

14. Donath, *Reform es forrdalom.*

15. Peto and Szakacs, *A hazai gazdasag.* Berend and Ranki, *A magyar gasdasag szaz eve.*

16. Ivan Volgyes, "Modernization, Collectivization, Production and Legitimacy: Agricultural Development in Modern Hungary," in *The Political Economy of Collectivized Agriculture: A Comparative Study of Communist and Non-Communist Systems,* ed. Ronald Francisco, Betty Laird and Roy Laird (New York: Pergamon Press, 1979), 120.

17. Joseph Held, *The Modernization of Agriculture: Rural Transformation in Hungary 1948-1975* (New York: Columbia University Press, 1980), 372. Sokolovsky, *Peasants and Power,* 91, 102.

18. For more details, see Pal Zavada, "Kulakpres," in *Medvetanc* (1984).

19. Peto and Szakacs, *A hazai gazdasag.*

20. Pal Zavada, "Kulakpres," in *Medvetanc* (1984).

21. Sokolovsky, *Peasants and Power,* 102.

22. Ivan Volgyes, "Dynamic Change: Rural Transformation 1945-1975," in *The Modernization of Agriculture: Rural Transformation in Hungary 1948-1975,* ed. Joseph Held (New York: Columbia University Press, 1980), 372.

23. Held, *The Modernization of Agriculture,* 373.

24. Held, *The Modernization of Agriculture,* 373.

25. Ferenc Fekete, Earl O. Heady, and Bob R. Holden, *Economics of Cooperative Farming* (Budapest: Akademiai Kiado, 1976), 31. Sokolovsky, *Peasants and Power,* 102. Peto and Szakacs, *A hazai gasdasag.*

26. Held, *The Modernization of Agriculture,* 374.

27. Peto and Szakacs, *A hazai gazdaság.*

28. Volgyes, "Dynamic Change: Rural Transformation 1945-1975," 119.

29. Volgyes, "Dynamic Change: Rural Transformation 1945-1975," 374.

30. Ivan T. Berend, *Gazdasági útkeresés* (Budapest: Magvetõ Könyvkiadó, 1983).

31. Held, *The Modernization of Agriculture,* 383.

32. Swain, *Collective Farms Which Work?* 196. Istvan Harcsa, Imre Kovach, and Ivan Szelenyi, "The Price of Privatization," *Sociological Review* (Budapest, 1995). Donath, *Reform és forrdalom.*

33. Donath, *Reform és forrdalom.* Ivan T. Berend, *Gazdasági útkeresés* (Budapest: Magvetõ Könyvkiadó, 1983). Peto and Szakacs, *A hazai gazdaság.*

34. Ronald Francisco, et al., *The Political Economy of Collectivized Agriculture: A Comparative Study of Communist and Non-Communist Systems,* ed. Ronald Francisco, et al. (New York: Pergammon, 1979), 119. Kozponti Statisztikai Hivtal (KSH) *A falu es a mezogazdasag (fobb gazdasagi es tarsadalmi jelzoszamai)* Budapest: KSH (1994).

35. Karl-Eugen Wadekin, *Agrarian Policies in Communist Europe: A Critical Introduction* (London: Allanheld, Osmun, 1982), 155.

36. Swain, *Collective Farms Which Work?* 197. Harcsa, Kovach, and Szelenyi, "The Price of Privatization," 31, 46. Kovach, *Termelok es vallalkozok.*

37. Kozponti Statisztikai Hivtal (KSH) *A falu es a mezogazdasag.*

38. Francisco, et al., *The Political Economy of Collectivized Agriculture,* 119.

39. Wadekin, *Agrarian Policies in Communist Europe*, 174. Held, *The Modernization of Agriculture*, 383.

40. Berend and Ranki, *A magyar gazdaság száz éve*. Peto and Szakacs, *A hazai gazdaság*.

41. Peto and Szakacs, *A hazai gazdaság*. Swain, *Collective Farms Which Work?* 49. Kovach, *Termelok es vallalkozok*. Pal Juhasz "Agrarpiac, kisuzem, nagyuzem," in *Medvetánc* (1982).

42. Kozponti Statisztikai Hivtal (KSH) *A falu es a mezogazdasag*.

43. Imre Kovach, "Rediscovering Small-Scale Enterprise in Rural Hungary in: Rural Entreprise," in *Critical Perspectives on Rural Change,* ed. S. Whatmore, P. Lowe, and T. Marsden (London: David Fulton Publishers, 1991). Kovach, *Termelok es vallalkozok*.

44. Wadekin, *Agrarian Policies in Communist Europe*, 86.

45. Swain, *Collective Farms Which Work?* 197.

46. Peto and Szakacs, *A hazai gazdaság*.

47. Peto and Szakacs, *A hazai gazdaság*. Volgyes, "Dynamic Change: Rural Transformation 1945-1975," 120.

48. Swain, *Collective Farms Which Work?* 57, 197.

49. Swain, *Collective Farms Which Work?* 51-54. Juhasz "Agrarpiac, kisuzem, nagyuzem."

50. Held, *The Modernization of Agriculture*, 416.

51. Wadekin, *Agrarian Policies in Communist Europe*, 87.

52. Kozponti Statisztikai Hivtal (KSH) *A falu es a mezogazdasag*.

53. Juhasz "Agrarpiac, kisuzem, nagyuzem." Kovach, *Termelok es vallalkozok*.

54. Swain, *Collective Farms Which Work?* 197. Istvan Harcsa, Imre Kovach, and Ivan Szelenyi, "A posztszocialista Atalakulasi valsag a mezogazdasagban es a falusi tarsadalomban," *Szociologiai Szemle* 2 (1994).

55. Harcsa, Kovach, and Szelenyi, "A posztszocialista Atalakulasi valsag a mezogazdasagban es a falusi tarsadalomban."

56. Kozponti Statisztikai Hivtal in *Magyar statisztikai evkonyv* (Budapest: KSH, 1993).

57. Kozponti Statisztikai Hivtal in *A magyar mezõgazdaság európai összehasonlításban* (Budapest: KSH, 1985).

58. World Bank, *Hungary, Economic Developments and Reforms* (Washington, D.C.: The World Bank, 1984), 72.

59. Kozponti Statisztikai Hivtal (KSH) *A falu es a mezogazdasag*.

60. Kozponti Statisztikai Hivtal (KSH) *A falu es a mezogazdasag*.

61. Gregory Lazarcik, et. al. "Agricultural Output, Gross Product, and Expenses in Eastern Europe 1975-1991," in Research Project on National Income in East Central Europe Occasional Paper 121 (New York: International Financial Research, Inc., 1992), 33.

62. Vienna Institute, *Comecon Data 1988* (New York: Greewood Press, 1989).

5

China: Farming Institutions and Rural Development

Justin Lin

Dramatic changes in farming institutions were a distinguishing feature of China's agricultural development following the socialist revolution in 1949. The traditional farming system in rural China had been characterized by small, independent household farms with less than one hectare of fragmented land-holding. The socialist government effected a land reform program in areas under its control before 1949, and completed the program nationwide in 1952. Under this program, land was confiscated from landlords and rich peasants without compensation, and redistributed freely to poor and landless peasants. However, individual household farms were collectivized under the provisions of the first five-year plan in 1953. This collective farming system prevailed until the household-based farming system reform in 1979.

Two of the most frequently mentioned achievements of the collective farming system are its ability to sustain an exploding population and to support a dramatic structural change in China's economy. When the socialist government was founded in 1949, the amount of cultivated land per capita was only 0.18 hectare, and due to rapid population growth, this figure had dropped to 0.1 hectare by 1978.[1] This collective system, nevertheless, was able to keep food production ahead of population growth. Meanwhile, the economy experienced a spectacular transformation, with industrial income expanding from 12.6 percent of total national income in 1949 to 46.8 percent in 1978.

An important issue that confronts most developing countries is how to develop agriculture rapidly in order to support urban industrialization and to meet the increased food demands brought on by explosive population growth. The small and fragmented holdings that characterize the landscapes in most developing countries are often regarded as a great obstacle to mechanization, irrigation, plant protection, and efficient allocation of inputs. Therefore, some economists have suggested that the institution of collective farming in China can provide a model of agricultural development for underdeveloped, densely populated economies.[2] However, recently released data do not seem to support this theory, as the data indicate that between 1952 and 1978 the growth rate in grain production was 2.4 percent per year, only 0.4 percent above the population growth rate for the same period. Per capita availability of grain, therefore, only increased 10 percent in more than a quarter century. In addition, the per capita income of farm population increased only about 50 percent in the same period. Compared to the remarkable economic transitions in East Asian economies—Taiwan, Hong Kong, Singapore, and Korea—China's economic performance in the 1960s and 1970s was disappointing.

Frustrated by their inability to substantially improve the welfare of the Chinese population after thirty years of socialist revolution, at the end of 1978 the veteran leaders, who were purged during the Cultural Revolution and came into power again after the death of Chairman Mao Zedong in 1976, initiated a series of sweeping reforms in agriculture, including the replacement of the collective system with a new household-based farming system. These reforms resulted in remarkable growth during the first half of the 1980s. Between 1978 and 1984, the value of the agricultural sector as a whole grew at a rate of 7.4 percent annually, and grain output at 4.8 percent. Both these rates are far above the 2.9 percent and 2.4 percent achieved during the previous twenty-six years. Meanwhile, the population growth rate dropped from an annual rate of 2 percent in 1952-1978 to 1.3 percent in 1978-1984. The availability of agricultural products and the overall living standard of both the urban and rural population had a substantial improvement for the first time in about three decades.

The success of agricultural reforms in 1978-1984, and especially the remarkable growth of grain output, greatly encouraged China's political leaders to implement further reforms. As a result, a series of more market-oriented reforms were undertaken at the end of 1984 in both the urban and rural sectors. Agriculture as a whole continued to grow at a respectable average rate of 4.1 percent per year after 1984. Grain production, however, stagnated after reaching a peak of 407 million tons in 1984. This was of some concern, since most political leaders in China gave a high priority to the principle of grain self-sufficiency.[3] Therefore, the optimism that robust agricultural development had generated during the first five years of rural reforms was swiftly replaced in the subsequent downturn by a pessimistic mood. Poor grain production from 1985 to 1988 gave some political leaders a strong reason to reemphasize more conservative, and plan-oriented agricultural policies. Some even advocated recollectivizing the individual household-based farming system under the banner of pursuing economies of scale in agricultural production. Although China's rural institutional reforms may have reached an irreversible point, poor performance in grain production will always be a political issue in China.

In the rest of this chapter, I provide an analytical description of the institutions and policies related to China's agricultural development. The first section, "Economic Development Strategy and the Role of Agriculture," briefly describes the role of agriculture in the overall economic development strategy after the adoption of the first five-year plan in 1953. The section entitled "Rural Institutional Change and Development Policies" is devoted to a discussion of the major institutional and related policy changes during the years 1952-1988. This period is divided into two subperiods: the collectivization period of 1952-1978, and the household responsibility reform period of 1979-1988. "Farming Institutions, Performance, and Income Distribution" describes the performance of Chinese agriculture in terms of output growth, yield changes, and total factor productivity. The impact of development policies on rural income distribution and rural-urban income disparity is also assessed in this section. The chapter concludes with a brief summary of the lessons to be learned from China's agricultural development.

Economic Development Strategy and the Role of Agriculture

To assess the performance of China's agricultural development after the socialist takeover in 1949, I start with a description of the role of agriculture in the socialist government's overall economic development strategy. It will become clear in the following discussion that the agricultural problems prior to the 1979 reforms stemmed from the development strategy that the Chinese government adopted in the early 1950s. The postreform problems also have their roots in this early development strategy.

At the founding of the People's Republic in 1949, the Chinese government inherited a war-torn agrarian economy in which 89.4 percent of the population resided in rural areas and industry made up only 12.6 percent of national income. A developed heavy-industry sector was considered to be the symbol of a nation's power and economic achievement at that time. The new political leadership in China, like the leadership in India and many other newly independent developing countries, certainly had every intention to accelerate the development of heavy industries. After China's involvement in the Korean War in 1950 and the resulting embargo and isolation from the Western camp, catching up with the industrialized powers also became a necessity for national security. Besides, the Soviet Union's outstanding record of nation building in the 1930s, contrasted with the Great Depression in the Western market economies, provided the Chinese leadership with both inspiration and experience for a heavy-industry-oriented development strategy. Therefore, in 1953, after the recovery from wartime destruction, the Chinese government adopted a Stalin-type development strategy. The goal was to build, as rapidly as possible, the country's capacity to produce capital goods and military materials.

This development strategy was shaped after 1953 through a series of five-year plans: table 5.1 shows the sector shares in state capital construction investment from the first five-year plan (1953-1957) to the sixth five-year plan (1981-1985). It is interesting to note that despite the fact that more than three-quarters of China's population participated in agriculture, agriculture received less than 10 percent of the investment in 1953-1985, while 45 percent went to heavy industry. Moreover, heavy industry received the lion's share of the investments under the heading "other," including workers' housing and infrastructure. At the same time most private initiative in economic activities was prohibited in China. This pattern in government investment is the best indicator of the bias in the official development strategy. As a result of this development strategy, industry grew at an average annual rate of 11 percent between 1952 and 1980, while agriculture's share in national income declined. In 1952, the year before the heavy-industry-oriented strategy was implemented, agricultural income constituted 57.7 percent of the total national income. In the 1970s and 1980s, though, agriculture's share dropped to around 40 percent. Meanwhile, the value of industrial output in national income grew from less than 20 percent in the 1950s to more than 40 percent in the 1970s and 1980s, as seen in table 5.2. Also, as a result of these investment priorities, fixed assets per industrial worker rose from 3,000 yuan per worker for 5.26 million industrial workers in 1952 to nearly 9,000 yuan per worker for 50.05 million industrial workers in the late 1970s, while a rural work force of 294 million in the late 1970s had only 310 yuan of fixed assets per person.[4]

In looking at the construction of a heavy-industry project, we can recognize that there are three distinct aspects that characterize such a project: (1) the project is likely to involve a long period of time, maybe ten years or more, until completion (2) each project requires a large initial investment; and (3) most heavy equipment for the project must be imported from more advanced economies. This last characteristic is specific to a developing economy.[5] For instance, when the Chinese government initiated the heavy-industry-oriented development strategy in the early 1950s, China was a poor, underdeveloped, capital-scarce, agrarian economy. The availability of credit in the market was very limited and the interest rate was high. Likewise, foreign exchange was scarce and expensive. Spontaneous development of capital-intensive industry in a capital-scarce economy was impossible. Therefore, to implement the heavy-industry-oriented development strategy in a capital-scarce economy, such as China's, a specific set of economic policies is required. To reduce the costs of interest payments and the costs of importing equipment for the priority industry, a low-interest-rate policy and an overvalued exchange rate policy were introduced at the beginning of the first five-year plan. Meanwhile, for the purpose of securing enough funds for the industrial expansion, a policy of low wages for industrial workers evolved alongside the development strategy. The assumption was that the state-owned enterprises would be able to generate large profits through low costs and to then reinvest the profits in infrastructure and capital construction. Therefore, although real gross national product (GNP) per capita tripled between 1952 and 1978, the real wage rate was kept almost constant, increasing only 10.3 percent during the same period.[6] The establishment of low prices for energy, transportation, and other raw materials, such as cotton, was instituted for the same reason.

To make the policy of low wages possible, the government had to provide urban residents with inexpensive food and other necessities, including housing, medical care, and clothing. To this end, a restrictive rationing system was instituted in 1953 to distribute the low-priced food and other basic necessities and remained in effect until the 1979 reforms.[7] At the same time, to secure the source of cheap supplies for urban rationing, a compulsory procurement policy was imposed in rural areas. The policy obliged peasants to sell to the state, at government-set prices, certain quantities of their produce, including grain, cotton, and edible oil. In doing so, the state practically monopolized the trade in grain and other major agricultural products. This monopoly completely insulated Chinese consumers from the impact of price fluctuations in domestic and international markets. Meanwhile, to prevent an influx of rural population to cities to be fed by the low-priced rations, the government instituted a rigid urban household registration system, which virtually closed the route of rural-urban

Table 5.1 Sector Share of State Capital Construction Investment, Five-Year Plans

	Agriculture	Light Industry	Heavy Industry	Other
	(%)	(%)	(%)	(%)
First	7.1	6.4	36.2	50.3
Second	11.3	6.4	54.0	28.3
1963-1965	17.6	3.9	45.9	32.6
Third	10.7	4.4	51.1	33.8
Fourth	9.8	5.8	49.6	34.8
Fifth	10.5	6.7	45.9	36.9
Sixth	5.1	6.9	38.5	49.5
1953-1985	8.9	6.2	45.0	39.9

Source: State Statistical Bureau, *Zhongguo gudingzichantouzi tonggiziliao (China capital construction statistical data 1950-1985)*, (Beijing: China Statistics Press, 1987), 97.

migration.[8] As a result, even though agriculture's share of the national income dropped from 57.7 percent to 39.1 percent due to rapid industrialization from 1952 to 1980 (see table 5.2), rural population only dropped from 87.5 percent of total population to 80.6 percent during the same period.[9]

In addition to providing cheap food for industrialization, the agricultural sector also enabled China to build up its weak industrial base, by generating the foreign exchange necessary for obtaining equipment and raw materials from abroad. In fact, agriculture remained the main source of scarce foreign exchange up to the 1970s, as seen in table 5.3. This dependence on agriculture's performance for the country's importation of capital goods can be recognized by noting that in the 1950s, agricultural products alone made up over 40 percent of all exports. If processed agricultural products are also counted, agriculture contributed more than 60 percent of China's foreign exchange earnings up to the 1970s. In addition, as table 5.4 indicates, except for the years during and immediately after the great agricultural crisis in the early 1960s, most of this foreign exchange was used to import machinery, equipment, and raw materials for industrial uses. Thus, in the early stage of development, the country's capacity to import capital goods for industrialization clearly depended on agriculture's performance. In short, agriculture played a supporting role in the heavy-industry-oriented development strategy in China.

However, although agriculture played this supporting role and the majority

Table 5.2 Sector Composition of National Income (Current Price)

Year	Agriculture %	Industry %	Construction %	Transportation %	Commerce %
1949	68.4	12.6	0.3	3.3	15.4
1952	57.7	19.5	3.6	4.3	14.9
1957	46.8	28.3	5.0	4.3	15.6
1962	48.0	32.8	3.5	4.1	11.6
1965	46.2	36.4	3.8	4.2	9.4
1970	41.3	40.1	4.1	3.8	10.7
1975	39.4	44.5	4.5	3.8	7.8
1980	39.1	45.8	5.0	3.4	6.7
1985	40.2	40.3	5.7	3.6	10.2

Source: State Statistical Bureau, *Guominshouru tongji ziliao huibian (A Compilation of National Income Statistics Data)* (Beijing: China Statistical Press), 9.

of the population resided in rural areas, the state invested only modestly in agriculture. Given the link between agriculture and industrialization and agriculture's meager initial state, agriculture's stagnation or poor performance would not only affect the food supply but also have an almost immediate and direct adverse effect on industrial expansion. Therefore, although agriculture assumed only a supporting role in the overall development strategy, the government could not ignore the importance of agriculture's growth. The central feature of China's agricultural development, however, was the reliance on organizational reforms, specifically collectivism, as a means of achieving development goals. The following sections will examine the effectiveness of this agricultural development strategy.

Rural Institutional Changes and Development Policies

This section discusses the features and evolution of China's agricultural institutions and development policies. The major changes in Chinese agriculture, following recovery from the war destruction, can be divided into two sub-periods: (1) the collectivization period of 1952-1978, and (2) the household responsibility system reform period spanning from 1979 to the present.

Table 5.3 Composition of Exports

		Share of		
Year	Total Value (Million US$)	Agricultural Products (%)	Processed Agricultural Products (%)	Industrial & Mineral Products (%)
1953	1,022	55.7	25.9	18.4
1957	1,597	40.1	31.5	28.4
1962	1,490	19.4	45.9	34.7
1965	2,228	33.1	36.0	30.9
1970	2,260	36.7	37.7	25.6
1975	7,264	29.6	31.1	39.3
1980	18,272	18.5	29.5	99.8
1985	25,915	17.5	26.9	55.6

Source: The Editorial Board of the Almanac of China's Foreign Economic Relations and Trade, *Almanac of China's Foreign Economic Relations and Trade 1986* (Beijing: Zhongguo Zhanwang Press, 1986), 954.

Collectivization and Agricultural Development Policies[10]

Although the priority sector in China's economic development strategy was
heavy industry, the pace of industrialization was nevertheless constrained by the
performance of agriculture. The government, however, was reluctant to divert
scarce resources and funds from industry to agriculture, which could have
improved agricultural performance. Therefore, alongside the heavy-industry-
oriented development strategy, the government adopted a new agricultural
development strategy that would not compete for resources with industrial
expansion. The core of this strategy involved the mass mobilization of rural
labor to work on labor-intensive investment projects, such as irrigation, flood
control, and land reclamation, and the use of traditional methods and inputs,
such as closer planting, more careful weeding, and the use of more organic
fertilizer to raise unit yields in agriculture. Collectivization of agriculture was
the institution that the government believed would best perform these
functions.[11]

The traditional farming institution in rural China for thousands of years
prior to the founding of the People's Republic had been the independent family
farm. Typically these farms were not only small but also fragmented. At the
dawn of the socialist revolution, nearly 40 percent of the cultivated land in rural
China was owned by landlords who leased land out to peasant families, as seen
in table 5.5. Rents were often as high as 50 percent of the value of the main
crops. Starting in the 1940s, a land reform program was implemented in areas
under the Communist Party's control, under which land was confiscated from
landlords and rich peasants without compensation, and distributed freely to poor
and landless peasants. This land reform program was continued after the success
of the revolution and completed nationwide in 1952. After the land reform, the
distribution of land in rural China was more egalitarian, as the information in
table 5.5 suggests. For instance, we can see that by 1954, the landholdings of the
poor had increased from 14.28 percent in 1950 to 47.1 percent, while that of the
landlords decreased from 38.26 percent in 1950 to only 2.2 percent, with the
1954 figures being more representative of the percentage of the population that
each class comprised.

As indicated by table 5.6, experiments with various forms of cooperatives
began even before the completion of land reform in 1952. Three main types of
cooperatives have been noticed. The first type of cooperative was the "mutual
aid team" in which 4 or 5 neighboring households pooled together their farm
tools and draft animals, and exchanged their labor on a temporary or permanent
basis, with land and harvests belonging to the individual households. This
mutual aid team was the predominant form of cooperative until 1955, after
which other types of cooperatives became more popular. In the second type of
cooperative, the "elementary cooperative," about 20 to 30 neighboring households pooled together farm tools and draft animals, as well as land, under

Table 5.4 Composition of Imports

| Year | Total Value (Million US$) | Machinery & Equipment (%) | Raw and Intermediary Materials | | Means of Sub-sistence (%) |
			For Industrial Use (%)	For Agricultural Use (%)	
1953	1,346	56.6	33.7	1.8	7.9
1957	1,506	52.5	34.6	4.9	8.0
1962	1,173	14.6	35.1	5.5	44.8
1965	2,017	17.6	40.1	8.8	33.5
1970	2,326	15.8	57.4	9.5	17.3
1975	7,487	32.1	45.7	7.6	14.6
1980	19,550	27.5	44.1	7.3	21.1
1985	34,331	31.9	46.6	4.3	17.2

Source: The Editorial Board of the Almanac of China's Foreign Economic Relations and Trade, *Almanac of China's Foreign Economic Relations and Trade 1986*, 958.

unified management. The net income of a cooperative was distributed in two categories: a payment for land, draft animals, and farm tools owned by each household; and a remuneration for work performed by each worker. Land, draft animals, and farm tools were still owned by member households. The third type of cooperative was the collective farm, or the "advanced cooperative," in which all means of production, including land, draft animals, and farm tools, were collectively owned. Remuneration in an advanced cooperative was based solely on the amount of work each member contributed, and took the form of work points. The income of a family in an advanced cooperative depended on the amount of work points earned by family members and on the average value of a work point. The latter, in turn, depended on the net production of the collective farm. The size of an advanced cooperative was initially about 30 households, and later evolved to include all households in a village, approximately 150-200 households.

The official approach to collectivization, initially, was cautious and gradual. Peasants were encouraged to join the different forms of cooperative on a voluntary basis. However, proponents for accelerating the pace of collectiviza-

Table 5.5: Class Structure and Land Holding

	1950		1954	
Peasant	Population (%)	Land (%)	Population (%)	Land (%)
Poor	52.37	14.28	52.2	47.1
Middle	33.13	30.94	39.9	44.3
Rich	4.66	13.66	5.3	6.4
Landlord	4.75	38.26	2.6	2.2
Other	5.09	2.86	—	—

Source: State Statistical Bureau, *Jianguo 30 nian chuanguo nongye tongji ziliao 1949-1979 (National Agricultural Statistics for the 30 Years Since the Founding of the Peoples' Republic of China 1949-1979)* (Beijng: State Statistical Bureau, 1980), 19.

tion won the debate within the party in the summer of 1955. That year there were only 500 advanced cooperatives, but by the winter of 1957, 753,000 advanced cooperative farms, with 119 million member households, had been established on a nationwide basis (see table 5.6).

Collectivization encountered no active resistance from the peasantry initially and was carried out relatively smoothly. The gross value of agriculture (measured at constant prices in 1952) increased 27.8 percent, and grain output increased 21.9 percent between 1952 and 1958.[12] This experience and blind belief in economies of scale greatly encouraged the leadership within the party and led them to take a bolder approach. This manifested itself in the "People's Commune," which was introduced in the fall of 1958 and which consisted of about 30 collectives of 150 households each and was introduced in the fall of 1958. From the end of August to the beginning of November, within only three months, 753,000 collective farms were transformed into 24,000 communes, which consisted of 120 million households, over 99 percent of total rural households in China in 1958. The average size of a commune was about 5,000 households with 10,000 laborers and 10,000 acres of cultivated land. Payment in the commune was made according to subsistence needs and partly according to the work performed. Work on private plots, which existed in the other forms of cooperatives, was prohibited.

Although, as expected, billions of person-days were mobilized, the commune movement ended in a profound agricultural crisis between 1959 and 1961. The gross value of agriculture, measured at 1952 prices, dropped 14 percent in 1959, 12 percent in 1960, and another 2.5 percent in 1961. Most important, grain output fell 15 percent in 1959, another 16 percent in 1960, remained at the same low level for another year, and did not recover to the level of 1952 until

1962. This dramatic decline in grain output resulted in a widespread and severe famine. The evidence available now suggests that this resulted in over thirty million deaths due to starvation and malnutrition.[13] This disaster is undoubtedly one of the worst catastrophes in human history.

Even after this terrible crisis, communes were not abolished. However, starting in 1962, agricultural operation was divided and management was delegated to a much smaller unit, the "production team," which consisted of about 20 to 30 neighboring households. In this new system, land was jointly owned by the commune, brigade, and production team. However, the production team was treated as the basic operating and accounting unit. Under the production team system, a peasant was awarded work points for each day's work. At the end of each year, the net team income, after deducting for tax, the public welfare fund, and distribution for basic needs, was distributed within the production team according to the work points that each peasant accumulated during the year. This remuneration system was similar to that in the advanced cooperative. After 1962, many attempts to improve the grading of work points were made. The production team, however, remained the basic farming institution until the household responsibility system reform began in 1979.

A more realistic approach toward agricultural development was adopted after the 1959-1961 crisis. While the mobilization of rural labor for public irrigation projects continued, greater emphasis was given to modern inputs. Irrigated acreage increased gradually from 30.55 million hectares (29.7 percent of total cultivated area) in 1962 to 44.97 million hectares (45.2 percent of total cultivated area) in 1978; but, as table 5.7 shows, most of this increase resulted from the spread of powered irrigation rather than from the construction of labor-intensive canals and dams. The utilization of chemical fertilizer was also accelerated. Starting from a very modest 22.5 kilograms per hectare in 1962, usage per hectare increased to 291 kilograms in 1978 (see table 5.7). Equally impressive was the expansion in the utilization of electricity, a 17.5-time increase between 1962 and 1978.

At the same time as the increases in the use of chemical fertilizers and other modern inputs, the government also initiated a program to establish an agricultural research and promotion system for modern varieties. As a matter of fact, agricultural research has been one of the Chinese government's most successful areas. The Chinese Academy of Agricultural Sciences was founded in Beijing in 1957, and, concurrently, each of the twenty-nine provinces also established its own academy of agricultural sciences. In the 1950s, the focus was on selection and promotion of the best local varieties. Later, the emphasis later shifted to the breeding of new, modern, high-yield varieties. First, a major breakthrough in rice breeding occurred in 1964, when China began full-scale distribution of fertilizer-responsive, pest-resistant dwarf rice varieties with high-yield potential, two years earlier than the release of IR-8, the variety that launched the Green

Many Shades of Red

Table 5.6 The Collectivization Movement in China, 1950-1958

	1950	1951	1952	1953	1954	1955	1956	1957	1958
Mutual Team:									
Teams (1,000)									
	2,724	4,675	8,026	7,450	9,931	7,147	850	—	—
Households per Team									
	4.2	4.5	5.7	6.1	6.9	8.4	12.2	—	—
Elementary Co-op:									
Co-ops (1,000)									
	0.018	0.129	4	15	114	633	216	36	—
Households per Co-op									
	10.4	12.3	15.7	18.1	20	26.7	48.2	44.5	—
Advanced Co-op:									
Co-ops (1,000)									
	0.001	0.001	0.01	0.15	0.2	0.5	540	753	—
Households per Co-op									
	32	30	184	137.3	58.6	75.8	198.9	158.6	—
Commune:									
Commune									
	—	—	—	—	—	—	—	—	24,000
Households per Commune									
	—	—	—	—	—	—	—	—	5,000

Source: Hanxian Luo, *Economic Changes in Rural China* (Beijing: New World Press, 1985), 59, and Agricultural Cooperativization in China Editorial Office, *Zhongguo nongye hezuoshi zilio (Historical Material of Agricultural Cooperativization in China)* no. 1 (February 1987), 6-7.

Revolution in other parts of Asia, by the International Rice Research Institute in the Philippines. At about the same time, hybrid corn and sorghum, improved cotton varieties, and new varieties of other crops were also released and promoted. These high-yielding varieties were accepted rapidly. A second major breakthrough in rice breeding occurred in 1976, when China became the first, and up to now the only, country to commercialize the production of hybrid rice. The innovation and commercial development of hybrid rice was heralded as the most important achievement in rice breeding in the 1970s.[14] By 1979, the percentage figures for areas sown with high-yielding varieties were 80 percent for rice, 85 percent for wheat, 60 percent for soybeans, 75 percent for cotton, 70 percent for peanuts, and 45 percent for rape.[15]

Despite the rapid increases in modern inputs and improvements in varieties in the 1960s and 1970s, the performance of agriculture continued to be poor, possibly as a result of the lack of market mechanisms, such as price signals, to guide the development of the rural economy. Planning prevailed as the adjustment measure in agriculture production, resulting from the emphasis placed on self-sufficiency in grain, which was a component of the Stalin-type heavy-industry-oriented development strategy that the Chinese government pursued from 1953. Two distinct prices, quota price and above-quota price, existed in the state commercial system. The quota price, also called the procurement price, applied to crops sold in fulfillment of procurement obligations; the above-quota price applied to crops sold in excess of the obligation. Because even the above-quota prices were kept at an artificially low level, the more grain an area exported, the more tax it effectively paid. Areas with a comparative advantage in grain production were thus reluctant to raise their level of grain output. Consequently, other areas, which lacked a comparative advantage in grain production and were therefore grain deficient, found it necessary to increase grain production themselves when population or income growth prompted increases in grain demand. National self-sufficiency thus degenerated into local self-sufficiency.

To guarantee that each region would produce enough grain for its needs, planning of agricultural production was thus extensive before the reforms. Mandatory targets often specified not only sown acreage of each crop but also yields, levels of inputs, and so forth. As grain was given priority in planning, insufficient attention was given to other economic considerations. To increase grain output to meet state procurement quotas and local demands, local governments were often forced to expand grain-cultivation area at the expense of cash crops, and to increase cropping intensity, even though these practices often resulted in net losses to farmers. Such measures undoubtedly caused land allocation to increasingly depart from the principle of comparative advantage. The loss of comparative regional advantages was especially serious in areas that traditionally depended on interregional grain trade to facilitate specialization in cash crops.[16] All these led to the failure in the goal of self-sufficiency; China changed from a net grain exporter in the 1950s to a sizable grain importer from the 1960s through the 1980s. The availability of grain per capita increased only 14 percent between 1952 and 1978 (see table 5.8). This dismal picture prompted dramatic institutional reforms in 1979.

The Household Responsibility System Reform[17]

The discouraging record of Chinese agriculture changed abruptly in 1978, when China started a series of fundamental reforms in the rural sector. Output growth accelerated to a rate several times the long-term average in the previous period. Specifically, the annual growth rates for the three most important agricultural products, namely, grain, cotton, and oil-bearing crops, averaged respectively 4.8 percent, 17.7 percent, and 13.8 percent between 1978 and 1984, compared to the average rates of 2.4 percent, 1.0 percent, and 0.8 percent per

Table 5.7 Irrigation, Tractor-plowed Area, Chemical Fertilizer, and Electricity

	Irrigation			Tractor-Plowed Area		Chemical Fertilizer		Electric-ity
Year	Total Irrigated Area (million hectare)	Irrigated Area in Total Cul-tivated Area (%)	Power-ed-Irriga-tion in Irrigated Area (%)	Total Area (million hectare)	Share in Sown Area (%)	Total Amount (million ton)	Per Hectare (kg/ ha)	(Million Kilo. watt. hr)
1952	19.96	18.5	1.6	0.14	0.1	0.08	2.25	50
1957	27.34	24.4	4.4	2.64	2.4	0.37	11.25	140
1962	30.55	29.7	19.9	8.28	8.1	0.63	22.50	1,610
1965	33.06	31.5	24.5	15.58	15.0	1.94	61.50	3,710
1978	44.97	45.2	55.4	40.67	40.9	8.84	291.00	25,310
1984	44.64	—	56.4	34.92	—	17.40	519.75	46,400
1988	44.37	—	58.8	40.91	—	21.42	616.49	71,200

Source: State Statistical Bureau, *Zhongguo tongji nianjian (China Statistical Yearbook)* (Beijing: China Statistiics Press,1989), 183; and Ministry of Agriculture, Planning Bureau *Zhongguo nongcun jingli tongli ziliao daquan (A Comprehensive Book of China Rural Economic Statistics* (Beijing: Agricultural Press,1984), 290-91; 189, 340-41).

year over the twenty-six years from 1952 to 1978. Average annual growth rates for the cropping sector and agriculture as a whole were equally impressive, rising from 2.5 percent and 2.9 percent to 5.9 percent and 7.4 percent (see table 5.9). In 1985, China was once again a net grain exporter, for the first time in a quarter of a century.[18]

This dramatic growth in output was a result of a package of reforms that reduced the function of ideology and planning and gave priority to the roles of individual incentives and markets. Broad changes in rural policy began at the end of 1978, when the importance of giving enough incentives to farmers in order to break the bottleneck of agricultural production was recognized. The original intention of the government, however, was to achieve this goal through raising the long-depressed government procurement prices for major crops, modifying management methods within the context of the collective system, and increasing budgetary expenditure on infrastructure, such as irrigation system, for agricultural development.

Table 5.8 Grain Output, Trade, and Availability

Year	Population (million) (1)	Grain Output (million tons) (2)	Grain* Trade (million tons) (3)	Grain Per Capita (kg) [(2) + (3)]/(1)
1952	547.8	163.9	-1.5	283
1957	646.5	195.1	-1.9	299
1962	673.0	160.0	3.9	244
1965	725.4	194.6	4.7	275
1978	962.6	304.8	5.7	322
1984	1,038.8	387.3	7.2	380
1988	1,096.1	394.1	8.2	367

* Positive figure indicates net export and negative figure indicates net import.
Source: State Statistical Bureau, *Zhongguo tongji nianjian (China Statistical Yearbook)* (1989), 87, 198, 639, 642. Ministry of Agriculture, Planing Bureau, *Zhongguo nongcun jingji tongji daquan (A Comprehensive Book of China Rural Economic Statistics)*, 520-22, 534-35.

Price Reform

The adjustment of procurement prices for major crops was envisioned, by the government, as the most important policy change at the beginning of the reforms. Thus, effective beginning in 1979, quota prices increased 20.9 percent for grain, 23.9 percent for oil crops, 17 percent for cotton, 21.9 percent for sugar crops, and 24.3 percent for pork, while average quota prices increased 17.1 percent.[19] In addition, the premium paid for above-quota delivery of grain and oil crops was raised from 30 percent to 50 percent of the quota prices, and a 30 percent bonus was instituted for above-quota delivery of cotton.[20] Regarding

Table 5.9 Average Annual Growth Rates of Agricultural Output

Year	Agri. Output Value	Crop Output Value	Grain Output	Cotton Output	Oil crops Output	Popula-tion
52-78	2.9%	2.5%	2.4%	2.0%	0.8%	2.0%
78-84	7.4%	5.9%	4.8%	17.7%	13.8%	1.3%
84-87	4.1%	1.4%	-0.2%	-12.9%	8.3%	1.3%

Source: Ministry of Agriculture, Planning Bureau *Zhongguo nongcun jingji tongji daquan (A Comprehensive Book of China Rural Economic Statistics)* (1989), 112-15, 146-49, 189-92; State Statistical Bureau, *Zhongguo tongji nianjian (China Statistical Yearbook)* (1988), 97.

state procurement prices, the average increase in prices was 22.1 percent.[21] However, if only the marginal prices, that is, the above-quota prices, are considered, the increase in the state prices was 40.7 percent (see column 1, table 5.10).

Corresponding to the increase in procurement prices, in 1979, retail prices were raised for pork, eggs, and fish; however, the retail prices for basic necessities such as grain and edible oils were not changed. To compensate for the rise in retail prices of pork, eggs, and fish, each city dweller was compensated 5 to 8 yuan a month, thereby increasing the government's expenditure on public subsidies.[22] This financial burden became especially unbearable when unexpected output growth began in 1982, resulting in an increase in price subsidies from 9.4 billion yuan (8.4 percent of the state budget) to 37 billion yuan (24.6 percent of the state budget) in 1984.[23] Therefore, in an effort to reduce the state's burden and to increase the role of markets, the mandatory procurement quotas were abolished, for cotton in 1984 and for grain in 1985, and replaced by procurement contracts that were to be negotiated between the government and farmers. The contract price was a weighted average of the basic quota price and above-quota price. This change resulted in a 9.2 percent decline in the price margin paid to farmers (see table 5.10). However, following the decline in grain and cotton production in 1985 and the subsequent stagnation thereafter, the contracts were made mandatory again in 1986.[24]

Institutional Reform

Unlike the price reform, the government did not intend to change the farming institution from the collective system to the household-based system, now known as the household responsibility system, at the beginning of the reforms. Although it had been recognized in 1978 that incentives might be improved by solving managerial problems within the production team system, the official position at that time still held that subdivision of collectively owned land and delegation of production management to individual households were a violation of the socialist principle and should be prohibited. Thus, the production team was to remain the basic unit of production management and accounting. Work points, which were supposed to reflect the quantity and quality of effort that each member performed, remained the effort measurement for peasants. Although theoretically the work-point system is not inherently inefficient, in practice, the degree of effort monitoring was very low because of the particular difficulty in monitoring in agricultural production. Due to this low degree of monitoring, the incremental income for an additional unit of effort was only a small fraction of the actual marginal product of effort. Consequently, the incentives for a peasant to work in a production team were also very low, resulting in disappointing productivity levels. Toward the end of 1978, to increase harvests, a small number of production teams, first secretly and later with the approval of local authorities, began to try out the system of dividing a team's land and the obligatory procurement quotas to individual households in the team. A year later these teams were producing yields far larger than those of other teams.[25] The central authorities later acquiesced to the existence of this new form of farming, but required that it be restricted to poor agricultural regions, mainly in hilly or mountainous areas, and to poor teams in which people had lost confidence in the collective. In most regions, these restrictions were ignored, and both rich and poor teams found their production performance improved after adoption of the new system. Eventually, full official recognition of the household responsibility system as an acceptable mode of farming institution was given in late 1981, exactly two years after the initial price increases. By that time, 45 percent of the production teams in China had already dismantled, substituting the household responsibility system. By the end of 1983, 98 percent of production teams in China had adopted this new system (see column 2, table 5.10). It is worth emphasizing that the household responsibility system was created initially without the knowledge or approval of the central government. It was developed by farmers themselves and spread to other areas because of its merits. In short, this institutional shift in Chinese agriculture was not brought about by any one individual's will, but evolved spontaneously in response to underlying economic forces.[26]

When the household responsibility system was originally introduced, the collectively owned land was leased to each of the individual households in a team for one to three years. Along with the land lease was a contract between the household and the team, specifying the household's obligations to fulfill state procurement quotas and to pay various forms of local taxes.[27] However, a household could retain any product in excess of the stated obligations. In the distribution of land leases, egalitarianism was generally the guiding principle. Therefore, collective land in most cases was allotted strictly in proportion to the size of a household. Interfamily differences in the size of the labor force were not taken into consideration, and thus efficient use of land was inhibited. Moreover, in the initial distribution, land was first classified into several different grades, and households were then given portions of each grade.[28] As a result, a household's holding, on average, was fragmented into nine tracts, though the total holding size was only about 1.2 acres. The short, one-to-three-year contract was also found to have detrimental effects on incentives for investment in land improvement and soil-fertility conservation.[29] To remedy the above problems, several new policies were introduced: (1) in 1983, households were allowed to exchange labor with other households and to employ a limited amount of labor for farm work; (2) in 1984, to provide better incentives for soil conservation and investment, leases were allowed to be extended to fifteen years; (3) to make land consolidation possible and to prevent land from being left idle when households engaged in nonfarm business, the subleasing of landholdings to other households, with compensation, was also sanctioned in 1984.[30] These policy reforms may eventually revive labor and land markets in

Table 5.10 Price, Crop Pattern, and Cropping Intensity

Year (1)	State Above-quota/ Contract Price (1978= 100) (1)	House-hold Respon-sibility System (%) (2)	Sown Area			Multiple Cropping Index (%) (6)
			Grain Crops (%) (3)	Cash Crops (%) (4)	Other (%) (5)	
65	84.1	0	83.5	8.5	8.0	138.3
70	97.2	0	83.1	8.2	8.7	141.9
71	98.4	0	83.1	8.2	8.7	144.7
72	98.4	0	81.9	8.5	9.6	147.0
73	98.1	0	81.6	8.6	9.8	148.2
74	98.4	0	81.4	8.7	9.9	148.7
75	98.7	0	81.0	9.0	10.0	150.0
76	99.4	0	80.6	9.2	10.2	150.6
77	100.0	0	80.6	9.1	10.3	150.5
78	100.0	0	80.4	9.6	10.0	151.0
79	140.7	1	80.3	10.0	9.7	149.2
80	140.4	14	80.1	10.9	9.0	147.4
81	145.1	45	79.2	12.1	8.7	146.6
82	144.3	80	78.4	13.0	8.6	146.7
83	144.9	98	79.2	12.3	8.5	146.4
84	142.5	99	78.3	13.4	8.3	146.9
85	129.4	99	75.8	15.6	8.6	148.4
86	130.1	99	76.9	14.1	9.0	150.0
87	130.2	99	76.8	14.3	8.9	151.3

Source: Column (1) is taken from Justin Lin, "Rural Factor Markets After the Household Responsi-bility Reform,". Column (2) indicates the percentage of production teams in China that had adopted the household responsibility system. The data for 1979-1981 are from *Jingjixue zhoubao* (Economic weekly) (January 11, 1982). Figures for 1982-1984 are taken from Editorial Board of China Agricultural yearbook (1984, 69; 1985, 120). Figures for 1985-1987 are inferred from the fact that no major change in the farming institution has taken place since 1984. Columns (3) to (7) are taken from Ministry of Agriculture, Planning Bureau (1984) 132; (1989), 130-31, 355-57; and State Statistical Bureau State Statistical Bureau, *Zhongguo tongji nianjian (China Statistical Yearbook)* (1988), 224, 243, 276.

rural China. So far, however, transactions in land only exist marginally in China, and labor hiring for farm work is mainly confined to particular regions in the coastal provinces.[31]

National policy so far still stresses the importance of maintaining the institutional stability of the newly established household farming system. However, the doctrine of equating big tractors with advanced technology and large farm size with efficiency is still deeply rooted in the minds of many scholars and prominent leaders.[32] Due to increasing discontent with the stagnation of grain production after 1984, the call for recollectivization has emerged under the guise of enlarging operational size in order to exploit returns to scale. In some localities, this call has resulted in contracts being disrupted before expiration without the consent of farmers.[33] Therefore, there is a concern that farmers may once again be deprived of the economic independence and increased freedom that they have enjoyed over the past ten years.[34] Nevertheless, the farming reforms may have reached a point of irreversibility, so that any attempt to change the institution back to a collective system might be doomed to fail.

Market and Planning Reform

The third important element of the reforms is the greater role given to markets, in place of planning, for guiding production in rural sectors. The loss of allocative efficiency caused by the self-sufficiency policy was conceded at the beginning of the reforms, and although planning was still deemed essential, more weight was given to market considerations. The decision to increase grain imports, cut down grain procurement quotas, and reduce the number of products covered by planning control reflected this intention.[35] Moreover, restrictions on private interregional trade in agricultural products were gradually loosened.[36] Special measures were also taken to encourage areas that traditionally had comparative advantage in cotton production to expand cotton acreage.[37]

Each of the above policy changes reduced the role of direct state planning intervention and increased the function of markets in guiding agricultural production. As a result, cropping patterns and cropping intensity changed substantially between 1978 and 1984. The area devoted to cash crops increased from 9.6 percent of total sown acreage in 1978 to 13.4 percent in 1984, a 41.6 percent increase; meanwhile, the multiple cropping index declined from 151 to 146.9 (see table 5.10).[38] Much of these changes in crop patterns was in conformity with regional comparative advantage. For example, between 1978 and 1984, the seven provinces traditionally specializing in cotton production increased their cotton acreage by 2.33 million hectares, while the rest of the provinces reduced theirs by 1.19 million hectares.[39] Cotton acreage increased only 25 percent nationally between 1978 and 1984, while total output increased 189 percent. A substantial portion of this dramatic output surge was attributable to gains in comparative advantage.[40]

The climax of the market reforms occurred at the beginning of 1985, when the state declared that it would no longer set any mandatory production plans in agriculture and that obligatory procurement quotas were to be replaced by purchasing contracts between the state and farmers.[41] The restoration of household farming and the increase in market freedom prompted farmers to adjust their production activities in accordance with profit margins. This caused the acreage devoted to cash crops to further expand from 13.4 percent of total acreage in 1984 to 15.6 percent in 1985, while grain acreage declined from 78.3 percent to 75.8 percent (see table 5.10). Expansion in animal husbandry, fishery, and subsidiary production was even faster. As a result of these adjustments, agricultural output still grew at a respectable rate of 3.4 percent in 1985, although the aggregate outputs of the cropping sector declined 1.9 percent. In 1985, among the three most important agricultural products, grain output declined 6.9 percent, and cotton 33.7 percent; only oil crops registered an increase of 33.3 percent.[42] Since 1985, this stagnation of the cropping sector has lingered (see table 5.9).

These market-oriented reforms aroused anxiety in some sectors of the government from their very beginning. Concern over "loss of control" was widely reported in the early 1980s.[43] Even so, in the wake of the unprecedented successes between 1978 and 1984, the pro-market group was able to push the reforms further toward the market direction. However, when growth rates slowed down and grain output declined in 1985 and thereafter, the government retreated from its position, and the voluntary procurement contracts were made mandatory again. The policy announced in 1985 has not since been formally reversed, and the government still hopes to rely on market measures to stimulate grain production.[44] Nevertheless, administrative intervention in markets and production has been increasing. For example, to facilitate the fulfillment of procurement quotas, local governments often set blocks on markets in grain, cotton, silk cocoons, tobacco, and so forth. Also, intervention in production is revealed by the fact that the acreage devoted to cash crops declined after 1985 and the multiple-crop index increased to 151.3 in 1987, a level even higher than that reached in 1978 (see table 5.10). The attempts to increase grain outputs, though, were not successful until 1990. Faced with the stagnation in grain production, the state monopolies in regional grain trade and markets in chemical inputs was instituted again in 1989.

The above three components of reforms all contributed positively to the remarkable output growth between 1978 and 1984. A careful econometric analysis, using province-level input-output data covering the period 1970 to 1987 and employing the production function approach found that of the 42.2 percent output growth in the cropping sector between 1978 and 1984, about 48.6 percent can be attributed to productivity growth resulting from the reforms. Specifically, concerning this productivity growth, 96 percent is attributable to the changes in the farming institution from the production team system to the household responsibility system, and the remaining 4 percent is attributable to changes in cropping patterns and cropping intensity. The latter two items are related to reforms in the role of markets and planning. The rise in state procurement prices also had a significant effect on output growth, but its effect was derived indirectly from its impact on input uses.[45]

Farming Institutions, Performance, and Income Distribution

For several decades before the socialist takeover in 1949, China's agriculture was ravaged by war. The success of the socialist revolution in 1949 brought peace to rural areas. Since most students of the Chinese economy agree that the Chinese economy had recovered from war destruction by 1952, in the following discussion we will use 1952 as a base year.

Farming Institutions and Agricultural Growth

To evaluate agricultural performance in China, we will divide the period after 1952 into four subperiods: 1952-1965, 1966-1978, 1979-1984, and 1985-1988. As discussed in the section on economic development strategy, the farming institution was changed from the household system to the collective system in the first subperiod. The collectivization movement resulted in a serious agricultural crisis in 1959-1961, and agricultural production did not recover to the precrisis level until 1965. While the focus was on traditional technology in the first subperiod, more emphasis was given to modern technologies in the second subperiod. In the third subperiod, the farming institution was shifted from the production team to the household responsibility system. The last subperiod is the postreform period.

In addition to farming institutions, many other factors may affect the performance of agriculture. The rates of increase and the reliability of supplies of modern varieties, chemical fertilizers, pesticides, irrigation, tractors, and other inputs also affected the rates of yield increase and output growth in each period. The best way to measure the impact of farming institutions on agricultural performance, then, is to compare total factor productivity in each period.[46] Figure 5.1 depicts Guanzhong Wen's estimates of changes in total factor productivity from 1952 to 1988.[47]

From figure 5.1, we can see that the total factor productivity indexes in 1952-1988 can be divided into four periods, namely, 1952-1958, 1959-1978, 1979-1983, and 1984-1988. Between 1952 and 1958, that is to say, during the period of voluntary collectivization, although the increments are very small, the total factor productivity shows a rising trend. The total factor productivity declined dramatically in 1959-1960, when compulsory collectivization was first imposed, and throughout 1961-1978 stayed at a level about 20 percent below the total factor productivity reached in 1952. The record then improved dramatically after 1978, during the period of de-collectivization. By 1983, total factor productivity had returned to its 1952 level. In 1985-1988, the postreform period, total factor productivity remained about 30 percent higher than the 1952 level, though the rate of increase slowed down.

Based on this data, there are two puzzling questions that need to be addressed before we can draw conclusions about the different effects of farming institutions on agricultural performance: (1) Why did total factor productivity collapse in 1959-1961 and maintain a low level throughout the period of 1961-1978? (2) Why were there increasing trends in total factor productivity during the transition periods both from the household farming system to the collective system from 1952 to 1958 and from the collective farming system to the household farming system from 1978 to 1984?

Addressing our first question, the commonly accepted explanations for the agricultural crisis of 1959-1961 are that there were three successive years of bad weather, bad policies and poor management in communes, and that there were incentive issues arising from the unwieldy size of communes.[48] As discussed in

Figure 5.1   Total Factor Productivity Index, 1952-1988 (Index 1952=100)

Source: Justin Lin , "Rural Reforms and Agricultural Growth in China," *American Economic Review* 83 no.1 (1992).

the previous section, all three of these conditions had been eliminated by the time that the commune system was replaced by the production team system in 1962. If these explanations were sufficient, then agricultural productivity should soon have recovered to its level before the disaster of 1958. The empirical evidence, however, indicates that total factor productivity did not return to its precrisis level until the production team system was abandoned.

Low productivity can be linked to incentive problems in collectives. In two recent papers, I argue that because supervising and monitoring agricultural work are difficult, the success of an agricultural collective depends on a commitment by each member to discipline himself.[49] Due to the fact that in China a household's landholding was often highly fragmented and of too small a size for a single household to raise a draft animal, certain gains could be obtained by pooling the land and farm tools of several households.[50] Gains from economies of scale, however, could also be overshadowed by incentive problems arising when a collective member attempts to put in less effort and still take a share of what everybody else has produced. Since supervision in agriculture is difficult, some effective substitute for supervision was required to make a collective an efficient institution.

A self-enforcing commitment among collective members to provide as much effort as on their own household farms is an effective alternative when supervision is too costly or difficult.[51] Under such an agreement, if others fail to fulfill their commitment, a member may decide to withdraw from the collective and resume household farming. If this member's quitting significantly reduces the gains from economies of scale, then the other members will also no longer find it advantageous to remain in the collective. They will withdraw their membership and the collective will disintegrate. This threat of the disintegration of the collective causes the would-be shirkers to rethink their position: if they they break their promise and let the collective collapse, they will lose their share of the productivity benefits the collective produced. The threat of a collective's collapse can greatly reduce the incidence of shirking.

Sustaining such a commitment requires, however, that the decision to join the collective not be permanent, but rather that this decision be repeated over time so that members not honoring their commitment can be threatened with collective disintegration. Such a situation existed during the voluntary collectivization up to 1958, when members could leave collectives if they were not satisfied with performance. But in the fall of 1958 this situation changed. The state revoked the right for an individual to withdraw from a collective, making the decision to join permanent.

This significantly changed the incentive structure in the collectives. When a collective is imposed and withdrawal is prohibited, it becomes impossible to use the disintegration of the collective as a threat and thus reduce the likelihood of shirking by members. The self-enforcing agreement cannot be sustained.[52] Supervision then becomes crucial in establishing work incentives and maintaining productivity levels in the collective.[53] With supervision, those failing to honor commitments will be more easily detected and can be punished by linking pay to observed work.

However, supervision is very costly. The supervision of agricultural operations is particularly difficult because agricultural processes typically involve many acres of land and can necessitate several months of work. Farming also requires peasants to shift from one kind of job to another throughout the production season. In general, the quality of work provided by a peasant does not become apparent until harvest time. Furthermore, it is difficult to determine each individual's contribution by simply observing outputs because nature can have random effects on production. The larger the size of a collective, the harder it is to monitor each peasant's effort. It is thus very costly to provide close monitoring of each member's effort contribution in agricultural production. Consequently, the level of monitoring chosen in a collective engaging in agricultural production is very low, and an individual's pay is not closely linked to effort. Work incentives for peasants in an imposed collective remain low, and agriculture in the collective system performs dismally.

In short, the collapse of agriculture in 1959-1961 and the dismal agricultural performance up to 1978 were brought about by the abolishment in 1958 of the right to withdraw from a collective, and the continuation of this collectivization as an imposed institution until 1978. Total factor productivity had improved in the period of 1952-1958 because collectivization was voluntary, and, later, in the period 1978-1984 because incentives to work were improved with the elimination of imposed collectivization.[54]

Farming Institutions and Income Distribution

Although collectivization was ineffective in terms of the performance of agriculture, one often-mentioned favorable effect was its impact on income distribution.[55] As table 5.5 shows, the land reform program in the early 1950s confiscated and redistributed the landlords' property to poor peasants. This program had a significant effect on the distribution of income in rural areas. The formation of collectives further eliminated differences in incomes resulting from variations in the amounts of land owned by individual households. However, in a country as large as China, there are substantial cross-regional variations in agro-climatic and natural resource endowments. Moreover, for historical reasons, the development of urban centers, markets, transportation, and so on varies significantly from region to region. Therefore, the major source of income differences in China is regional disparity, which cannot disappear by way of collectivization. A study based on simulations found that the Gini coefficient before and after collectivization was, respectively, .227 and .211.[56] This estimate is supported by a recent study based on nationwide household survey data, which found that the Gini coefficient in 1978 was .2124 (see table

5.11). These estimated Gini coefficients suggest that collectivization left nationwide income inequality basically unchanged.

The first row of table 5.11 shows that inequalities in income distribution worsened after the rural reforms in 1978, as the Gini coefficient increased from .2124 in 1978 to .3014 in 1988.[57] Since land owned by production teams was more or less equally distributed among team members in the household responsibility reform, the increasing disparity of household income after the reform may have been due to sources other than the distribution of operational land. Table 5.11 shows that accompanying the reform were substantial changes in the composition of household income. Also, in 1978, 85 percent of income derived from agricultural production, but by 1988 this share dropped to 63.4 percent. Meanwhile, the share from nonfarm sources, including rural industry, transportation, construction, and commerce, increased from 7 percent in 1978 to 27.3 percent in 1988. Since the opportunity to engage in nonfarm activities exhibits large regional variation, and the ability to capture such opportunity differs from household to household due to differences in human capital and other endowments, the worsening of income inequality may have arisen from policies that encouraged nonfarm activities rather than from the household responsibility reform itself. However, without more detailed and careful studies, the main sources of the increase in income disparities cannot be ascertained.

The most important disparity in China is the gap in living standards between the urban and rural populations, which existed at the beginning of the first five-year plan. A natural way to reduce this disparity would be to allow the poor rural population to migrate into cities. However, the employment opportunities created by the heavy-industry-oriented development strategy were not sufficient to absorb the increasing urban labor force. Thus, in the 1960s and 1970s, there was even a program to send urban youth to rural areas, and the rural to urban migration was effectively blocked by the government. The restrictions on this migration relaxed only slightly during the 1980s.[58] As a result, the gap between urban and rural areas has persisted throughout the past four decades. Figure 5.2 depicts the relative annual per capita consumption levels of peasants and nonpeasants. The consumption level of peasants was only about 40 percent that of nonpeasants throughout the period from 1952 to 1990. The situation reached its worst during the 1959-1961 agricultural crisis and again in 1978, the year before the household responsibility system reform began. Although the gap was narrowed substantially during the reforms up to 1984, it started to worsen again in 1985. By 1990, the disparity in the relative consumption between peasants and nonpeasants returned to the prereform level.

Although rural reforms did not reduce the consumption gap between peasants and nonpeasants, it did significantly improve peasants' absolute level of consumption. Figure 5.3 depicts the index of peasant's per capita consumption in 1952-1990. Here, we find that between 1952-1978 peasants' per capita consumption, measured at comparable prices, increased only 57.6 percent, with

Table 5.11 Gini Coefficient and Average Per Capita Net Income of Agricultural
Household

	Year						
	1978	1980	1984	1985	1986	1987	1988
Gini Coefficient							
	.2124	.2366	.2577	.2635	.2848	.2916	.3014
Average Per Capita Net Income (Yuan)							
	133	191	355	398	424	463	545
Share (%)							
	100	100	100	100	100	100	100
Agricultural income							
	85.0	78.2	70.5	66.3	65.8	65.0	63.4
Non-agricultural income							
	7.0	8.8	18.2	21.7	22.6	25.4	27.3
Non-productive income							
	8.0	13.0	11.3	12.0	11.6	9.6	9.3

Note: Agricultural income refers to income from crops, animal husbandry, forestry, fishery, and
household handicraft production. Nonagricultural income refers to the income from township- and
village-industry, construction, transportation, commerce, and catering trade. Nonproductive income
refers to remittance and transfers from the collectives and government.
Source: Gini coefficient is taken from State Statistical Bureau Agricultural Household Survey Team,
A Study on Agricultural Household Income Difference. Beijing: State Statistical Bureau, mimeo-
graph, 1989. The rest of the data is taken from State Statistical Bureau, State Statistical Bureau,
Zhongguotongji nianjian (China Statistical Yearbook) (1989), 743.

an annual growth rate of only 1.8 percent. In contrast, the consumption level
more than doubled between 1978-1988, increasing 8.1 percent per year. Similar
improvement is also found by comparing peasants' per capita net income before
and after the reforms. Sixty-five percent of households in 1978 had per capita
net incomes of less than 150 yuan, and only 2.4 percent had per capita incomes
of more than 300 yuan. In 1988, though, only 2 percent of households had per
capita incomes of less than 200 yuan while more than 80 percent of households
had per capita incomes of higher than 300 yuan. Even though the price index for
consumption goods in rural periodic markets increased 112 percent between
1978 and 1988, the increase in per capita income still represents a substantial
improvement.[59] It is thus safe to conclude that, in terms of absolute level and
rate of growth of consumption and income, peasants are much better off in the
period of the household-based farming system than in the period of the collective system.

Figure 5.2 Ratio of Consumption Levels Between Peasant and
Non-peasant

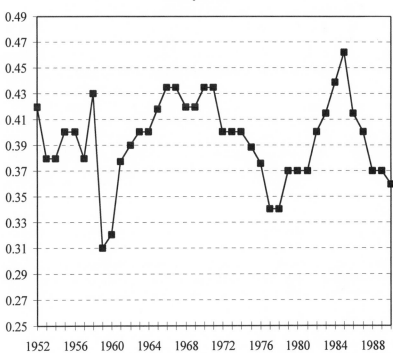

Source: Statistics Bureau of China, *Zhongguo Tongji Nianjian* (Statistical Yearbooks of China), (1991), 270.

Conclusion

China's experience in agricultural development, both its successes and its failures, provides many valuable lessons for other developing countries. It is remarkable that China has been able to feed over one-fifth of the world's population with only one-fifteenth of the world's arable land, and to transform a predominantly agrarian economy into an industrial power. China, however, paid a very high price for these achievements before the 1979 reform. The Chinese experience in 1952-1957 showed that the collective farming itself was not a barrier for rural development if the institution was adopted by farmers volun-tarily. However, when the collective farming system became forced, it was so detrimental to work incentives that, despite sharp improvements in technology and increases in modern inputs in the 1960s and 1970s, grain production in China barely kept up with population growth, just matching the performance of agriculture in the six centuries before the socialist revolution.

The individual household-based farming system reform in 1979 greatly improved peasants' work incentives. Grain production and the agricultural sector as a whole registered unprecedented growth between 1979 and 1984. The increase in work incentives resulting from the farming institutional reform, however, had mainly a one-time, discrete impact on agricultural productivity. While the average annual growth rate of 4.1 percent for Chinese agriculture from 1984 to 1988 is still very remarkable compared to the agricultural growth rates of other developed and developing countries, grain production in China has stagnated since reaching its peak in 1984. This stagnation is mainly due to the fact that food policy reform has lagged behind farming institutional reform. Individual households have been given more autonomy in production decisions, so that farmers in the household system will allocate more resources to crops that command higher profits. Reforms have freed the marketing of most cash crops and other products of animal husbandry and fishery. Grain, however, remains among the exceptions, as farmers are still required to meet grain quota obligations at government-set prices. In addition, local governments often impose blockades on grain markets, thus reducing grain prices in areas with comparative advantages in grain production. The stagnation of grain production in the postreform period, contrasted against the sizable growth of agriculture as a whole, can be attributed mainly to the decline in profitability of grain compared to other crops.

Most people in China, including political leaders and economists, are grain fundamentalists. Whenever there is a fall or stagnation in grain production, the optimism about Chinese agriculture will be quickly replaced by pessimism. The small farm size and the fragmentation of cultivated land in the household-based farming system are often wrongly blamed for the poor performance in grain production. This results in pressure for recollectivizing the household-based farming system, under the guise of pursuing economies of scale in agricultural production.[59] This practice is especially appealing to local officials, because it simplifies the task of procuring grain under state quotas.

The lessons of the period prior to the reform demonstrate that forced collectivization is not a solution to the increasing demand for grain arising from population growth and industrial expansion. The final way to break the current stagnation of grain production is to let prices carry the right signal to farmers. As long as the grain price brings farmers profits as attractive as those from other crops, the individual household-based farmers in China will be able to produce enough grain to feed the Chinese population. However, grain is a land-intensive production, and China's land endowment is extremely scarce. This makes grain self-sufficiency a very costly policy. A better policy for China would be to rely on comparative advantage and to allow the nation to produce other labor-intensive crops in exchange for part of the grain requirement through international trade. However, this policy will not be conceivable until the government gives up the ideology of grain self-sufficiency and allows urban residents to face, at least partially, world price fluctuations.

Agriculture is a supporting sector in the existing development strategy, receiving public attention only when a poor harvest becomes a constraint on industrial development. Under such a strategy, the contribution that agriculture makes to modern economic growth is systematically undervalued, and a cyclic pattern in agricultural production is inevitable. Sustained agricultural growth will be possible only when China replaces the traditional heavy-industry-oriented strategy and its related policy environment with a strategy that stresses regional as well as international comparative advantage. Such a strategy requires that both the prices of commodities and factors of production reflect their relative scarcities in the economy, and this can be achieved only in undistorted markets that allow demand and supply to take their parts in price determination.

Notes

1. The cultivated land and population were, respectively, 97.9 million hectare and 541.7 million in 1949, and 99.4 million hectare and 962.2 million in 1978.

2. Joan Robinson, "Chinese Agricultural Communes," *Co-Existence* (May 1964): 1-7. Reprinted in *The Political Economy of Development and Underdevelopment*, ed. Charles K. Wilber (New York: Random House, 1973).

3. This political wisdom, shaped through many dynastic transitions in millennia of history, is capsuled in an often-cited motto *"wu nong bu wen"* (without a strong agriculture, the society will not be stable) in the agricultural policy debates in China.

4. Dwight Perkins and Shahid Yusuf, *Rural Development in China* (Baltimore, Md.: Johns Hopkins University Press, 1984), 16.

5. Otherwise, it is not a developing economy anymore.

6. SSB (State Statistical Bureau), *Zhongguo laodong gongzi tongji ziliao*, China Labor and Wage Statistics, 1949-1985 (Beijing: China Statistics Press, 1987 c), 151.

7. In addition to grain, edible oil, pork, sugar, cotton cloth, and other living necessities were also rationed. At the peak, the items of rationed goods for each urban residence were more than 100. After the reforms in 1979, the government has attempted to abolish the ration system. So far, the only remaining items are grain and edible oil. It is likely that these last two items will also be eliminated.

8. The urban residents were entitled to all kinds of subsidies, which were estimated to be as high as 80 percent of their wage earnings, whereas the rural population had none of those benefits. The urban residents in effect became a new vested-interest class. They often were a barrier for market-oriented reforms in urban sector.

9. SSB (State Statistical Bureau), *Zhongguo tongji nianjian, 1981-1989*, China Statistical Yearbook, 1981-1989 (Beijing: China Statistical Press, 1981-1989 annual), 87.

10. This subsection draws heavily on Justin Yifu Lin, "Rural Reforms and Agricultural Growth in China." See Justin Yifu Lin, "Rural Reforms and Agricultural Growth in China" *American Economic Reform* 82 (March 1992).

11. The government also viewed collectivization as a convenient vehicle for effecting the state's procurement program of grain and other agricultural products. As an economist noted: "A still more fundamental reason for the collectivization of agriculture . . . was the fact that China had embarked on the construction of a planned socialist economy in 1953. For large-scale development of the national economy, it was imperative that changes be effected in the small peasant economy to enable it to provide the large quantities of grain, cotton, oil-bearing crops, sugar crops and other industrial raw materials needed by developing industry. . . . the solution of which could only be found in the collectivization of agriculture." See Hanxian Luo, *Economic Changes in Rural China* (Beijing: New World Press, 1985), 53.

12. Ministry of Agriculture, Planning Bureau, *Zhongguo nongcun jingji tongji ziliao daquan, 1949-1986,* A Comprehensive Book of China Rural Economic Statistics, 1949-1986 (Beijing: Agriculture Press, 1989), 112, 143, 522, 535.

13. Basil Aston, Kenneth Hill, Allan Piazza, and Robin Zeitz, "Famine in China, 1958-61," *Population and Development Review* 10 (December 1984): 613-45.

14. Randolph Barker and Robert W. Herdt, *The Rice Economy of Asia* (Washington, D.C.: Resources for the Future, 1985), 61.

15. Ministry of Agriculture, Planning Bureau, *Zhongguo nongcun jingji tongji ziliao daquan, 1949-1986,* A Comprehensive Book of China Rural Economic Statistics, 1949-1986 (Beijing: Agriculture Press, 1989), 348-49.

16. Cotton acreage dropped 16 percent nationally between 1957 and 1977/1978. However, the northern provinces that initially had substantial comparative advantages in cotton production declined by a larger proportion. For example, cotton acreage in Hebei, the province initially with the strongest comparative advantage, fell 58 percent between 1957 and 1977. Consequently, north China ceased to export cotton in the late 1970s. See Nicholas R. Lardy, *Agriculture in China's Modern Economic Development* (Cambridge, Mass.: Cambridge University Press, 1983), 62-63.

17. This subsection draws heavily on Lin, "Rural Reforms and Agricultural Growth in China."

18. In 1985, China exported 9.33 million tons of grain and imported 5.97 million tons (State Statistical Bureau 1986, 569 and 572). The net export in 1986 was 1.69 million tons. However, because of the decline in grain output in 1985 and stagnation afterward, China began to import grain again in 1987. The net grain imports for 1987 and 1988 were 8.81 million and 8.15 million tons, respectively (State Statistical Bureau 1989, 639-642).

19. SSB (State Statistical Bureau), *Zhongguo maoyi wujia tongji ziliao 1952-1983,* China trade and price statistics 1952-1983 (Beijing: China Statistics Press, 1984 a), 404 -6.

20. For a detailed chronology of the price changes in 1979 and thereafter, see Terry Sicular, "Plan and Market in China's Agricultural Commerce," *Journal of Political Economy* 96, no. 2 (1988): 283-307.

21. SSB (State Statistical Bureau), *Zhongguo maoyi wujia tongji ziliao 1952-1983,* China trade and price statistics 1952-1983 (Beijing: China Statistics Press, 1984 a), 401.

22. *Quanguo wujia gongzi huiyi jiyao* (Summary of National Conference on Wage and Price) in State Statistical Bureau, Urban Sampling Survey Team (1988, 8-14).

23. SSB (State Statistical Bureau), Urban Sampling Survey Team (1988), 747, 763.

24. Sicular, "Plan and Market in China's Agricultural Commerce," 283-307.

25. It was found recently that a village in Guizhou Province had adopted the household-based farming system secretly for more than ten years before the reforms. The villagers did not admit it until the new policy was announced. See Runsheng Du, *China's Rural*

Economic Reform (Beijing: Social Science Press, 1985), 15. Anyway, several production teams in Chuxian County, Chuxian Prefecture, Anhui Province, which was frequently victimized by flood and drought, were reported to be the initiator of the household responsibility system. Chuxian County reported a 12.5 percent increase in grain output, whereas production teams in Chuxian County that used the household responsibility system increased grain output by 35.7 percent. Similarly, the ratio of increase in grain output was 12.4 percent against 35.7 percent in Quanjiao County, 0.7 percent against 37.1 percent in Laian County, and 0.3 percent against 31.0 percent in Jiashan County, all of the same prefecture. See Yizi Chen, "The Dawn for the Rural Area, the Hope for China: Report of a Survey on the Implementing of 'Baochan Daohu' in the Rural Area in Anhui Province," in *Rural Area, Economics, and Society*, a collection of papers by the Institution of Rural Development Problems in China (Beijing, 1981), 100.

26. This change provides empirical evidence for the induced institutional innovation hypotheses.

27. Crook provided a detailed analysis of a model contract. See Frederick W. Crook, "The 'Baogan Daohu' Incentive System: Translation and Analysis of Model Contract," *China Quarterly* 102 (June 1985): 291-305.

28. Reeitsu Kojima, "Agricultural Organization: New Forms, New Contradictions," *China Quarterly*, no. 116 (December 1988): 706-35.

29. Wen provides a theoretical investigation of the possible impact of tenure insecurity on long-term farm investments. See Guanzhong James Wen, *The Current Land Tenure and Its Impact on Long Term Performance of Farming Sector: The Case of Modern China*, Ph.D. dissertation, University of Chicago, 1989.

30. Yak-Yeow Kueh, "The Economics of the 'Second Land Reform' in China," *China Quarterly*, no. 101 (March 1985): 122-31.

31. Justin Yifu Lin, "Rural Factor Markets in China after the Household Responsibility Reform," in *Chinese Economic Policy*, ed. Bruce Reynolds (New York: Paragon, 1989a).

32. For an insightful critique of this doctrine, see Theodore Schultz, Transforming Traditional Agriculture (New Haven, Conn.: Yale University Press, 1964), chap. 8.

33. Yaping Jiang, "Wo men bu gou yao zhong di: beijing shunyixian yiqi chengbao tudi hetong jiufeng jishi" (All we want is to cultivate land: an on-the-spot report of a dispute of land contract in Shunyi County, Beijing), in *Renmin ribao* (People's Daily), October 26, 1988.

34. D. Gale Johnson, "Economic vs. Noneconomic Factors in Chinese Rural Development," Paper No. 89:13 (Chicago, Ill.: Office of Agricultural Economics Research, University of Chicago, June 1989).

35. The net grain import increased from 6.9 million tons in 1978 to 14.9 million tons in 1982. See Ministry of Agriculture Planning Bureau, *Zhonggau nongcun jingji tongji ziliao daquan, 1949-1986*. The grain purchase quota was reduced 2.5 million tons in 1979. See Robert F. Ash, "The Evolution of Agricultural Policy," *China Quarterly*, no. 116 (December 1988): 529-55. For example, the numbers of planned product categories and obligatory targets were reduced from twenty-one and thirty-one, respectively, in 1978, to sixteen and twenty in 1981 and further to only thirteen categories in 1982. See Yak-Yeow Kueh, "China's New Agricultural-Policy Program: Major Economic Consequences, 1979-1983," in *Journal of Comparative Economics* 8 (1984), 353-75.

36. Sicular, "Plan and Market in China's Agricultural Commerce," 283-307.

37. In 1979, a policy was instituted that awarded above-quota delivery of cotton with low-priced grain sale. This policy made a huge expansion of cotton area possible in the traditional cotton producing region.

38. Because the cropping intensity might have exceeded a reasonable level in certain areas, the reduction in multiple cropping may increase the net revenue to farmers in those areas, though the gross output may decline.

39. The seven provinces traditionally specializing in cotton production are Hebei, Shanxi, Jiangsu, Shandong, Henan, Hubei, and Xinjiang. See Lardy, *Agriculture in China's Modern Economic Development*, 58. The cotton acreage data are taken from the State Statistical Bureau (see SSB, *Zhongguo maoyi wujia tongji ziliao 1952-1983*), and the Editorial Board of Agricultural China Yearbook, *Zhongguo nongye nianjian, 1980 - 1989* (China Agriculture Yearbook, 1980 - 1987) (Beijing: Agriculture Press, 1985), 150.

40. Another reason for this rapid growth was the introduction and diffusion in the early 1980s of a new high-yield variety called *lumian yihao*.

41. "Zhonggong zhongyang guowuyuan guanyu jinyibu huoyue nongcun jingji de shixiang zhengce" (Ten Policies of the CCP Central Committee and the State Council for the Further Invigoration of the Rural Economy) in Editorial Board of China Agriculture Yearbook (1985, 1-3).

42. However, the output of oil crops also declined sharply after 1985.

43. Sicular, "Plan and Market in China's Agricultural Commerce," 283-307.

44. The government further reduced the quantity of grain procurement contracts by 22 percent in 1986, and again by 10 percent in 1987. This measure increased the quantity of grain sold to government at "negotiated prices," which are higher than contract prices and closer to market prices. The government also instituted a policy called "three-link ups," awarding subsidized credit, chemical fertilizer, and diesel for grain, cotton, and selected crops. See Sicular, "Plan and Market in China's Agricultural Commerce," 283-307.

45. Estimates using Solow-Denison-type growth accounting by Mcmillan et al and Wen also find the household responsibility system reform to have been the main source of productivity growth in 1978-1984. See John McMillan, John Whalley, and Li Jing Zhu, "The Impact of China's Economic Reforms on Agricultural Productivity Growth," *Journal of Political Economy* 97, no. 4 (1989), and Wen, *The Current Land Tenure and Its Impact on Long Term Performance of Farming Sector*. Lin, "Rural Reforms and Agricultural Growth in China," *American Economic Reform* 82 (March 1992).

46. This approach first uses factor shares as weights to compile individual input series into a total input series, and then divides the aggregate output series by the total input series to obtain the total factor productivity index.

47. Wen, "The Current Land Tenure."

48. Dennis L. Chinn, "Cooperative Farming in North China," *Quarterly Journal of Economics* 95 (March 1980): 279-97. Perkins and Yusuf, *Rural Development in China*, 16. Alexander Eckstein, *Communist China's Economic Growth and Foreign Trade: Implication for U.S. Policy* (New York: McGraw-Hill, 1966).

49. Justin Yifu Lin, "Collectivization and China's Agricultural Crisis in 1959-1961," *Journal of Political Economy* 98 (December 1990): 1228-52. Justin Yifu Lin, "Exit Rights, Exit Costs, and Shirking in Agricultural Cooperatives: A Reply," *Journal of Comparative Economics* 17, no. 2 (June 1993): 504-20.

50. Chinn, "Cooperative Farming in North China," 279-97.

51. Self-enforcing agreement does not require a third party to enforce the agreement, to determine whether there have been violations, or to impose penalties. When the costs of third-party intervention are too high, a self-enforcing agreement is an effective substitute and guarantees the continuing of the transaction. However, a self-enforcing agreement is sustainable only if the game is repeated. For further discussion of self-enforcing agreements, see L. G. Telser, "A Theory of Self-enforcing Agreements" *Journal of Business* 53 (1980): 27-44.

52. Telser, "A Theory of Self-enforcing Agreements."

53. The supervision and monitoring of each member are an incentive tool since the return on a member's additional effort has two components: the member gets a share of the increase in the collective output, but also a larger share of the total net collective income when the member supervision allows recognition for contributing a larger share of total effort. If there is no monitoring of effort, a member will not get more work points for the additional contribution of effort. In this case, the return on a member's increase in effort is only the share of the increase in team output, which in itself may be an insufficient incentive.

54. For more discussion on the theoretical and empirical issues about the agricultural crisis in 1959-1961, see the symposium on my 1990 *Journal of Political Economy* article, which appeared in the *Journal of Comparative Economics* 17, no. 2 (June 1993).

55. Carl Riskin, *China's Political Economy* (New York: Oxford University Press, 1987), 225-32. Nicholas R. Lardy, *Economic Growth and Income Distribution in the People's Republic of China* (New York: Cambridge University Press, 1978). Victor D. Lippit, *The Economics Development of China* (Armonk, N.Y.: Sharpe, 1987), 159-60.

56. Quoted in Perkins and Yusuf, *Rural Development in China*, 110. Robert C. Roll, "The Distribution of Rural Income in China: A Comparison of the 1930s and the 1950s," Ph.D. diss., Harvard University, 1974.

57. Two studies using recently released provincial-level data also confirm that the regional disparities were not reduced in the collective period, and the inequality increased after the reform. See Thomas P. Lyons, "Interprovincial Disparities in China: Output and Consumption, 1952-1987," in *Economic Development and Cultural Change* 39 (1991): 471-506, and Kai Yuen Tsui, "China's Regional Inequality, 1952-1985," in *Journal of Comparative Economics* 15 (1991): 1-21.

58. Peasants are now allowed to find temporary jobs in the cities. However, they are not entitled to any of the subsidies given to the regular urban residents. Moreover, they are often forcibly sent back to rural areas when the urban economy suffers depression.

59. See the report by Jiang Yaping, "Wo men bu guo yao zhong di: beijing shungyixian yiqi chengbao tudi hetong jiufen jishi" (All we want is to cultivate land: an on-the-spot report of a dispute of land contract in Shungyi County, Beijing), *Renmin ribao* (People's Daily), October 26, 1988.

6
Cuba: Successful Voluntary Collectivization

*Carmen Diana Deere and
Niurka Perez*

Cuban agricultural policy has always differed from that of other centrally planned economies. From the early years of the 1959 revolution, the government focused on state farms, rather than collectives (production cooperatives), as the goal of "socialist" agriculture. But the Cuban agrarian reform also created a landed peasantry. Moreover, not until the late 1970s—almost twenty years into the revolution—did the Cuban leadership begin to encourage its private farmers to pool land to form production cooperatives. The pooling of individual peasant farms to form production cooperatives (what we term "collectivization") is an extension of the Cuban leadership's long-standing concern to exert control over the agricultural sector, given the importance of sugar exports to the Cuban economy and of basic needs fulfillment to government legitimacy. For the first two decades of the revolution, this control was primarily exerted through the creation of a huge state farm sector, characterized by a high degree of centralization and little worker participation in decision making. For this reason, we do not view state farms as collectives, even though they were created upon nationalized land and, theoretically, they were run in the interests of all the Cuban people.

Political considerations, as well as ideological ones, resulted in collectivization taking place relatively late in the Cuban socialist project. Even then, collectivization was weighed against the alternative of incorporating private farms directly into the state sector—not against increased support for a viable peasant farming sector.

Nonetheless, in contrast to the earlier collectivization drives of many centrally planned economies, the Cuban experience is notable for its relatively voluntary and successful nature. It has been voluntary in that some real choice has always existed for peasants. The majority of farmers have exercised their right to continue farming individually, while others have resigned their cooperative membership when such has suited them, given the availability of alternative employment opportunities.

The Cuban collectivization process can also be deemed to be successful in that a modern, economically viable cooperative sector was created without great political costs. This sector has steadily contributed to government goals of increasing the flow of foodstuffs to the urban population. This successful experience is partly explained by its timing: by the late 1970s the Cuban state had invested considerable resources in social services in rural areas, winning the confidence of the peasantry, and had built up a sizable agriculturally oriented capital goods sector, enabling it to use the lure of mechanization as a stimulus for cooperative development.

Moreover, the cooperative movement was judged to be so successful that in 1993, as the Cuban economy was reeling from the effects of the demise of the Socialist trading bloc (a process that began in 1989), the huge state agricultural sector was decentralized and cooperativized, in the hopes of emulating the relative success of the private sector production cooperatives.

This chapter focuses on the economic and political conditions supporting the successful Cuban collectivization process and on how these conditions, as well as the response of the peasantry, changed over time. While the analysis is driven by national-level data, the chapter also attempts to illustrate how local conditions—the inherited class structure, the natural environment, and differences in the implementation of state policy—have influenced the relative success of the cooperative movement in different regions of the country.

Our analysis of the Cuban experience suggests that under certain economic and political conditions, collectivization can be done voluntarily, and that it can be used to create a viable agricultural sector. Our study also indicates that democratic control of cooperatives by their members and relative autonomy from the state are essential to achieving the benefits of this form of production. While state support is crucial to successful cooperative development, too much state control tends to lessen cooperative autonomy and weaken the commitment of the membership to the success of the enterprise.

The regional analysis suggests that production cooperatives are much more successful in the more well-endowed regions of the country, where differential rents from soil fertility and irrigation may accrue to the private sector. In addition, production cooperatives tend to be more successful if they are largely peasant based, rather than made up primarily of former wage workers, and where kinship ties among the membership are strong.

The next section of this chapter provides a brief description of land tenancy and class relations in prerevolutionary Cuba and introduces the three regions where our fieldwork has been based. The subsequent section presents an overview of the 1959 agrarian reform and of peasant-state relations through 1977, the first year of the collectivization drive. Subsequent sections are organized around a detailed periodization of the collectivization process—based upon the changing mix of incentives, the performance of the new cooperatives, and peasant responses.

Cuba's Agrarian Structure Prior to 1959

At the time of the 1959 revolution, Cuba was the classic agroexport economy. One product, sugar, made up 81 percent of its total exports; moreover, it was heavily dependent on one country, the United States, for over two-thirds of its exports and imports.[1] Its agrarian structure was characterized by the dominance of large sugar cane plantations and cattle haciendas, with many of the former in the hands of U.S. capital. Its class structure was dominated by the presence of a large landless proletariat, which far exceeded property-owning peasants in number.

Table 6.1 illustrates the degree of concentration of land. Whereas farms smaller than 5 hectares constituted 20 percent of the total number of farms in 1945, these held less than 1 percent of the nation's farmland. On the other hand, less than 8 percent of the total number of farms held over 70 percent of the farmland, with farms greater than 500 hectares in size holding 47 percent.

This highly unequal distribution of landholdings was largely an early twentieth-century phenomenon, associated with the accelerated growth of sugar production and sugar latifundia between 1900 and 1925. At the moment of the Cuban revolution, the twenty-eight largest sugar mills owned or controlled over two million hectares of land, corresponding to approximately 20 percent of the nation's farmland. U.S. sugar interests controlled 13 percent of the area in farms.[2]

The Case Studies

The three municipalities in which our fieldwork has been based span the three main regions of Cuba: the municipality of Guines, in the western province of Havana; the municipality of Santo Domingo, in the central province of Villa Clara; and the municipality of Majibacoa, in the eastern province of Las Tunas (see map 6.1). The three are broadly representative of Cuba's main agricultural rubrics: sugar cane, livestock, and mixed cropping of grains, *viandas* (a Caribbean term for root crops and plantains), and vegetables. They also represent different stages in the development of sugar cane production—which spread from the western to the eastern part of the island over the nineteenth and early twentieth century—and of the different levels of development reached in the prerevolutionary period.

The province of Havana was the site of the initial development of the sugar industry in the seventeenth and eighteenth centuries and of efforts to develop a modern sugar industry in the nineteenth century. The first sugar mills in Guines date from the eighteenth century; by 1827 there were forty-seven small mills in the municipality. After Cuba's first railroad was completed in 1838, which connected the sugar cane plantations of Guines to Havana city, the number of small mills

Table 6.1 Cuban Farms by Size Groups, 1945

Hectares	Number of Farms	Percent of Total	Hectares (000s)	Percent of Total	Average Size
to 4.9	32,195	20.1	86	0.9	2.67
5-24.9	79,083	49.5	935.8	10.3	11.83
25-99.9	35,911	22.5	1,608.1	17.7	44.78
100-499.9	10,433	6.5	2,193.6	24.2	210.26
500-999.9	1,442	0.9	992.5	10.9	688.28
1,000+	894	0.5	3,261.1	36	3,647.76
Total	159,958	100	9,077.1	100	56.75

Source: Dudley Seers, Andres Bianchi, Richard Jolly, and Max Nolff, *Cuba: The Economic and Social Revolution*, (Chapel Hill, N.C.: University of North Carolina Press, 1964), table 6; Sergio Aranda, *La Revolucion Agraria en Cuba*, (Mexico City: Siglo Veintiuno, Eds., 1968), table 69; based on *Memoria del Censo Agricola Nacional, 1946*.

increased to eighty-nine in 1857.[3] But by 1901 only two large, modern mills were left. Through the continual concentration of land, in 1959 these two mills owned or controlled (through milling contracts), 23,357 hectares of land, presenting approximately 52 percent of the land surface and 65 percent of the farmland of this municipality.[4]

Along with the neighboring province of Matanzas, Havana province was the site of the most important agricultural infrastructure investments, particularly in irrigation, well into the twentieth century. It is also one of the better endowed areas of the country in terms of natural resources (fertile land, average rainfall). In addition to sugar cane production, Guines has always been part of the breadbasket of Havana city, providing an important share of its fruits, vegetables, grains, and *viandas*. It is located only 45 km. from the nation's capital.

The province of Villa Clara was the site of the second wave of expansion of the sugar industry in the late nineteenth century and of its subsequent moderniza-tion. In the later part of the second decade of the twentieth century, three mills dominated the landscape in the municipality of Santo Domingo, one owned by U.S. interests, another by Spanish, and a third by Cuban interests. In the late 1950s these mills owned or controlled slightly over one-quarter of the farmland; twenty-four large cattle haciendas controlled much of the remaining land. Santo Domingo is located 260 km. southeast of Havana city.

Until the twentieth century, today's province of Las Tunas was a marginal, cattle-producing region. At the northern edge of former Oriente province (located some 694 km. from Havana city), it was not developed for sugar export production

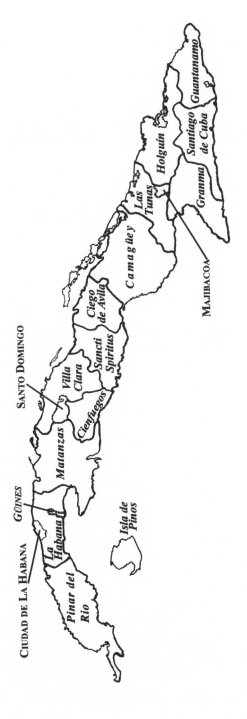

Map 6.1 Cuban Municipalities

until the early decades of this century. Between 1899 and 1916, U.S. capital built six large sugar mills in the province. None of these mills was located in the municipality of Majibacoa, differentiating it from the other two regions we study. Nonetheless, beginning in the 1920s the lands of this region were also subjected to a steady process of deforestation (which continued through the 1980s), and the best lands turned over to sugar cane production. The fact that a mill was not built in this area until the revolutionary period, however, accounts for it exhibiting quite different relations of production from the other two municipalities in the prerevolutionary period.

The development of Las Tunas as a sugar cane producer did not bring much prosperity to its inhabitants; in 1959 it was considered to be one of the most backward regions of the island.[5] Guines, given its highly favorable natural conditions and location, was among the most developed. Santo Domingo is illustrative of a midpoint with respect to prerevolutionary economic development.

The Relations of Production

The last agricultural census carried out in prerevolutionary Cuba, in 1945, is indicative of both the degree of concentration of land and of the relative insignificance of a landed peasantry. As table 6.2 demonstrates, less than one-third of the nation's farms were worked by their owners. Plantations and haciendas administered by absentee landowners and corporations accounted for 6 percent of the total number of farms and 26 percent of the land. The overwhelming number of farmers, with almost 50 percent of the land, held land in pre- or noncapitalist relations of production, being *arrendires* (renters who paid rent in cash) (30 percent), sharecroppers (6 percent), squatters (3 percent), or *subarrendires* (2 percent).

The preponderate size of the agricultural proletariat within the economically active population (EAP) in agriculture also distinguishes Cuba from other socialist countries at the eve of revolution. According to the 1953 census, agricultural wage workers comprised 61 percent of the agricultural EAP.[6] This may be an overestimation, as Brian Pollitt has argued, since "landless" wage workers sometimes had access to a small plot of land for self-provisioning. But it is clear that the majority of agricultural semiproletarians and proletarians were dependent upon the sugar sector for their livelihood. Nevertheless, this sector offered steady employment less than four months of the year, during the cane harvest.

Retrospective survey data are helpful in distinguishing the three regions in terms of the predominant class relations. Table 6.3 illustrates the predominant form of access to land of the parents of the 475 agricultural workers surveyed by us in our three case study municipalities. As can be seen, the greatest number (31 percent) were landless prior to the 1959 agrarian reform, followed by those who owned land (21.5 percent) and *arrendires* (18 percent). But there were striking differences by region.

In Guines, the greatest number of families of today's agricultural workers were

Table 6.2 Distribution of Farms and Farmland by Form of Tenancy, 1945

Tenancy	Percent of Farm	Percent of Land
Owners	30.5	32.4
Administrators	5.8	25.6
Arrendires	28.8	30.0
Subarrendires	4.4	2.4
Sharecroppers	20.7	6.1
Squatters	8.6	2.7
Others	1.2	0.8
Total	100.0	100.0
	(n=159,958)	(9,076,458 has.)

Source: Valdez Paz, *La Reforma Agraria en Cuba* (Havana: Centro de Estudios sobre America, 1990), ms.; based on data from the *Memoria del Censo Agricola Nacional, 1946.*

arrendires (31 percent) before the 1959 agrarian reform. In Santo Domingo, the landless predominated (39 percent); in Majibacoa, the sample was equally divided among those who owned property and those who were landless prior to 1959.

In Guines, those who were *arrendires* were usually cane farmers who rented land from one of the two mills in this municipality. Most of these *arrendires* farmed between 13 and 27 hectares of cane. Those who were sharecroppers tended to be situated on medium-sized properties dedicated to grain, *vianda*, and vegetable production and had access to relatively small plots of land, ranging from 3 to 5 hectares.

In Santo Domingo, cane farms (or *colonias*, as these were called, irrespective of the relations of production) tended to be larger than in Guines, particularly those rented from a mill. For example, on the Central Washington in 1939, the *colonias* averaged 110 hectares.[7] Rarely were these farmed by a peasant household, but rather, they were usually rented to members of the petty bourgeois strata who employed wage labor. Moreover, in the early decades of this century, "administration cane" (land worked directly by the mill) was more common than in Guines, giving rise to fewer *arrendires* overall and the predominance of landless households in the class structure of this municipality.

Majibacoa appears as the municipality where peasant landowners were relatively more numerous prior to 1959, perhaps because a sugar mill was not built in this zone until after the revolution. While numerous cane *colonias* were developed in the 1920s to supply mills in other municipalities, land here never became as concentrated. As in Santo Domingo, few peasants had cane *colonias*, with the majority of these owned or leased by professionals and others from the provincial capital who relied on wage labor to work them.

Table 6.3 Form of Access to Land before the Cuban Agrarian Reform—Total Sample, Parents of Interviewees

	Arrendire	Share-cropper	Squatter	Land-less	Other	Property	Un-known	Total
GUINES								
	30.4%	6.3%	—	21.5%	1.9%	15.2%	24.7%	100% (n=158)
SANTO DOMINGO								
	17.7%	—	1.9%	38.6%	1.9%	16.5%	23.4%	100% (n=158)
MAJIBACOA								
	6.9%	13.2%	3.1%	32.1%	0.6%	32.7%	11.3%	100% (n=159)
TOTAL								
	18.3%	6.5%	1.7%	30.7%	1.5%	21.5%	19.8%	100% (n=475)

Source: 1991 Agricultural Household Survey of the University of Havana

There was a high degree of semiproletarianization among the landed peasantry in Majibacoa. With relatively poor lands, most peasants migrated to the *colonias*, both nearby and far away, during the cane harvest to seek work. Work was usually available for only the harvest months, and if one was lucky, for the weeding of the cane fields. Particularly prized was obtaining a permanent job on one of the *colonias*, which entitled the worker to year-round work. These positions were often sold. For example, in 1956, the going rate for a full-time job was 280 pesos.

Also, in Majibacoa the landless frequently lived on the farms where they were wage workers; they usually were given a small plot, rent free, to farm for their own self-provisioning. While technically "squatters" (although they had the landowner's permission), these workers tended to consider themselves among the landless, and so report themselves in the survey. A recurring feature of the decades of the 1940s and 1950s, were evictions of these workers since they had no security of tenure.

In Guines, landless agricultural workers were more likely than those in Majibacoa or Santo Domingo to live in a town, since the municipal capital of Guines was a bustling city of 22,669 in the 1940s. In contrast, the municipal capital of Santo Domingo had only 3,880 inhabitants in 1943 and no town in Majibacoa had a population of over 3,000.[8] Santo Domingo and Majibacoa would continue to be much more rural than Guines up to the current period. The differing pre-

Table 6.4 Distribution of Cuban Farmland by Form of Tenancy, 1959-1993 (000s hectares)

Year	Total	State	Individuals	CPAs
1959[a] (after first Agrarian Reform)	9,070.0	3,628.0 (40%)	5,442.0 (60%)	—
1963 (before second Agrarian Re-form)	9,110.4	4,737.4 (52%)	4,373.0 (48%)	—
1963 (after second Agrarian Re-form)	9,092.4	6,419.2 (71%)	2,673.2 (29%)	—
1974[b]	9,721.9	7,760.0 (80%)	1,961.9 (20%)	—
1985	10,325.7	8,589.2 (83%)	727.7 (7%)	1,008.8 (10%)
1989[c]	11,016.4	9,065.2 (82%)	1,083.0 (10%)	868.2 (8%)

Note: After 1974, the total refers to the total land surface, defined as including agricultural land, forests, lands not apt for agriculture, and lands with buildings and other constructions. Estimates of the distribution of land between the state and private sector reported in the literature often differ, depending on whether they refer to Cuba's land surface, the land claimed by farms, agricultural land, or cultivated land. The data on the private sector also differ depending upon whether nonpeasants (wage workers who own land parcels and others who are not member of the peasant organization, ANAP) are included in the estimate. Not until 1987 was the first census of private sector land use and tenancy carried out, revealing that the amount of land held by this sector had been previously underestimated in official data, particular the land held by nonpeasants. This readjustment was not included in the official data until the 1989 Statistical Yearbook was published. That revealed that members of the CCSs held 7.5 percent of the land surface, and dispersed individuals, 2.3 percent. The decrease in the land held by the production cooperatives between 1985 is 1989 is largely explained by the large amount of state land that many of the CPAs initially held in usufruct.
Sources:
[a] Figures for 1959-1963 based on Oscar V. Trinchet, *La Cooperativizacion de la Tierra en el Agro Cubano* (Havana: Ed. Politica, 1984), graph 6, 22-23.
[b] Data for 1974 and 1985 from CEE, Direccion de Agropecuaria y Silvicultura, "Distribucion y uso de la tierra del Fondo Agricola y Forestal por formas de tenencia, Octubre 31, 1987," June 1988,13.
[c] 1989 data from CEE, *Anuario Estadistico de Cuba, 1989*, table 8, 3.

revolutionary class structure and land tenure in the three municipalities was to yield quite different patterns of agrarian development in the postrevolutionary period.

Cuba's Agrarian Reform

The first agrarian reform law of May 1959 limited the size of all landholdings to

401 hectares. It also guaranteed all tenants—whether *arrendires*, sharecroppers, or squatters—the right to the land that they worked directly. The second agrarian reform law, of October 1963, reduced the maximum size landholding still further, to 67 hectares.

The 1959 and 1963 agrarian reform decrees brought approximately 70 percent of the nation's farmland into the state sector (see table 6.4). That such a huge state farm sector was constituted so quickly is largely explained by the prerevolutionary land tenancy, since the majority of Cuba's farmland was concentrated in large sugar cane plantations and cattle haciendas. The text of the 1959 law provided for the expropriated estates to remain intact and to be worked as cooperatives. There was little question of dividing these up, due both to the perceived economies of scale of large-sized production units and the fact that it was not a demand of the rural proletariat. While in theory, the workers were to elect their own councils to play a role in the administration of the enterprises, participatory forms of management never were consolidated and the managers of these estates were appointed by the National Institute of Agrarian Reform (INRA), with little worker participation in decision making.[9]

Among the reasons cited for the subsequent decision to operate the large estates as state farms rather than as production cooperatives was the fear that the heterogenous production conditions and productivity of the estates would lead to severe inequality between rich and poor cooperatives. Moreover, it was felt that cooperatives run by permanent workers would do nothing to ameliorate the seasonal unemployment problem of temporary workers, exacerbating income inequalities among the rural work force. Further, the lack of experienced administrators and technicians at the local level favored the centralization of production decisions within INRA. This, combined with the state's concern to ensure sufficient exports and food supplies, led to the conversion of the cane cooperatives into state farms in late 1961-1962.[10]

Less attention has been given in the literature to the fact that, in addition to creating a huge state farm sector, the Cuban agrarian reform also created a large landed peasantry. By granting every tenant, sharecropper, and squatter the right to claim the land that they worked (up to a maximum of 67.1 hectares), the number of small property owners in rural Cuba more than tripled. By the end of 1963, the private sector in Cuban agriculture consisted of some 154,000 peasant households who held approximately 26 percent of the nations' farmland; another 3 percent was held by nonpeasant households.

Our survey of 475 agricultural households indicates that the families of 34 percent of Cuba's 1991 agricultural labor force benefited directly from the agrarian reform, receiving land as private property. The regional differences were marked, as seen in table 6.5. The greatest number of beneficiaries, 42 percent, were found in Guines, where *arrendire* arrangements predominated prior to 1959. The fewest were found in the municipality of Santo Domingo (29 percent), which also had the highest proportion of households reporting to have been landless prior to 1959 (see

Table 6.5 Beneficiaries of Cuba's Agrarian Reform

Municipality/ Sector	Households in Which Interviewee or Parent Received Land	Amount of Land Titled
GUINES		
State Wageworker	14* (16.7%) (n= 84)	17.51 (n=13)*
Cooperative Member	19 (59.4%) (n= 32)	20.17 (n=19)
Peasant	36 (85.7%) (n= 42)	18.67 (n=36)
Subtotal:	69 (43.7%) (n=158)	18.60 (n=68)
SANTO DOMINGO		
State Wageworker	18 (17.8%) (n=101)	9.79 (n=16)
Cooperative Member	9 (29.0%) (n= 31)	19.47 (n= 9)
Peasant	19 (73.1%) (n= 26)	22.62 (n=19)
Subtotal:	46 (29.1%) (n=158)	17.31 (n=44)
MAJIBACOA		
State Wageworker	27 (26.7%) (n=101)	5.33 (n=25)
Cooperative Member	12 (35.3%) (n= 34)	10.51 (n=12)
Peasant	12 (50.0%) (n= 24)	8.19 (n=12)
Subtotal:	51 (32.1%) (n=159)	7.30 (n=49)
TOTAL		
State Wageworker	59 (20.6%) (n=286)	9.58 (n=54)
Cooperative Member	40 (41.2%) (n= 97)	17.11 (n=40)
Peasant	67 (72.8%) (n= 92)	17.91 (n=67)
Total:	166 (34.9%) (n=475)	14.92 (n=161)

* The totals differ on the number of state wageworkers reporting that they or their parents were beneficiaries of the agrarian reform from the number reporting the amount of land titled to their families, since not all interviewees remembered the precise amount of land that their families received. This problem only affected state wageworkers, who were less likely to be agrarian reform beneficiaries themselves (as opposed to their parents), due to the differing age composition of the three sectors.
Source: 1991 Agricultural Household Survey of the University of Havana

table 6.3). In Majibacoa, the share of agrarian reform beneficiaries (32 percent) significantly exceeded the share of households reporting themselves to have been engaged in pre- or noncapitalist relations of production prior to 1959, confirming that a good number of landless households were incorporated among the beneficiaries of the 1959 agrarian reform. These data suggest that the 1959 agrarian reform law was implemented with different criteria in the three municipalities, and that it benefited a much greater number of landless, rural workers in the eastern region of Cuba.

As might be expected, the greatest number of beneficiary families are found among those who today constitute the peasantry, fully 68.5 percent of these households having been beneficiaries (see table 6.4). This figure supports the contention that Cuba's landed peasantry was, in fact, largely created by the revolution. Moreover, 41 percent of today's cooperative members belonged to families who were beneficiaries of the reform. A not insignificant number of today's wageworkers on state farms, 21 percent, were either agrarian reform beneficiaries themselves or belonged to families that were beneficiaries.[11]

Also worth noting is the relatively large amount of land that the beneficiaries received through the reform. The mean was 13.74 hectares, approximately equal to the traditional Cuban land measure of a *caballeria* (equal to 13.47 hectares). As can be seen in table 6.5, the former *colonos* of Guines received much larger farms (19.23 hectares), compared with beneficiaries in Santo Domingo (12.93 hectares) and Majibacoa (7.30 hectares).

In Majibacoa as in Santo Domingo, some peasant farmers were also affected negatively by the agrarian reform. In Majibacoa, three of the peasant interviewees lost some land as a result of the reform, and in Santo Domingo, one household lost some land. These cases were of families who owned between 27 and 40 hectares and who sharecropped or rented some land to other peasants. In the reform, their tenants were deemed beneficiaries of the plots that they directly worked.

Of the three provinces where our case studies are located, only in Villa Clara were a good number of peasants expropriated totally for being involved in counterrevolutionary activity, which centered in the Escambray mountains of the province. In the municipality of Santo Domingo, two households in the sample lost all of their land, presumably for this reason; today, they are state wageworkers. The period of counterrevolutionary activity has left a mark upon the Communist Party (PCC) in Villa Clara, which continued to play roughshod over the peasantry in subsequent decades.

In contrast, in Majibacoa, where there was no counterrevolutionary activity, no peasants where expropriated totally and the agrarian reform process showed considerable flexibility. There were even cases of peasants who owned over 67 hectares who were not affected negatively by the agrarian reform. Moreover, in later years, there is less evidence of state coercion in its relations with the peasantry. And in Guines no households in the sample were partially or totally expropriated of their lands.

Peasant-State Relations to 1977

Most of the new agrarian reform beneficiaries, as well as prior peasant landowners, became members of ANAP, the National Association of Small Producers, which was constituted in 1961. As stated at ANAP's founding congress by its secretary general, Jose Ramirez, the goal of ANAP and "the road to the socialist transformation of agriculture, is the road of cooperation"; i.e., the formation of various types of cooperatives.[12] But Fidel Castro also made clear at that time that membership in any type of cooperative was to be strictly voluntary, that "peasants will never be forced to join an agrarian cooperative."[13]

In contrast to other socialist agrarian reforms that quickly collectivized the peasantry, the Cuban government early on abandoned attempts to encourage peasants to pool their private property to form production cooperatives. This decision responded as much to political exigencies as to the economic need to consolidate the huge state farm sector. Although ANAP had organized some 345 production cooperatives (*Sociedades Agropecuarias* or agricultural societies, as they were known) and 587 credit and service cooperatives (CCSs) amongst the peasantry by 1963, it was decided in that year that conditions were not propitious for further cooperative development.[14]

At this point, some 10,000 medium to large-sized farmers still existed in the Cuban countryside and, reportedly, they were attempting to draw the peasantry into a coalition to defend private property by spreading rumors that cooperatives were the first step toward the expropriation of peasant lands.[15] To counter this political offensive, the Cuban leadership decided to no longer encourage the formation of production cooperatives. Thus, in his closing speech to the Second ANAP Congress in May 1963, Fidel Castro again assured the peasantry that small farmers would never be forced to join any type of cooperative and that after the passage of the October 1963 agrarian reform decree—which expropriated farms larger than 67 hectares—there would be "no more agrarian reforms."[16]

By 1967 the number of agricultural societies nationally had dwindled to 136 with only 1,707 members, and a decade later, to only 44, primarily as a result of state indifference.[17] ANAP's political work, however, remained focused on the principle of cooperation, and by 1967 some 1,119 credit and service cooperatives were in existence with a membership of 77,933.[18]

In the mid-1960s peasant producers were integrated into the national planning system, being required to make delivery contracts with the state procurement agency for their principal crop. They were allowed to set aside 3 hectares for their own self-provisioning. Moreover, until 1967, peasants could legally sell above-plan surpluses to urban residents. In that year, in tandem with the "Revolutionary Offensive" (which closed all private retail and service outlets), peasants could no longer engage in such above-plan sales.

State-peasant relations took on a more coercive turn in this period, since the state also began a concerted effort to integrate the lands of peasant producers into state enterprises.[19] Carried out with the intention of more fully specializing and modernizing agricultural production, peasants residing near state farms were encouraged to lease or sell their land to the state and to become wageworkers on these enterprises.

ANAP's self-criticism of the period supports the argument that peasants were sometimes forced to lease their land to the state under duress. According to Martin Barrios, a member of the ANAP national committee at the time, "although Fidel had stressed that this [incorporation into state farms] had to be a gradual process, based on persuasion . . . many state functionaries, in their desire to carry out the plan, substituted the necessary discussion for the bureaucratic method of *ordeno y mando* (order and rule)."[20]

The integration of peasant lands into state enterprises, nevertheless, was also based on material incentives. The state built modern communities on the state farms, communities that included modern housing with electricity, and water and sewer systems, as well as a primary school, a health post, a day care center, and other amenities. By 1971, 212 of these communities had been built; priority access to the housing units—which were rent free—was given to peasants who rented their land to the state.[21]

Between 1967 and 1971 at least 24,500 peasant farms nationally were integrated into the state farms, while additional private land was purchased by the state as a result of the death of the owner or old age and a lack of heirs willing to work the land.[22] While figures differ on the number of households that ceded their land to the state over this period, by 1974 the private sector occupied only 20 percent of Cuba's land surface as compared with 29 percent a decade before (see table 6.4).

Here again, our fieldwork in three municipalities illustrates the process. As Cuban planners moved toward the goal of achieving a ten-million-ton harvest in 1970, it was decided that the municipality of Majibacoa showed great potential as a cane producer. As a result, the sugar cane enterprise of Majibacoa more than doubled in size between 1964 and 1976. Part of this expansion came from turning previous pastures into cane and from deforestation, as new land was brought into production. In addition, farmers residing in the area where the state cane plan was being developed were encouraged to sell their lands to the state. In this municipality nine households (6 percent of the sample) reported that they or their parents sold their land to the state in this period. Here, these sales seemed quite voluntary.

According to the son of one former *arrendire* who had been a beneficiary of the agrarian reform, "all of our lives we wanted to have a permanent job that would give us the right to a pension; this is what was in people's heads." His family thus sold its lands to the state cane plan in the late 1960s and moved to the town of Las Parras; he became a permanent wageworker on the state cane farm.[23]

Social mobility and the lack of apparent heirs also played a role in peasants' voluntarily renting or selling their land to the state. In another peasant family, long-time property owners, not one of the eight brothers and sisters wanted to stay on the farm; in the 1960s they all went to work for the state in various capacities. The father finally sold his 13.47 hectares to the state cane enterprise in return for a monthly pension.[24]

In Santo Domingo, the families of six current state wageworkers sold land to the state in this period; one other household had rented lands to a state cane enterprise, receiving a rental payment for this land. In addition, another five peasant families sold part of their land to the various state sugar enterprises, remaining with approximately 3 hectares for their own self-provisioning. These latter households remained officially categorized as "peasants" and members of ANAP, forming part of what are known as peasant associations (*Asociaciones Campesinas*). Two other peasant households were forced to sell their land to the state when a major dam was built in this municipality. They were able to exchange 3 hectares of their total land area to maintain their self-provisioning. They, too, continue to be officially listed as "peasants" and belong to a peasant association. Overall, Santo Domingo's agricultural workers seem the most negatively affected by state intervention in agriculture, with 11 percent of those interviewed having been expropriated or having sold or rented land to the state. In interviews, they also seemed the most disgruntled over having lost access to land.

In Guines only 4 percent of the households interviewed lost access to land. Here fewer wageworkers were beneficiaries of the agrarian reform, and only two state wageworkers reported selling their land to the state during this period. The main group of peasants affected by state plans were those in the area of the livestock plan "El Cangre." Four peasant households interviewed rented their land to the state to form this dairy enterprise, most subsequently becoming wageworkers on it. All four were agrarian reform beneficiaries and two of these had already pooled their land to form an agricultural society. All four maintained their self-sufficiency areas of approximately 3 hectares each, with the area varying according to family size. These peasants remain members of ANAP as part of a peasant association.[25]

It is evident that in the late 1960s the Cuban leadership expected the private sector to eventually disappear as peasants abandoned independent production for the security and modern production conditions on state farms. Little was done, therefore, to modernize private farming, which continued to rely on ox plow and family labor while state farms mechanized. Despite their relative neglect, private producers benefited greatly from the rural development emphasis of revolutionary policy. During the 1960s thousands of rural schools and health posts were built, along with roads and rural electrification. This maintained a certain amount of trust of the state on the part of private producers, even while it became increasingly apparent that most remaining family farmers had no intention of becoming wageworkers on state farms.

The role of ANAP in national policy formation and execution, along with that of the other mass organizations, had diminished considerably in the late 1960s and early 1970s.[26] Apparently, growing peasant discontent with the manner in which they were being incorporated into the state enterprises led ANAP to take on a greater advocacy role on their behalf subsequent to the 1971 ANAP National Congress. These changes would boost ANAP's prestige among the peasantry and contribute to its steadily growing membership.[27] While for several more years Fidel Castro continued to insist that the incorporation of peasants into state farms was the primary way of integrating peasants into socialist production, the importance of voluntary incorporation was reiterated. But not until the First Congress of the Cuban Communist Party (PCC) in 1975 was there a major change in the Cuban leadership's vision of what constituted a socialist agricultural sector.

While state farms had been relatively successful in increasing sugar cane as well as rice, meat, and milk production, they had been less so in meeting the demand of the population for root crops, plantains, vegetables, and fruits, which remained limited and of poor quality. As Cuban incomes rose in the mid-1970s, this became increasingly problematic. Private farmers continued to be the main source of these products, and the slow growth in private sector sales to the state became a central concern.[28] Peasants were accused of not pulling their weight in the economy, of profiteering in the black market, while simultaneously taking advantage of social services financed by the state.[29]

Growing awareness that most peasants would not voluntarily turn over their land to the state, and of the need to modernize the private sector, combined with the desire to more fully control this sector, finally led the Cuban leadership to reconsider the role of production cooperatives. Thus, in a major speech in May 1974 Fidel Castro argued that there were two paths to a socialist agriculture: state farms and collectivization.[30] His speech formed the basis for the elaboration of the "Thesis on the Agrarian Question," which was approved at the First Party Congress the next year. The most important point of the thesis was that the collectivization process was to be gradual, based on the voluntary decisions of peasants, with the rhythm of the process dependent on the demonstration effect of successful production cooperatives and on the political consciousness of the peasantry.[31] Moreover, ANAP was given the responsibility for promoting the new production cooperatives, the CPAs.

The Beginning of Collectivization: 1977-1980[32]

At its Fifth Congress in 1977, after sixteen months of discussion of the party thesis among its membership, ANAP formally adopted collectivization as the long-term goal of the association and pledged itself to carry such out. The congressional resolutions again stressed that collectivization was to be strictly voluntary, based on the power of persuasion regarding the benefits of this "superior" form of production.[33]

ANAP had an impressive array of political, ideological, and material resources at its disposal to carry out the task. Its political capital came from its fifteen years of work among the peasantry—and, particularly, its ability to project peasant interests during periods of stress in peasant-state relations—and its ample membership. In 1976 it had 213,035 members (151,169 of whom were landowners, the remainder being family members), organized into 4,470 base-level organizations (CCSs and peasant associations).[34] Moreover, ANAP's drive to collectivize was backed by the relatively strong support for the revolution in rural areas, a product of the transformations described earlier.

ANAP also relied upon a strong package of material incentives, targeted at meeting peasants' concerns with collectives as well as at making sure that the CPAs were economically viable and thereby more attractive than individual farming. Among the former incentives was the ANAP guideline that peasants be compensated fairly for the full value of land, animals, and other means of production that they brought into the cooperative. Local commissions set up for this purpose included peasant representatives. Peasants were to be compensated for the means of production that they pooled out of cooperative profits, with the payments spread out over five to ten years, depending upon cooperative performance.

A further inducement was the promise that each cooperative would strive to guarantee the basic consumption requirements of its membership through collective self-provisioning, replicating, in part, the typical pattern of peasant production under the planning system. As noted earlier, from the time that peasants were first incorporated into the national planning apparatus in the mid-1960s, they had been allowed to maintain an area not subject to the plan (or delivery quotas)—a maximum of 3 hectares—for self-provisioning. Perhaps one of the most important inducements was the pledge that, for the first time, the national social security system would be extended to peasants when they joined the production cooperatives. This system provides old-age security through a guaranteed pension as well as paid sick leave, accident and death compensation, and paid maternity leave for women.

A further material incentive was the promise that the cooperatives were to be given priority access to construction materials to build new communities similar to those built in the previous decades for workers on state farms. However, these new communities were to be built by the cooperative members themselves, and in the beginning, the housing was expected to be quite modest. Moreover, in contrast to the pattern on state farms, cooperative members were to purchase their own housing units.[35]

The potential resources that the state pledged to the development of the production cooperatives were substantial. In addition to building materials, they would be given preferential access to machinery, inputs, and technical services as well as credit. Whereas independent farmers paid interest rates of 6 percent, the CPAs would pay only 4 percent on their loans. Moreover, the lion's share of private sector investment credit—the level of which was to increase significantly—would now be channeled to the new cooperatives.

Finally, the new cooperatives were to be managed in a democratic fashion, with the membership electing its own leadership from among its members. The executive council of the CPA was to be accountable to the general assembly, which was required to meet at least once a month.

ANAP inaugurated the collectivization effort by focusing on the leadership of the credit and service cooperatives. Monthly seminars on cooperative development were held with CCS leaders and local ANAP activists throughout the country. The need for the collectivization process to be voluntary, based not only on the power of persuasion but also on knowledge of how well production cooperatives functioned, was highly stressed in the training program.[36] Hundreds of CCS leaders were taken to visit the remaining agricultural societies, to see the benefits of collective farming firsthand.

ANAP's strategy was to initially try to organize the greatest number of production cooperatives, even if small in size. These were then to be consolidated, to prove their economic viability, so that other peasants would be encouraged to join. In a second phase, the aim would be to encourage growth in cooperative size both through new memberships and the fusion of smaller cooperatives to reach optimal size.[37]

At the beginning of 1977, only 44 production cooperatives (the former agricultural societies) existed in all of Cuba; by the end of that year 136 production cooperatives had been constituted, a number that doubled in 1978 and again in

Table 6.6 The Evolution of the Agricultural Production Cooperatives

Year	#CPAs	Members	Hectares (000s)	Ha/CPA	Members/ CPA
1978	343	9,103	n.d.	n.d.	n.d.
1979	725	16,692	104.3	143.9	23
1980	1,035	29,535	212.9	205.7	29
1981	1,128	39,519	383.4	339.9	35
1982	1,416	63,285	690.5	487.2	45
1983	1,472	82,611	938.2	637.4	56
1984	1,414	72,297	988.3	698.9	51
1985	1,378	69,896	1,008.8	732.1	51
1986	1,368	67,672	1,011.5	739.4	49
1987	1,418	69,604	977.0	689.0	49
1988	1,398	66,014	907.7	649.3	47
1989	1,353	63,838	877.5	648.6	47
1990	1,305	62,130	833.7	638.9	48
1991	1,227	60,432	786.9	641.3	49
1992	1,188	59,941	782.1	658.3	50
1993	1,160	60,442	778.4	671.0	52
1994	1,155	61,722	715.7	619.7	53

Note: The data presented in Cuban Statistical Yearbook (CEE/AEC) differ slightly from the data kept by the National Directorate of ANAP, "Composicion de los asociados de la ANAP por tipo de organizacion de base desde 1973" (handwritten ms., no date), for the years 1978-1989. We report the Statistical Yearbook data since it is the only source that reports hectarage in addition to the number of CPAs and CPA members.

Sources: 1978 from BNC, Banco Nacional de Cuba "El Credito Bancario en Apoyo al Desarrollo Rural Cooperativo" (Havana: BNC, May 1982): 20; 1979 from CEE/AEC, Comite Estatal de Estadisticas. *Anuario Estadistico de Cuba* (Havana: CEE, 1982), 210; 1980-1989 from CEE/AEC *Anuario Estadistico de Cuba* (Havana: CEE, 1989), 184; 1990-1994 from ANAP, "Resumen del Registro de Asociados de la ANAP" (as of December 31, respective years).

1979.[38] As table 6.6 shows, by 1980 there were 1,035 CPAs with a membership of 29,535. At that point the CPAs held 13 percent of the landholdings of the ANAP membership.[39]

As planned, these first cooperatives were relatively small, averaging 29 members and slightly over 200 hectares of land. Approximately one-third were dedicated primarily to sugar cane production; another one-third engaged in mixed vegetable, grain, and tuber production, while the remainder specialized in either tobacco or coffee production. The sugar cane cooperatives had the most members (33 percent of the total) and were the largest, averaging 271 hectares.[40]

Although in this initial stage the cooperatives had relatively underdeveloped systems of accounting, very basic forms of work organization (no work norms, for example), and comparatively few resources, they performed relatively well. For 239 CPAs that carried out the year-end exercise known as *balance economico* in 1980, the average per peso cost of production was 0.69, implying that these cooperatives earned a profit of 0.31 pesos per peso of output.[41]

Although a national regulation guided profit distribution within the CPAs, cooperative members themselves decided on the level of the "advance" that members would earn for their work on the cooperative. Since the level of the advance determined whether the cooperatives would be profitable, ANAP and the state encouraged the CPAs to maintain these levels relatively low, below the prevailing wage for state workers. According to the regulation, up to 50 percent of the profits could be distributed among the membership. Twenty-five to 30 percent of the profits would go into a fund to reimburse members who had pooled their means of production. The remaining profits were to be distributed as follows: not less than 15 percent should go into investment goods; not less than 15 percent into a fund for working capital; and not less than 5 percent each for cultural, sports, and social activities, and for social benefits.[42]

The Expansion of the Cooperative Movement: 1981-1983

As ANAP envisioned, the real growth in cooperative membership came once the cooperatives had been constituted. Membership doubled between 1980 and 1982 while the number of CPAs increased by one-third. Cooperative membership reached a peak in 1983 with 82,611 members, 28 percent of whom were women, organized into 1,472 CPAs, as seen in table 6.7.

The Financial Commitment of the State

The amount of credit channeled by the Cuban National Bank (BNC) to the private agricultural sector tripled between 1979 and 1983, with a total of 722 million pesos lent in this five-year period. The lion's share of the credit, 62 percent, went to the production cooperatives, with only 38 percent to individual farmers. Moreover, whereas almost half of the credit directed to the cooperatives consisted of medium or long-term credit for new investment, only 18 percent of that channeled to individual farmers consisted of investment credit, with the remainder consisting of working capital.[43] The medium and long-term credit includes the credit extended for housing construction on the cooperatives, which amounted to 11 percent of the total between 1981 and 1983. While credit for housing construction was extended only to the CPAs, credit for the purchase of machinery went almost entirely to the cooperatives as well, with private farmers receiving only 1.5 million pesos out of 61.2 million disbursed for this purpose between 1981 and 1983.[44]

As a result of this massive channelling of resources, the level of new investment per cooperative increased from 7,211 pesos in 1979 to 46,099 in 1984.[45] By 1981, 36 percent of the CPAs had irrigation systems covering at least 50 percent of the area dedicated to their principal crop.[46] The level of mechanization reached by the CPAs was also impressive. For example, the number of tractors per

Table 6.7 CPA Retention Rates

Year	Net Change Members	Retirements	Separations	Resignations	Total Losses
1984	- 10,314		n.d		n.d.
1985	- 2,401	3,914	620	2,355	6,889
		(57%)	(9%)	(34%)	(100%)
1986	- 2,224	2,489	554	3,146	6,189
		(40%)	(9%)	(51%)	(100%)
1987	+ 1,932	2,473	1,097	3,311	6,881
		(36%)	(16%)	(48%)	(100%)
1988	- 3,590	2,709	940	4,886	8,535
		(32%)	(11%)	(57%)	(100%)
1989	- 2,176	1,953	831	3,786	6,570
		(30%)	(13%)	(58%)	(100%)
1990	- 1,708	1,006	654	4,480	6,140
		(16%)	(11%)	(73%)	(100%)
1991	- 1,699		n.d.		n.d.
1992	- 490		n.d.		n.d.
1993	501		n.d.		n.d.
1994	+ 1,280	900	1,294	2,495	7,643*

Note: * Total losses in addition to retirements, separations, and resignations, include other reasons such as passed to state employment (1,740), military service (341), and deaths (205). It is unclear how these "other reasons" were categorized in the pre-1991 data, but they may be included with resignations. The increased pace of collectivization can be attributed to the massive state resources channeled to the cooperative sector, to the reasonable performance of the CPAs in this period, and to the passage of the 1983 Social Security Law for the CPAs.
Sources: 1978 from BNC (1982:20); 1979 from CEE/AEC (1982:210); 1980-1989 from CEE/AEC (1989:184); 1990-1994 from ANAP "Resumen del Registro de Asociados de la ANAP (al cierre de 31 de diciembre), for respective years.

CPA increased from 3.1 in 1982 to 5.9 in 1985; the number of tractor-trailers from 2.6 to 4.7; and the number of sugar cane combines from 0.5 to 1.1 in those years.[47]

The degree of mechanization that was attained was facilitated by the development of Cuba's capital goods industry over the decade of the 1970s.[48] The majority of Cuba's new import-substituting industries produced machines for the agricultural sector, including plows, harrows, trailers, tractors, combines, and irrigation and planting equipment.

State policy also encouraged the prioritization of the CPAs over individual farmers in the delivery of inputs and technical assistance. Finally, the cooperatives also benefited in this period by the policy of granting the CPAs the best land as land was traded by state farms and cooperatives in order to consolidate contiguous land areas (a process known as *compactacion*).

With such levels of support, the CPAs reported good financial results. Cooperative costs per peso of output remained well below those of state farms throughout the early 1980s, on the order of 0.64 peso in 1982, whereas state farm costs per peso of production were reported to remain above 1.00 peso.[49] For the cooperatives, this meant profits available for distribution at year end and that the income of cooperative members would increasingly exceed that of state wage-workers.[50]

The Legal Framework

The growth in cooperative membership was also facilitated by the passage of three laws in this period. The 1982 cooperative law gave legal status to most of the principles followed by ANAP in constituting the cooperatives.[51] The principle of voluntary association was reaffirmed as well as the relative autonomy of the cooperatives vis à vis the state. Also, the norms were established for the distribution of CPA assets, should a CPA disintegrate. Their land and other means of production could only be sold to the state or another cooperative. Upon liquidation of their assets, the CPAs were to honor their debts first (including any remaining payments for means of production that had been pooled, outstanding advances that had not been paid, and debts contracted with the Cuban National Bank). The remaining sum could be divided among the membership according to their labor contributions.

While the cooperative law consolidated the legal status of the production cooperatives, the passage of the 1983 social security law for the CPAs was more important in inducing peasants—particularly older farmers—to join the cooperatives, and in demonstrating that the state would follow through on its promises.[52]

The social security law officially established the age of retirement for cooperative men as sixty-five and for women as sixty, above that required for state wageworkers (sixty and fifty-five, respectively). Members who pooled their means of production would receive a minimum pension in the range of 60 to 90 pesos a month, depending on the value of these means of production; other members would receive a minimum monthly pension of 40 to 60 pesos, comparable to that of state farm workers.[53] The other benefits of the Cuban social security system, mentioned earlier, were also officially extended to CPA members.

A third law passed in this period provided a somewhat different economic incentive for peasants to join the CPAs. Under the tax law of April 1983, the production cooperatives received preferential tax treatment.[54] Both CPAs and individual farmers were now to be subject to a progressive income tax on their sales to the state, to range from 5 percent to a maximum of 20 percent of the value of sales. But whereas the cooperatives would be taxed on the value of their *net* sales income, individual farmers would be subject to a tax on their *gross* sales income. Opposition to the progressive taxation structure was so vehement among individual farmers that in 1984 the tax was reduced to a flat 5 percent of gross sale income. The progressive taxation of CPA profits was rescinded at the same time, although they maintained the advantage of being subject to a 5 percent tax of net, rather than gross, sales income.[55]

Peasant Response

Few systematic studies were carried out on the process of collectivization in this early period. Interviews by one of the authors with members of two CPAs in June 1980 revealed that what most motivated peasants to collectivize was the promise of better living conditions.[56] Most peasant households lived on scattered, isolated farms, often distant from most urban amenities. The new communities that were being built on the CPAs at that time were, indeed, quite attractive, providing not only modern apartments with indoor plumbing and electricity but also services, such as a primary school, a health care unit, a day care center, a communal laundry, store, and recreational facilities. Not surprisingly, given the potential of these communities to reduce domestic work, women often reported that they had been the most enthusiastic of the family members in the decision to pool private property. Moreover, peasant wives were guaranteed membership and employment in the cooperatives, giving them access to their own income. Women represented over one-quarter of the CPA membership during the early 1980s, attesting to their interest in earning their own income, even though many of them had not always participated in field work.[57]

In these interviews, young people were also credited with playing an important role in the household's decision to collectivize. With the majority of rural youth having completed the ninth grade by 1980, and many with technical skills, they were often quicker to grasp the potential benefits of mechanization that collectivization offered and to consider individual family farming as backward and out of step with the revolution.[58]

ANAP's political work was very intense in this period, and besides the use of mass communications, included thousands of seminars throughout the country, in all of ANAP's base-level organizations.[59] The goal was to personally reach every single ANAP member. An unpublished sample survey of 1,428 CCS members undertaken for ANAP in 1983 found that 80 percent of the CCS members had been personally visited by ANAP activists or the leadership of a neighboring CPA.[60]

The combination of economic and political factors in the decision to collectivize is apparent in the responses of 872 CPA members also surveyed for ANAP in 1983. The largest number (34 percent) of CPA members indicated that they had joined the CPAs because of the advantages these offered in terms of income-generating possibilities and living standards; 16 percent joined because they considered the production cooperatives to be more productive than individual farming, while 10 percent cited the privileged position of the CPAs with respect to machinery and other investments. The other responses very much reflected the official discourse: 13 percent indicated that the CPAs constituted a superior form of production, while 9 percent noted that by joining the cooperatives they were contributing to the development of the country.

In terms of the actual benefits that the members perceived from their membership in a CPA, most noted (by 36 percent) was an increased standard of living or an enhanced level of self-provisioning (23 percent); 11 percent noted that they now had access to electricity for the first time. These results are not surprising since it has often been noted that those peasants who joined the production cooperatives were generally those characterized by the worst socioeconomic conditions, frequently living at great distances from social services and other amenities.[61]

Cooperative membership significantly increased household income in certain regions. In the 1983 survey, 27.5 percent of CPA members reported earning over 5,000 pesos a year, with these primarily concentrated in the provinces of Matanzas and Camaguey. In comparison, a wageworker on a state farm earned an average 2,004 pesos in 1983.[62]

The prospect of retiring on a pension—and one that was deemed relatively high in this period—also served as an inducement to collectivize.[63] While most CPA retirees received pensions on the order of 60 to 90 pesos per month, on some cooperatives the monthly pension could reach as high as 150 pesos, if the CPA decided to contribute to such out of its profit distribution (the social welfare fund).[64] In other cases, retirees continued to work on the cooperative part-time, usually earning an advance and the right to continue purchasing subsidized food generated from the self-provisioning plot.

The level of education and age also played a role in the decision to pool private property. In the 1983 ANAP survey, members of production cooperatives were slightly better educated than those peasants who remained members of credit and service cooperatives. While the majority of members of both groups had studied through the sixth grade, a larger percentage of CPA members (14 percent) had completed the ninth grade than had CCS members (6 percent). The higher level of education of CPA members is also related to the fact that, overall, they were younger than the CCS members. Whereas 68 percent of CPA members were under

50 years of age, only 45 percent of CCS members fell into this category. Thus, in contrast to the CPA members, the majority of peasants not joining production cooperatives were already adults at the time of the revolution.

While there is little doubt that peasants who were most predisposed to the revolution were among the first to join the CPAs—responding to the "call to collectivize"—ANAP's political work among the peasantry also played an important role in convincing many to join.[65] In our field interviews, peasants and CPA members alike considered the visits by ANAP activists and the cooperative leadership to have been positive. Respondents noted that these stressed the voluntary nature of collectivization, the benefits of joining a cooperative, and discussed peasant fears with respect to joining a CPA—principally, that they would "lose their land" and "lose their liberty," and that, perhaps, all of the promises of the state might not be kept.[66]

As a result of the strong incentive package and ANAP's political work in rural areas, by 1983 41 percent of ANAP's membership of 201,551 had been incorporated into the production cooperatives and 56 percent of their land had been collectivized.[67] The cooperatives accounted for a slightly higher percentage of ANAP land than membership, because sometimes farmers sold their land to a CPA without actually joining the cooperative.[68]

The most frequently cited reason given by the 1,428 CCS members surveyed in 1983 for not joining a production cooperative (44 percent) was that they did not like the idea of working land collectively; another quarter responded that they did not like having someone boss them around. Thirty percent considered that they were too old to change their ways and work collectively. As noted above, age was an important variable differentiating those who did and did not join the CPAs in this period. Other peasants did not see many advantages in becoming a CPA member, noting that cooperative members received fewer products in self-provisioning than they themselves produced on their own farms or believed that they earned higher incomes than CPA members. Others noted that the cooperatives were paid the same price for their products as were individual farmers, and that the state provided the same services to both sectors, suggesting that economic coercion to join a CPA was minimal.

In our field interviews, some peasants reported that they thought others "had been forced to join" or "had given in" because of the low prices being paid for sugar cane or the increasing cost of services provided to individual producers by the state.[69] The 1983 attempt to impose a progressive income tax on individual farmers could also be considered a form of economic coercion, but at most a very mild one, since the progressive tax structure was to apply to CPAs as well. But, in fact, the state was not very successful in maintaining any of these economic pressures. For example, it was forced to raise sugar cane prices several years later in response to declining sugar cane yields among individual farmers.

From the 1983 survey, it is also clear that the cooperative movement had not yet exhausted the pool of peasants potentially willing to join a production cooperative. Thirty-four percent of the CCS members interviewed noted that they preferred to wait and see the results of the production cooperatives before deciding whether to join. Only 43 percent felt that they had any idea of how the cooperatives were functioning; of these, the great majority indicated that they thought the cooperatives were functioning relatively well. The most negative perceptions were concentrated in the tobacco region of Pinar del Rio, long a stronghold of peasant smallholders and where, in fact, the CPAs were performing very poorly. The generally favorable opinion of cooperative performance would change substantially over the next few years as the economic difficulties of many CPAs became increasingly apparent.

The 1983 survey interviews with CPA members indicated that the cooperatives were not without problems at this time. While 98 percent of the members expressed their satisfaction with membership, the great majority (77.5 percent) also noted that their cooperatives were experiencing some difficulties. Almost two-thirds reported that the main problem was the lack of building materials for the promised new housing, while one-third reported production-related difficulties.

Notwithstanding the difficulties, the CPAs were providing a growing share of private-sector sales to the state. In 1983 they were contributing 39 percent of *viandas*, 27 percent of vegetables, and 42 percent of grains sold through official channels. By 1985 they were contributing 46 percent of total non-sugar cane sales by the private sector, up from 15 percent in 1981.[70]

The Period of Reflection: 1984-1987

Between 1983 and 1984 there was a sharp drop in cooperative membership, as table 6.6 shows. In one year, the production cooperatives experienced a net loss of 10,314 members, principally through retirements. But more alarming to the ANAP leadership was that net membership continued to fall until 1987—a year in which there was a short recovery in net membership—and increasingly, not through retirements, but rather through resignations. Moreover, it became increasingly difficult to convince individual farmers to join the CPAs.

Both the surge in new memberships in 1983 and the rapid plunge in numbers in 1984 is explained by the 1983 Social Security Act. A total of 19,399 CPA members retired during 1984, to receive a pension; by 1987 the cooperatives had some 35,000 pensioners. The state was reportedly paying some 58,000 pesos a year in pensions while the CPAs were contributing 25,000 pesos.[71] Not surprisingly, the growing pension burden began to affect the profitability of some of the cooperatives.

Table 6.7 illustrates how the reasons for dropping CPA membership changed over this period. In contrast to 1985, in the late 1980s less than half of those leaving the CPAs did so through retirement, while an increasing percentage were either resigning or losing their memberships as a result of disciplinary actions (noted as separations in the table).

Our fieldwork in a number of provinces suggests that membership has been less stable among three, sometimes overlapping, groups of members: youth, women, and those who entered the CPAs without means of production to pool. This latter group includes former workers on state farms, skilled workers who have been especially channeled to the CPAs to upgrade their technical capabilities, and urban workers attracted to the CPAs by the promise of better housing. According to national statistics for 1984, 59 percent of CPA members joined the cooperatives without means of production to pool.[72] This figure greatly overstates the number of nonpeasants among the membership, since it includes the adult children of those who pooled land as well as their wives. Nonetheless, a growing concern has been precisely the "proletarianization" of the cooperatives.[73]

Peasants who have pooled land are much more committed to the success of the cooperative than others, partly because if they resign from the cooperative, while paid in full for the means of production that they have pooled, they cannot get their land back. Those from a proletarian background, particularly young people, have much less attachment to the land and are more likely to get discouraged if the cooperative is not functioning well, with few profits to distribute. They also have greater alternative employment opportunities than traditional peasants, contributing to their greater instability as CPA members.

While up through 1983 the number of women cooperative members continued to grow, their relative share in CPA membership fell from 35 percent to 28 percent between 1979 and 1983. And they were overrepresented in the 1984 drop in membership, so that in 1985 they constituted 25 percent of the members. While the latter drop may be explained by the fact that women can retire at an earlier age than men, women have also dropped their CPA membership when they were unable or unwilling to work on the cooperative full-time, as is required of all cooperative members.[74] Women members also tend to be concentrated in the coffee and tobacco cooperatives, the CPAs experiencing the greatest difficulties in this period. Both the coffee and tobacco cooperatives lost a higher percentage of members in the 1984 drop—the coffee CPAs losing 31 percent of their membership that one year, and tobacco CPAs 17 percent—than the national average of 12.5 percent. The growing number of CPA resignations was undoubtedly related to the financial difficulties of many of the cooperatives.

Changing Economic Incentives

Two factors affected the economic incentives with respect to CPA member retention and in terms of enticing additional peasant farmers to pool their land: (1) a fall in the profitability of the cooperatives; and (2) the enhanced standard of living of individual farmers as a result of sales in the free peasant market. In 1982 only 11 percent of the CPAs did not earn a profit; this figure rose to 30 percent by 1985. Moreover, average costs per peso of production increased from 0.64 in 1982 to 0.82 in 1985.[75] Part of the reason for the apparent financial deterioration might be that over time, more cooperatives were actually capable of keeping track of costs and performing the year-end financial exercise. But the evidence suggests that the problems of the cooperatives were real, associated with the very expansion in cooperative membership and heavy capitalization of the CPAs of the early 1980s.[76]

The rapid expansion of cooperative membership and the associated land area held by the CPAs exacerbated the organizational problems of many cooperatives. Peasants were simply inexperienced at managing large-scale extensions of land, and the cooperative management at coordinating the work of a large number of workers.[77] It is one thing to coordinate the work of 23 members on 144 hectares of land, as in 1979, but quite another to do so well with 51 members and some 732 hectares to attend to, as in 1985.[78] Notwithstanding the fact that the cooperative leadership tended to include the better educated members, and the many ANAP training seminars, their preparation was often less than adequate given the growing complexity of cooperative operations.[79]

Also, the skill level of the cooperative membership, while steadily increasing, was still quite low. The CPAs had only 553 middle-level technicians in agronomy and veterinary services, and 140 university-trained agronomists and veterinarians in 1985.[80] While efforts had been made to train cooperative members themselves as middle-level technicians, all too often these positions were filled by bringing in new members from a nonpeasant background, causing other problems, such as lack of cohesion among the membership, in addition to the previously cited instability in its numbers.

Another explanation for the declining performance of the CPAs can be found in rising investment costs. While the cooperatives initially relied on traditional production methods while developing collective methods of work, in the early 1980s most cooperatives undertook major investments. Many replanted permanent crops, for example, replacing fifty-year-old coffee plantations on which productivity had declined seriously. As noted in the previous section, many cooperatives, especially cane CPAs, mechanized heavily. These investments may take years to yield returns, as cooperative members must learn to use the new technology and plants must mature. Moreover, some of the inexperienced cooperatives made investments in machinery or crops not adapted to their soil or climate, or simply overinvested, and among these, debt burdens weighed particularly heavily.[81] The BNC, aware of these problems, began to reduce the amount of investment funds lent to the cooperatives in the mid-1980s.

Another problem resulted from CPA reliance on the Ministry of Agriculture or the Ministry of Sugar for the provision of inputs and services allocated to the cooperatives through the plan. The ministries, according to some reports, prioritized deliveries of materials and services to the state farms, for whose performance it is directly responsible. Some cooperatives thus suffered from inadequate or untimely provision of services, and sometimes also from their arbitrary pricing, all factors that affected cooperative profitability.[82]

Lack of profitability was also related to the practice that cooperatives, as socialist enterprises, were sometimes required to plant crops that were unprofitable, given state pricing policy. Moreover, when the free peasant markets were opened in 1980 the CPAs were expected to sell their above-plan surpluses at prices lower than those being charged by individual farmers. And after new regulations were passed to control the high prices and excesses of the free market in 1983, the CPAs were strongly discouraged from selling in the free peasant market at all. A new state-run parallel market was created to procure above-plan CPA surpluses at prices higher than those governing planned production. While the dual procurement and price structure was aimed at maintaining incentives for the cooperatives, it led to a growing disparity in the profitability of cooperative production as compared with that of individual farmers who could still sell their above-plan production in the free peasant market.[83]

There was also growing concern that the free peasant markets were corrupting cooperative members and state functionaries alike, while acting as a disincentive for the remaining individual producers to collectivize. Some cooperatives, in an effort to maintain profitability, continued to sell their surpluses, and in some cases, even planned production, in the free peasant market. The high prices individual farmers and others could earn in the free peasant market reportedly led them to bribe state firms into diverting services and inputs that had been allocated to cooperative development, further undermining the performance of the cooperatives.[84] Not surprisingly, with net cooperative membership continuing to fall through 1986, there was growing concern that the free peasant markets were a hindrance to the collectivization effort.[85]

The high incomes individual farmers could earn, combined with the relaxed market for construction materials in this period, also diluted the incentive for collectivization provided by the cooperative housing construction program. Individual farmers, particularly in Havana province, were building themselves what were considered to be "palaces," houses of five to eight rooms with mosaic floors and tiled bathrooms. But in addition, the cooperative housing construction program was moving slower than expected. While an average 1,860 new units had been built each year between 1981 and 1985, this was considerably below housing needs.[86] Part of the problem was that members were often not satisfied with the prefabri-cated apartment units that had been planned, but rather were insisting on building independent houses, similar to those being constructed by prosperous CCS farmers.[87] This development increased the amount of construction materials required, raised costs, and slowed the pace of construction. Considerable progress had been made with respect to rural electrification, however. By 1985, 967 cooperatives, with 26,351 members, had been connected to the national electrical system or had their own generating system.[88]

While a range of problems persisted, strides had been made in consolidating the cooperatives politically. By 1985, 25 percent of the membership of the CPAs were members or aspirants of either the Communist Party or the Union of Communist Youth, up from 17 percent in 1983.[89] The persistent problems, however, led the party and ANAP to a major evaluation of the cooperative movement, and a number of new measures.

The New Measures

The new measures of 1986 and 1987, in tandem with the broader rectification process of these years, were designed to improve the functioning of the cooperatives while increasing the incentives for individual peasants to join the CPAs, and to ensure that the CPAs performed according to their original purpose, as a socialist form of production.[90] The new measures resulted in greater state control over the activities of the cooperatives, which subsequently generated a different set of problems in the late 1980s.

The new party guidelines—particularly, the recommendation that the free peasant market be closed—were discussed in detail at the Second Congress of the CPAs in May 1986. A change in market policy was clearly on the agenda, but the actual decision to close the markets appears to have been heavily influenced by CPA members themselves. ANAP's president, Jose Ramirez, noted at the start of the two-day meeting that while the majority of the CPA members favored closing the peasant markets, the markets would have to remain open until an alternative national system of distribution was functioning. By the end of the meeting, so many CPA delegates had reportedly demanded that the peasant markets be shut immediately that Fidel Castro, in his closing speech, announced that the free peasant markets would be closed that same day.[91]

In addition, Fidel Castro noted that "the day will come . . . not too far in the future when we will be able to say that 100 percent of the peasantry belong to the cooperatives, that 100 percent of peasant lands are cooperativized."[92] It is clear that, at this point, full collectivization of the peasantry was still the goal.

Henceforth, above-plan production of both individual peasants and the CPAs was to be sold in the state-controlled parallel market and a new procurement agency, *Frutas Selectas*, was created for this purpose. To maintain producer incentives, procurement prices in the parallel market would remain considerably higher than prices paid for planned production through *Acopio*, the main state procurement agency. Nonetheless, it was thought that at least one impediment to the incentive scheme for individual farmers to join the CPAs had been eliminated—the possibility of earning superprofits as a result of shortages or advantages of farm location or access to transport.

To ensure that the cooperatives performed according to their original purpose, the 1986 party guidelines also required CPA sales to be more closely monitored, and the CPAs were prohibited from engaging in secondary activities, such as artisan production. This new restriction received much less attention at the CPA congress than did the issue of the peasant markets, and would end up having a negative effect on the profitability of some cooperatives. It would also have the unintended consequence of reducing the possibility for women's participation in the CPAs, since women cooperative members were often responsible for these sideline activities.[93]

To cope with rising debt burdens and other financial problems, a plan of action, comprised of 194 "tasks," went into effect at the Seventh ANAP Congress in 1987. The often-noted task #26 called for a study to be done of each CPA with financial problems, to lead to a specific plan to improve the performance of the cooperative, including debt restructuring. It was also stipulated that debt repayment could not exceed 35 percent of cooperative profits, to ensure that profits be available for distribution to the membership. A commission composed of representatives of ANAP, the Ministries of Agriculture and Sugar, and the BNC was subsequently formed to study the problems of the 692 cooperatives having financial difficulties—i.e., those that were either unprofitable or generating very low profits.[94]

At the Third Party Congress later that year, a special program, known as the Plan Turquino, was launched for the mountainous areas of the country, to spur coffee and cacao production. Aiming to slow the out-migration from these regions as well as to promote CPA development, the program placed priority on the construction of housing and social infrastructure on the CPAs. In addition, these cooperatives were exempted from paying taxes as well as interest payments on loans from the BNC. The price paid for coffee by the state procurement agency was also raised to stimulate production.[95]

These initiatives, as we noted, were a response to unsatisfactory cooperative performance and the slowing pace of collectivization. Many of them also reduced cooperative autonomy, however. Combined with continued extension of closer state planning and the implementation of technical norms in the cooperatives during this period, some of the changes reduced the cooperatives' ability to determine how their own resources would be used.[96] As working conditions on CPAs became more like those on state farms, peasants were more likely to feel alienated from the cooperative, to have weaker work incentives, and to lose their commitment to the survival of the cooperative.

Persisting Problems of the Cooperative Movement: 1988-1991

Even before the disintegration of the socialist bloc in 1989 and 1990—which disrupted Cuba's traditional trading relationships and, hence, internal production—and the development of Cuba's National Food Program—intended to rapidly deepen food import substitution—it seemed as if the state was running out of positive incentives to offer individual farmers to join the cooperative movement.[97] Peasants continued to resist pooling their land for economic and ideological reasons, and increasingly, because they believed that the cooperatives were unprofitable. Particularly worrisome to Cuban officials was the apparent growing lack of interest among rural youth in joining the CPAs or remaining as CPA members.

Why Peasants Won't Collectivize

By the late 1980s ANAP was left with an increasingly difficult group to work with, as those peasants predisposed to joining the cooperatives had already done so. A study in four municipalities of Havana province in 1988-1989, which included in-depth interviews with eighty-three CCS members, found that not one was interested in joining a CPA.[98] Moreover, a number of peasants noted that they would not join a production cooperative under any conditions.

The attitude noted above was influenced by two factors: the possibilities for reproduction of the peasantry and the level of retirement incomes. Most of the CCS members interviewed in this 1988-1989 study had heirs, grown children or other family members, who helped out on the farm and were interested in taking it over once the household head was ready to retire. According to these CCS members, their children were not any more interested in joining the production cooperatives than they were. Also, most CCS members interviewed considered the pension granted to cooperative retirees to be quite low. Greater state supervision over cooperative activities and particularly retirements in the late 1980s did, indeed, reduce the privileges and income cooperative pensioners could receive.

What stands out most clearly is that many individual farmers earned quite high incomes and enjoyed a relatively high standard of living. Because of the need to maintain price incentives for production, the closing of the peasant markets had little detrimental effect on their incomes, since peasants could sell their above-plan production to the state at higher prices.[99] Peasants could still make a comfortable living working alone, raising labor-intensive crops. For example, CCS members in the municipality of Mariel in Havana province estimated that they earned around 10,000 pesos a year, five times as much as the average cooperative member.[100]

Access to modern technology and economies of scale on the cooperatives thus did not constitute significant enough incentives for these farmers to collectivize. Neither did the possibility of living in the communities being built on the cooperatives. The great majority of CCS members interviewed in Havana province live in quite good conditions, in houses built of wood with tile roofs and cement or terraced floors.[101] Less than one-quarter of the eighty-three CCS members did not have access to electricity, about the same proportion characterizing CPA members nationally.[102]

Notwithstanding the fact that not all the CCS members had electricity, the accumulation of appliances among them was impressive. Over 90 percent of the households interviewed in Havana province in the late 1980s had a refrigerator, washing machine, television, radio, and a number of smaller appliances. A significant number of them also owned vehicles.[103] As one of these farmers pointed out, "the CPA can't offer us anything better."[104] Of course, the standard of living of the peasantry of Havana province is much higher than in many other regions of the country, as our regional case studies will subsequently demonstrate.

The opinions of individual farmers regarding the functioning of the cooperatives had also deteriorated over time. In Havana province, for example, CCS members argued that they worked more and had better results than the production cooperatives, even with fewer resources. They noted that the cooperatives were heavily indebted as a result of buying too much equipment, that they wasted resources, and that they did not do a good job of cultivating their land. For all these reasons, they asserted that the cooperatives were running losses and certainly were not as profitable as individual farming.[105]

As one of these farmers in Havana province was quick to point out, however, "just because we continue as independent farmers doesn't mean we aren't revolutionary," explaining that most farmers met their annual plans, selling their crops to the state procurement agencies, and many participated in the militias.[106] Moreover, most individual farmers were either agrarian reform beneficiaries or their heirs, and they continued to be intensely loyal to Fidel Castro and the revolution. As another CCS member noted, only Fidel, himself, could make them part with their land, for Fidel gave the land to them: "Fidel se las dio y solo el puede quitarselas."[107]

Cooperative Performance

Paradoxically, while individual farmer opinion of the CPAs became increasingly negative in the late 1980s, cooperative financial performance improved substantially in this period. Whereas in 1985, 30 percent of the CPAs did not earn any profits, and in 1987, 692 CPAs (49 percent of the total) were considered to be in financial difficulty (unprofitable or earning low profits), by 1990 only 200 (15 percent) remained in this latter category.[108] The performance of the sugar cane CPAs, in particular, had improved dramatically, with only 9 percent being unprofitable in 1988 and 8 percent in 1989. Moreover, the average cost per peso of production dropped from 0.80 in the 1981-1987 period, to 0.76 and then 0.74 in succeeding years.[109]

In addition, the CPAs were contributing a growing share of food sales to the state. In the late 1980s, the CPAs were contributing approximately 55 percent of *vianda* sales (compared to 39 percent in 1983), almost two-thirds of rice sales, and had increased their share of vegetable sales to one-third of total private-sector sales.[110]

Other problems, besides financial ones, overshadowed discussions in the late 1980s, partly as a result of increased state control over the cooperatives and their functioning.[111] The economic controls imposed in the effort to make the CPAs financially viable were often difficult for peasant members to understand. Where the style of management and work of the state farms was reproduced (following strict norms of how much work was to be accomplished per day), peasant members sometimes felt the organization of work to be irrational. In addition, in an effort to make the cooperatives profitable, frequently unprofitable CPAs were merged with ones that were profitable, with only the tacit agreement of the membership of the latter. This usually reduced the profits earned by the profitable cooperative, since the new, fused cooperative had to assume the debt of the unprofitable cooperative. Such mergers also reduced the degree of cohesion of these CPAs as they became larger and more unwieldy.

Moreover, it seems that even within the degree of autonomy retained by cooperatives, many failed to consolidate participatory management styles and collective decision making. This has oftentimes reduced the interest and commitment of the membership—one of the keys to good cooperative performance.

The Problem of Youth

Whereas in the late 1970s it seemed as if young people were pivotal in the development and expansion of the cooperative movement, in the late 1980s there was growing concern about the inability of the CPAs to attract and retain youth. In a number of cooperatives the aging of the membership led—in addition to a growing pension burden—to worries over the possibility of the cooperatives reproducing themselves over time. In the CPAs of the province of Villa Clara, for example, 10 percent of cooperative members were over sixty-five years of age, and would be retiring shortly. And while 41 percent of the members were over fifty years old, only 15 percent were less than thirty years of age.[112]

An in-depth study of the role of young people in six CPAs and three CCS in the provinces of Pinar del Rio, Sancti Spiritus, and Granma found that the principal reason that youth were not being attracted to and retained on production cooperatives was due to the poor performance of the CPAs and the attendant low income levels of cooperative members.[113] This study also noted that the CPAs had not always given sufficient attention to increasing the skills of young members, something in which young people were very interested. Meanwhile, the cooperatives had to import skilled labor, which often was not very stable. The lack of emphasis on training, combined with the absence of amenities on many cooperatives and the low level of the advance, gave young people few incentives to keep working on the cooperatives.

If the CPAs have no profits to distribute, the members earn only the stipulated advance as well as the opportunity to purchase self-provisioning products at cost. The advance in the late 1980s was usually in the range of 4.5 to 5.0 pesos per day, somewhat less than the daily wage of a state agricultural worker.[114] And the advance was much less than what young people could earn as temporary wageworkers working for individual peasants—in Havana province the latter were reported to pay as much as 20 pesos per day.

The above-mentioned study concluded that many of the problems of retaining and attracting youth to the CPAs were associated with the growing state control over the cooperatives and, hence, the lack of sufficient cooperative autonomy. For where the participation of young people in decision making had been encouraged, they had been eager to help in solving the problems of the cooperatives; in cooperatives where member participation in decision making was not stressed, youth were often disinterested in cooperative problems.[115] Thus one explanation for the different attitude among youth between the late 1970s and the late 1980s could have to do with a slackening of cooperative autonomy over time.

Ironically, the harsh conditions of the Special Period in Cuba, particularly after 1992, when food supplies in urban areas became increasingly tight, seems to have produced a turnaround in CPA membership recruitment and in the stability of their membership (see table 6.6). As we will demonstrate below, drawing on our case studies in three municipalities, the CPAs have proven quite resilient in the face of extreme shortages in petroleum and other farm inputs and many continue to generate quite high levels of membership income as well as foodstuffs from their self-provisioning efforts.

Cooperative Development Viewed from Below

Between 1977 and 1982 ten CPAs were constituted in Majibacoa and nine each in Santo Domingo and Guines. The majority (59 percent) of cooperative members in our 1991 sample survey joined their CPA in its initial years, 1977-1982. In Guines, in particular, most current cooperative members were founding members, 78 percent. Membership in the CPAs in Santo Domingo and Majibacoa has been much less stable, partly because they contained a smaller percentage of peasants.

The production cooperatives were also a much more important social and productive force in Guines, where the CPA membership constituted 16 percent of the agricultural EAP in 1991, than in Santo Domingo (where they constituted 4 percent) or Majibacoa (6 percent). As we will demonstrate, the CPAs have also been much more successful in Guines than in the other two municipalities, partly because of their natural and infrastructural endowment and because of the composition of their membership.

While the CPAs were initially formed by peasants who pooled their own means of production, the majority of members in 1991 were nonpeasants. In terms of previous occupation, 39 percent of CPA members in the sample had been individual peasant producers prior to joining a production cooperative; 29 percent had been state agricultural workers and 9 percent state industrial workers, with the remainder students, housewives, or in other occupations. As table 6.8 also illustrates, regional differences were significant.

The majority of cooperative members in Guines, 62.5 percent, were once individual peasant farmers. In contrast, in Majibacoa the largest number of members, 44 percent, were agricultural wageworkers prior to joining the CPA; this same tendency is apparent in Santo Domingo, where ex-agricultural workers constituted 32 percent. Santo Domingo also stands out for the relatively large

Table 6.8 Previous Occupations of Members of Agricultural Production Cooperatives before Joining the CPA

Occupation	Guines	Sto Domingo	Majibacoa	Total
Ag Wageworker	9.4%	32.3%	44.1%	28.9%
Industrial Wageworker	9.4%	16.1%	2.9%	9.3%
Peasant	62.5%	29.0%	26.5%	39.2%
Cooperative Member	—	—	2.9%	1.0%
Housewife	3.1%	—	8.8%	4.0%
Own-account	3.1%	—	—	1.0%
Mid-level Technician	—	6.5%	—	2.1%
Service Sector	3.1%	3.2%	5.9%	4.1%
Student	6.3%	12.9%	8.8%	9.3%
Military Service	3.1%	—	—	1.0%
Total	100.0%	100.0%	100.0%	100.0%

Source: 1991 Agricultural Household Survey of the University of Havana

number of industrial wageworkers (many from the sugar industry), 16 percent, among the CPA membership.

As table 6.9 shows, 39 percent of the sample of cooperative members pooled their own land when they joined the CPA. This was a much more frequent occurrence in Guines, where 56 percent pooled land. Less than one-third of the membership of the CPAs in Santo Domingo and Majibacoa had private property to pool. A better measure, however, of both the peasant base of the cooperatives and of the importance of the weight of land-pooling members to the success of the cooperatives is provided by taking into account those cases where other family members (besides the survey interviewee) contributed land to the CPA. By this measure, 55 percent of the current membership belong to families who pooled land. This figure is highest in Guines, 72 percent, and lowest in Santo Domingo, 39 percent. It is an important variable in explaining the commitment of the membership to the success of the cooperative and in terms of the different productive outcomes among CPAs.

The average amount of land pooled was 17.3 hectares, and much larger in Guines and Santo Domingo than in Majibacoa, where the average was only 7 hectares. The value of land and other means of production contributed to the production cooperative was highest in Guines, averaging 4,062 pesos. In Santo Domingo, where the average amount of land contributed was similar to Guines, the mean value was only 3,032 pesos, reflecting both poorer quality land and the fact that peasants were much more capitalized in Guines and had other means of production besides land to contribute to the cooperatives.

In terms of the motivations for joining a production cooperative, what previous studies did not reveal was whether agrarian reform beneficiaries were more likely to voluntarily pool their land to form a CPA than those peasants who were property owners before the revolution. In our sample, of the farmers who pooled their land, 51 percent were agrarian reform beneficiaries, suggesting that nonbeneficiaries were just as likely as beneficiaries to collectivize.

However, in Guines, where the CPAs have been most successful, the majority of cooperative members who pooled land were agrarian reform beneficiaries. This is consistent with the earlier finding that this was the municipality that had the largest number of beneficiaries. In contrast, in Santo Domingo, which had by far the fewest number of agrarian reform beneficiaries, the CPAs were constituted by peasant farmers who pooled the private property that they owned before the revolution.

In Santo Domingo, one of the main motivations for many in joining the cane CPA Niceto Perez was that living conditions in their zone were still quite bad. Most members lived in a settlement some 13 kilometers away from a main road, in dispersed houses constructed of wood floors and roofs made of palm. They were promised by ANAP that if they pooled their land to form a CPA, they would be given the materials to construct modern houses outside of the small town of Manacas. Moreover, their land would be exchanged for contiguous state lands near their new community. These promises were kept and the members feel that they are now much better off. The CPA has been profitable and it has also attracted new members, growing from 17 in 1980 to 49 in 1993.

As noted earlier, in the late 1980s, as part of the attempt to consolidate the CPAs, there was a move to merge smaller and/or less profitable cooperatives with larger and more successful ones. In Santo Domingo, the first merger was in 1981, when two CPAs were fused due to problems with the leadership in one of these; subsequently, four others were fused to form two CPAs in 1989 because they were

Table 6.9 Landpooling among Cuban Peasants to form CPAs

Municipality	Percentage of Interviewees who Pooled	Average Amount of Land Pooled (has.)	Percentage whose Families Pooled
GUINES			
(n=32)	56.3%	21.80%	71.9%
SANTO DOMINGO			
(n=31)	29.0%	21.26%	38.7%
MAJIBACOA			
(n=34)	32.6%	7.01%	52.9%
TOTAL	39.2%	17.29%	54.6%

Source: 1991 Agricultural Household Survey of the University of Havana

not profitable. This merger created problems for at least one of these, the CPA Martires del Moncada, a cane cooperative that had been profitable until it was merged with another CPA.

In Majibacoa, between 1988 and 1990 six CPAs were fused into three at the initiative of municipal authorities. For example, the CPA Waldemar Diaz was merged with the CPA Manuel Cordero in 1988. The former was small and in debt due to poor management. As a member of the latter puts it, "It really was not in our interest to merge . . . but the Party discussed it with us and we accepted."[116] In this case, the merger worked out. The state agreed to an exchange of lands so that all of the cooperative lands would be contiguous, and the CPA ended up with better lands and a slightly larger area. But in other cases (the CPA Ramon Naranjo) these fusions have caused the merged CPAs to be unprofitable for a number of years, much to their membership's dissatisfaction.

The largest CPAs in terms of members in 1992-1993 were those of Guines, whose seven cooperatives averaged 116 members with 629 hectares of land. The smallest were the seven CPAs in Majibacoa, which averaged 34 members and 520 hectares of land. The six CPAs of Santo Domingo were the largest in area, averaging 797 hectares and 51 members.

The Guines cooperatives are by far the most successful. Household income survey data for 1991 indicate that in Guines 100 percent of the cooperative members interviewed earned a profit distribution in that year, as compared with only 71 percent in Santo Domingo and 79 percent in Majibacoa. Most significant was the difference in the level of profits generated by the CPAs in the three municipalities. The average profit distribution in Guines of 2,535 pesos was ten times the level generated in Santo Domingo, 246 pesos, where the average profit distribution was the lowest. In Majibacoa the average profit distribution in 1991 was 410 pesos.[117]

The level of profit distribution in Guines was slightly higher than the average level of the advance (or implicit wage) that the cooperative members pay themselves over the course of the year. The average level of the advance was also highest in Guines, as was the implicit value of the food subsidy, the latter measured as the difference between the price cooperative members pay for the products the CPA sells them from the self-provisioning effort, and the retail price of these products.

The value of the food subsidy is quite high in all three municipalities—ranging from 866 pesos in Majibacoa to 1,018 pesos in Guines, indicative of the high degree of self-sufficiency generated by the cooperatives. In fact, this is one of the greatest accomplishments of the CPAs. Many, including CPAs dedicated primarily to cane production, have been able to renounce the ration card for many products. In contrast, self-provisioning efforts on the state farms in 1991 were comparatively meager; the implicit subsidy of self-provisioning purchases ranged from 33 pesos in Santo Domingo to 71 pesos in Majibacoa. Undoubtedly, in that year CPA members were eating much more abundant, diverse, and higher quality foods than state wageworkers, a difference that was exacerbated after 1992.

Overall, the average income of cooperative members in Guines from their work in the CPAs, 5,800 pesos, was almost double the average income of those in Santo Domingo (3,239) and in Majibacoa (3,061). The profitability of the Guines cooperatives can be attributed not only to their more favorable initial conditions—better land and greater access to irrigation, as well as location—but also to the fact that the CPAs in this municipality are much more peasant based. This in turn is related to the fact, noted earlier, than in Guines there were more agrarian reform beneficiaries than in the other municipalities. Moreover, the Guines CPAs are characterized by a much higher share of peasants who pooled land, bringing large numbers of family members into the CPAs with them. The extremely strong family ties among the membership appears to have committed them to the successful outcome of the cooperative venture.

An indicator of the success of the cooperative movement, in general, is that in all three municipalities the mean, net household income of cooperative members exceeds that of state wageworkers, a difference that is statistically significant. As table 6.10 shows, the difference in the income levels attained is particularly acute in Guines.

In all three regions the highest net household incomes were reported by peasant households. However, the difference in the average household income of cooperative members and peasants was not statistically significant. This suggests that the process of collectivization has not severely hampered the income-generating possibilities of those peasants who pooled their land compared with those who did not, particularly in terms of those peasants who sell the bulk of their production to the state at official prices.[118]

The CPAs in the Special Period

Our fieldwork in the three municipalities suggests that the production cooperatives have fared relatively well under the harsh conditions of the Special Period, providing one of the explanations why after thirty-four years of viewing state farms as the "superior" mode of production, the Cuban leadership decided to cooperativize the state farms in September 1993.

First, the membership of the production cooperatives had stabilized or increased by 1993 in all three municipalities, following the national trend. In Guines, which has by far the largest number of CPA members, the problem is that too many people are eager to join them, particularly state farm workers. These CPAs do not want too many additional members and are quite selective in whom they admit to membership, generally preferring only to add family members. Since membership implies a commitment on the part of the cooperative to provide permanent, year-round employment, and to remunerate such with the basic advance, the CPAs prefer to rely on temporary wage labor during peak periods.

The attractiveness of the CPAs in all three regions in the current period is largely due to the high level of self-provisioning that they offer their members. Moreover, with growing unemployment in the cities as a result of the economic crisis, more rural youth are opting to remain in the countryside, and prefer to work on the CPAs rather than on the state farms.

In terms of production, notwithstanding the shortfall in inputs, in the first quarter of 1992 Havana province CPAs increased their deliveries to the state of root crops, plantains, and vegetables by 17 percent compared with the same period in 1991. The Guines ANAP president informed us that the production cooperatives surpassed their production plan during 1992, delivering more than 600,000 quintals of vegetables, grains, root crops, and plantains to the state procurement agency. Deliveries were somewhat lower in 1993 due to losses that this municipality sustained at the hands of an unusual tropical storm (termed "the Storm of the Century") in March 1993.

The Guines CPAs have been able to increase or at least sustain production levels while using fewer inputs primarily by bringing more land into food pro-

Table 6.10 Net Household Income by Sector and Region
(annual in current Cuban pesos)

State Wageworkers (n=286)	4,901.62
Guines (n=84)	5,068.24
Sto. Domingo (n=101)	5,131.39
Majibacoa (n=101)	4,533.27
Cooperative Members (n=97)	6,642.68
Guines (n=32)	8,619.50
Sto. Domingo (n=31)	5,965.83
Majibacoa (n=34)	5,399.28
Peasants (n=92)	7,897.75
Guines (n=42)	9,245.75
Sto. Domingo (n=26)	6,250.59
Majibacoa (n=24)	7,323.17
Total (n=475)	6,897.96
Guines (n=158)	6,897.96
Sto. Domingo (n=158)	5,479.28
Majibacoa (n=159)	5,139.57

Source: 1991 Agricultural Household Survey of the University of Havana

duction. One cane cooperative, the CPA Antolino Rojas, has now become a "mixed" cooperative, with some 145 hectares going from cane to mixed cultivation. Another cane cooperative, the CPA Alberto Torres, was to be given 27 hectares of state land (in usufruct) to plant onions. There were also plans to transfer land from state farms to the very best mixed-cropping cooperatives. The CPA Amistad Cubano-Hungara was to receive 135 hectares in usufruct to plant vegetables and another CPA was to receive half that amount to do the same. According to a functionary of the Ministry of Agriculture, the planned transfer of land is indicative of the fact that it is finally being recognized that the cooperative sector is much more productive than the state sector in terms of root crop and vegetable production.

In terms of the cane cooperatives in Guines, yields have fallen drastically since 1990 due primarily to the lack of fertilizers. The 1992-1993 harvest was characterized by a 40 percent drop in supplies of chemical inputs compared with 1990. To give an example of its effect, yields on the CPA Antolino Rojas went from 119,000 *arrobas* per *caballeria* in 1990 to 51,800 in 1993. At the nearby state farm (the Amistad Agro-Industrial Complex), however, yields had fallen to 36,400 *arrobas* per *caballeria*.[119]

In Majibacoa, for the first time in 1993, all seven of its cooperatives were profitable. Two of these had been almost at the point of disintegrating in 1991 due poor management and their excessive debt burden. Under new management, one of these, the CPA Ramon Naranjo, was now considered to be one of the best CPAs in the province of Las Tunas. Moreover, here, too, the cane CPAs continued to outperform the state farm of the Majibacoa Agro-Industrial Complex.

In sum, in our fieldwork in these municipalities during 1993 it was apparent that the CPAs were adjusting to the shortage of modern inputs in a more successful fashion than the state farms. In addition, there was growing recognition among state farm managers that the CPAs were much more efficient and productive than the state farms. Although the state farms had been experimenting with various new forms of decentralization and worker incentives for several years, the new schemes had not reversed falling production trends.[120] This was the context for the subsequent decision to form basic units of cooperative production (UBPCs, *Unidades Basicas de Produccion Cooperativa)* on the state farms.

Conclusion

We began this chapter by claiming that the Cuban experience with collectivization is notable for its relatively voluntary and successful nature. The Cuban experience can be judged successful in that (1) peasants responded to the mix of economic and political incentives, pooling over half of the landholdings of this sector to form the new production cooperatives; (2) notwithstanding the many problems in cooperative development, the great majority of CPAs have been consolidated as profitable enterprises; and (3) over time, the CPAs have been contributing a growing share of private-sector foodstuff production as well as export crops.

Probably the greatest measure of success, and the one differentiating the Cuban experience from other collectivization processes, is that collectivization was accomplished while adhering to the principle of voluntary membership. Perhaps the best measure of the voluntary nature of the process is the fact that in 1990 123,505 ANAP members continued to farm some 82,240 holdings as individual farmers.[121] Another is the very fact that cooperative members have felt free to drop their CPA membership when it suited them.

In addition, a sufficiently broad range of field studies have now been carried out in rural Cuba to confirm the voluntary nature of the process, with ANAP's political work based less on the power of persuasion than in the demonstration principle: that the CPAs do in fact work and may offer better living and working conditions for segments of the peasantry.[122]

The differential treatment of CPAs and individual farmers with respect to interest rates, taxes, access to equipment and construction materials, and so on, was, of course, an economic incentive designed to make the CPAs more attractive and viable than individual farming. As we have attempted to demonstrate, while state support for the cooperative movement has been crucial to its success, the differential treatment of individual farmers was neither very onerous nor able to undermine the viability of this form of production. Even with the closing of the free peasant markets, individual farmers could still make a good living, since the state increased wholesale prices to maintain production incentives. And given the important productive role that individual farmers still play in labor-intensive crops such as vegetables, the state has had to continue to ensure this sector adequate levels of inputs and credit.

ANAP is also aware that many CCS members have simply made up their minds that they do not want to join a production cooperative, under any conditions. Cognizant of this, in recent years, there has been less political work among the peasantry, with the number of visits by ANAP activists and the CPA leadership to convince CCS members to join the CPAs decreasing in the late 1980s and coming to a halt after 1990. Since then, given the urgency of Cuba's National Food Program, ANAP's work has centered on strengthening the credit and service cooperatives to ensure that peasant farmers maintain or even increase their sales of foodstuffs to the state.

In terms of the factors promoting successful collectivization, on a national level it appears that cane, livestock, and mixed cropping production cooperatives have been much more successful than those in coffee or tobacco. This trend is partly associated with geography, with the former dominating Cuba's plains, whereas coffee production is confined to the mountainous regions, which also have the poorest infrastructure. But in addition, there appear to be few economies of scale in coffee and tobacco production, two labor-intensive crops based on family farming throughout Latin America.

Our regional analysis of three municipalities characterized by a similar crop structure (cane, livestock, and mixed cropping) suggests that the natural and infrastructural environment is also a major factor explaining the differing degree of profitability and success of Cuba's production cooperatives. As we have shown, through the analysis of incomes earned by CPA members, Guines CPAs earn differential rents from their much more favorable natural endowment and infrastructure.

But in addition, social and political factors must also be taken into account in explaining the relative success of the Guines CPAs. These cooperatives are much more peasant based, with a much larger share of the membership having pooled their land than in the other municipalities. This, in turn, is associated with land tenure patterns in the prerevolutionary period, with *arrendires* predominating in Guines, and then, with the agrarian reform, which resulted in a higher proportion of agricultural households being beneficiaries here than in the other municipalities. In addition, a large number of cooperative members are related to each other through kinship ties. All these factors combine to make the Guines CPAs more cohesive units of production, with strong membership commitment to their success. Finally, the fact that most of the CPAs have also been profitable since their founding serves to bolster the commitment of the membership to this form of production.

In our view, the future of the cooperative movement may very well depend on a clarification of the relationship between centralized state control and cooperative autonomy. Many of the problems of the cooperatives before the Special Period seemed to be linked to a slackening of member participation in decisionmaking. While greater state control may have been a consequence of the attempt to ensure the financial viability of the CPAs, greater control has reduced cooperative autonomy. Less autonomy and member participation in decision making, in turn, are associated with a lower commitment among the membership to cooperative viability, a "proletarianization" of the members, and, undoubtedly, is associated with defections among the CPA membership.

In the Special Period, given the weakened ability of state functionaries to exercise their monitoring role over CPA activities (largely because of the scarcity of petroleum to make regular visits to the field), and the urgency that the CPAs maximize production however they see best, there is a tendency emerging in favor of more cooperative autonomy. This tendency is favored by the recognition that the state sector no longer constitutes (if it ever did) "the highest form of socialist production," and the recent move to convert the state farms to production cooperatives. Cooperative autonomy in the context of a broader decentralization of the Cuban economy may represent the only way forward for the Cuban collectivization experiment in the 1990s.

Notes

This chapter is based on Deere, Meurs, and Perez (1992), but is updated and revised to include data from the 1991 Agricultural Household Survey of the University of Havana and other *fieldwork* in three municipalities of Cuba between 1991-1994. The latter research has been directed by Deere, Perez, and Ernel Gonzales. The coauthors are grateful to the Rural Studies Team of the University of Havana, and particularly to Ernel Gonzales, Myriam Garcia, and Cari Torres for their contributions to the analysis of the three municipalities highlighted here, and to Mieke Meurs and Mark Selden for insightful comments on earlier versions of this chapter.

1. Dudley Seers, Andres Bianchi, Richard Jolly, and Max Nolff, *Cuba: The Economic and Social Revolution* (Chapel Hill, N.C.: University of North Carolina Press, 1964), 19-20.

2. Sergio Aranda, *La Revolucion Agraria en Cuba* (Mexico City: Siglo Veintiuno, Eds., 1968), 170.

3. Hugh Thomas, *Cuba: The Pursuit of Freedom* (New York: Harper and Row, 1971), 122.

4. *Anuario Azucarero de Cuba* (La Habana: Ed. Cuba Economica y Financiera, 1959).

5. Republica de Cuba, "Proyecto de Fomento de la Produccion de Alimentos y Conservacion del Medio Ambiente en la Provincia Las Tunas: Solictud al PMA," vol. 1 (Havana: 1990), 14-16.

6. Brian Pollitt, "Some Problems in Enumerating the 'Peasantry' in Cuba," *Journal of Peasant Studies* 4, no. 2 (1977): table 1.

7. *Anuario Azucarero de Cuba* (La Habana: Ed. Cuba Economica y Financiera, 1939).

8. Leui Marrero, *Geografia de Cuba* (Havana: Ed. Alfa, 1950), app. 8.

9. Arthur MacEwan, *Revolution and Economic Development in Cuba* (London: Macmillan Press, 1981), 48. Carlos Rafael Rodriguez, "The Cuban Revolution and the Peasantry," *World Marxist Review* 8, no. 10 (1965): 64.

10. MacEwan, *Revolution*, 49 - 81.

11. As a result of the different way that the agrarian reform was applied regionally, many more wageworkers in Majibacoa have access to land today, as well as more land, than in Guines and Santo Domingo. According to the results of the 1991 Agricultural Household Survey, state wageworkers in Majibacoa had access to an average 1.45 hectares, as compared to 0.36 hectares in Santo Domingo and 0.08 hectares in Guines.

12. Adelfo Martin Barrios, *La ANAP: 25 Anos de Trabajo* (Havana: Editorial Politica, 1987), 25.

13. Martin Barrios, *La ANAP*, 42.

14. Martin Barrios, *La ANAP*, 53.

15. Rodriguez, "The Cuban Revolution and the Peasantry," 69.

16. Martin Barrios, *La ANAP*, 59.

17. In the initial years of the agrarian reform, four agricultural societies each were formed in Majibacoa and Santo Domingo and five in Guines. Only one, in Majibacoa, survived to the mid-1970s, becoming one of first agricultural production cooperatives (CPAs) in the new wave of collectivization.

18. Martin Barrios, *La ANAP*, 74-75.

19. Rene Dumont, *Is Cuba Socialist?* (London: Andre Deutsch Ltd., 1974), 63-66. Susan Eckstein, "The Socialist Transformation of Cuban Agriculture: External and Domestic Constraints," *Social Problems* 29, no. 2 (1981): 192-93.

20. Martin Barrios, *La ANAP*, 81-84.

21. Juan Luis Martin, "Nuevas Vias en la Politica de Construccion de Viviendas para Area Rural en Cuba," in paper prepared for the Seminar on Housing in Latin America (Caracas: 1979), 6-7.

22. Martin Barrios, *La ANAP*, 94. Under the terms of the initial agrarian reform law,

peasant property can be inherited but sold only to the state.

23. Life history interview conducted in Las Parras, Majibacoa, in June 1992.

24. Life history interview conducted with a state wageworker on the Majibacoa Sugar Complex, Farm #4, June 1992.

25. As a result of these rentals and sales, in 1991 there were more peasants associated with peasant associations (459) than CCSs (379) in Santo Domingo, indicative of the depth of this process in this municipality. In contrast, in Guines, there were far more CCS members (621) than those belonging to peasant associations (432). In addition, by 1991 a much larger share of the peasantry in Guines had pooled their land to form production cooperatives than in Santo Domingo, since the peasant sector was so much larger at the advent of the 1977 collectivization movement.

26. MacEwan, *Revolution*. Dominguez, Jorge, *Cuba: Order and Revolution* (Cambridge, Mass.: Harvard University Press, 1978).

27. Martin Barrios, *La ANAP*, 82, 86-87, 96-98.

28. In 1975 the private sector accounted for 40 percent of the value of non-sugar cane output sold to the state, including 57 percent of the vegetables, 65 percent of the legumes, and 44 percent of the tubers. See CEE/AEC, Comite Estatal de Estadisticas, *Anuario Estadistico de Cuba* (Havana: CEE, 1988): 319-21. While in the first half of the 1970s, the growth rate of private sector output recovered from the plummet of the late 1960s, throughout the 1970s, such would be far below that of the state sector. See Carmen Deere, Mieke Meurs and Niurka Perez, "Toward a Periodization of the Cuban Collectivization Process: Changing Incentives and Peasant Response" *Cuban Studies* 22 (1992): tables 1 and 2.

29. Medea Benjamin, Joseph Collins, and Michael Scott, *No Free Lunch: Food and Revolution in Cuba Today* (San Francisco, Calif.: Institute for Food and Development Policy, 1984), 87.

30. Martin Barrios, *La ANAP*, 126-27, 138.

31. Martin Barrios, *La ANAP*, 128.

32. This section draws heavily on Deere, Carmen, Mieke Meurs, and Niurka Perez, "Toward a Periodization of the Cuban Collectivization Process: Changing Incentives and Peasant Response," *Cuban Studies* 22 (1992): 115-49.

33. Asociacion Nacional de Agricultores Pequenos, "Material de Estudio, Documentos que norman y orientan las CPAs" (Havana: Department of Revolutionary Orientation of the PCC, 1978). Martin Barrios, *La ANAP*, 129, 137.

34. Martin Barrios, *La ANAP*, 114.

35. Martin Barrios, *La ANAP*, 137-38.

36. Asociacion Nacional de Agricultores Pequenos, "Material de Estudio, Documentos que norman y orientan las CPAs." Jose Ramirez, "El Sector Cooperativo en la Agricultura Cubana," *Cuba Socialista* 11 (1984): 1-24.

37. Martin Barrios, *La ANAP*, 53.

38. Martin Barrios, *La ANAP*, 183.

39. Martin Barrios, *La ANAP*, 154.

40. CEE/AEC, *Comite Estatal de Estadisticas, Anuario Estadistico de Cuba* (Havana: CEE, 1987), 306.

41. Also, according to the Cuban National Bank, between 1979 and 1981 the average cost of production of the CPAs nationally was 0.70 per peso of output. See BNC, Banco Nacional de Cuba, "El Credito Bancario en Apoyo al Desarrollo Rural Cooperativo" (Havana: BNC, May 1982): 12. Martin Barrios, *La ANAP*, 154.

42. "Reglamento General de las Cooperativas," Gaceta Oficial, no. 8, 20 September

1990.

43. BNC, Banco Nacional de Cuba, "El Credito Bancario a las Cooperativas y a los Agricultores Pequenos," report prepared for the Second Meeting of Technicians on Agricultural Financing (Havana: BNC, 1984), 40.

44. BNC, "El Credito Bancario a las Cooperativas y a los Agricultores Pequenos," 43.

45. *Granma*, the official newspaper of the Cuban Communist Party (18 March 1985).

46. BNC, Banco Nacional de Cuba, "El Credito Bancario en Apoyo al Desarrollo Rural Cooperativo" (Havana: BNC, May 1982), 3.

47. Dharam Ghai, Cristobal Kay, and Peter Peek, *Labour and Development in Rural Cuba* (London: Macmillan Press, 1988), table 5.3. ANAP, Asociacion Nacional de Agricultores Pequenos, "Analisis del Movemimiento Cooperativo Hasta Diciembre 31 de 1985" (Mimeo: ANAP, February 1986).

48. Andrew Zimbalist and Claus Brundenius, *The Cuban Economy: Measurement and Analysis of Socialist Performance* (Baltimore, Md.: The Johns Hopkins University Press, 1989), 87-91.

49. ANAP, Asociacion Nacional de Agricultores Pequenos, "Informe Central al VII Congreso de la ANAP" (Havana: ANAP, May 1987), 12. Benjamin, Collins, and Scott, *No Free Lunch: Food and Revolution in Cuba Today,* 171. Since costs of production for the cooperative include only part of labor costs, the advance, these figures are not strictly comparable. While a rigorous study of comparative productive efficiency remains to be done, the available data on costs of production indicate that the CPAs are more cost-efficient than state farms under existing conditions.

50. This proposition was confirmed in the 1991 Agricultural Household Survey; the results are presented in table 6.10, discussed subsequently.

51. Law No. 36 of 22 July 1982.

52. Decree Law No. 65 of 23 January 1983; see *Gaceta Oficial*, no. 4, 1983: 9.

53. The final amount of the pension is to be based on 40 percent of the average annual income of the cooperative member over five of the last ten years, plus 1 percent per year worked on the cooperative. The cooperatives were to contribute 3 percent of the value of their gross sales to the general social security fund, and, initially, were permitted to increase the amount of the pensions offered out of their general social funds. The cooperative social funds (generated by a 3 percent profit distribution) were also to provide for sick leave, accident, and maternity leave pay.

54. Decree Law 66 of 1 April 1983; in Facultad de Derecho, *Legislacion y Documentos sobre Derecho Agrario Cubano.* Vol. 2 (Havana: Universidad de la Habana, 1986): 233.

55. Martin Barrios, *La ANAP*, 209.

56. Carmen Diana Deere, "Rural Women and Agrarian Reform in Peru, Chile, and Cuba," in *Women and Change in Latin American*, ed. June Nash and Helen Safa (South Hadley, Mass.: Bergin & Garvey, 1986).

57. Jean Stubbs and Mavis Alvarez, "Rural Women on the Agenda: The Cooperative Movement in Cuba," in *Rural Women and State Policy: Feminist Perspectives on Latin American Agricultural Development,* ed. Carmen Diana Deere and Magdalena Leon (Boulder, Colo.: Westview, 1987), table 1.

58. Deere, "Rural Women and Agrarian Reform in Peru, Chile, and Cuba."

59. Oscar Trinchet V., *La Cooperativizacion de la Tierra en el Agro Cubano* (Havana: Ed. Politica, 1984), 38-39.

60. This survey was carried out by the National Team of Public Opinion Studies of the PCC. Its sample was drawn from seven provinces: Pinar del Rio, Matanzas, Villa Clara, Las Tunas, Holguin, Camaguey, and Granma.

61. Niurka Perez, Miriam Garcia, Barbara Jorrin, Mabel Menendes, Joaquina Cruz, and Caridad Dacosta, "Algunos Aspectos de la Composicion Socio-Economica y Demografica de Campesinos Individuales Caneros en Cuatro Municipios de Provincia Habana" (Mimeo: University of Havana, 1990c), 15. Niurka Perez, Ernel Gonzalez, Miriam Garcia, Joaquina Cruz, and Caridad Dacosta, "Informe del Estudio sobre las Relaciones Politico Economicas del Campesinado con el CAI Azucarero 'Antonio Guiteras' Municipio Puerto Padres, Provincia Las Tunas" (Mimeo: Research Group on the Sugar Sector CAIs of the Province of Havana, University of Havana, May 1990a), 3, 33.

62. CEE/AEC, *Comite Estatal de Estadisticas, Anuario Estadistico de Cuba* (Havana: CEE, 1987), 306.

63. Perez, Garcia, Jorrin, Menendes, Cruz, and Dacosta, "Algunos Aspectos de la Composicion Socio-Economica y Demografica de Campesinos Individuales Caneros en Cuatro Municipios de Provincia Habana," 13.

64. Interview with Mavis Alvarez, ANAP National Committee, Havana, February 2, 1991.

65. Perez, Garcia, Jorrin, Menendes, Cruz, and Dacosta, "Algunos Aspectos de la Composicion Socio-Economica y Demografica de Campesinos Individuales Caneros en Cuatro Municipios de Provincia Habana," 3.

66. Niurka Perez, Joaquina Cruz, Caridad Dacosta, Miriam Garcia, and Barbara Jorrin, "Valoraciones acerca del proceso cooperativo canero en cuatro municipios de la provincia de la Habana" (Mimeo: University of Havana, October 1989a).

67. BNC, "El Credito Bancario a las Cooperativas y a los Agricultores Pequenos," 16. Ramirez, "El Sector Cooperativo en la Agricultura Cubana," 6.

68. In the provinces of Havana and Las Tunas it was observed that peasants were often allowed to keep a small parcel (usually the 3 hectares dedicated to self-provisioning) when they sold their sugar cane lands to the production cooperatives. See Perez, Garcia, Jorrin, Menendes, Cruz, and Dacosta, "Algunos Aspectos de la Composicion Socio-Economica y Demografica de Campesinos Individuales Caneros en Cuatro Municipios de Provincia Habana," 13, and Perez, Gonzalez, Garcia, Cruz, and Dacosta, "Informe del Estudio sobre las Relaciones Politico Economicas del Campesinado con el CAI Azucarero 'Antonio Guiteras' Municipio Puerto Padres, Provincia Las Tunas," 39. Some of these peasants considered that sugar cane was more trouble than it was worth and preferred to dedicate themselves to the more lucrative production of vegetables and basic grains. Surely a good number of these were not predisposed to collective farming.

69. Perez, Cruz, Dacosta, Garcia, and Jorrin "Valoraciones acerca del proceso cooperativo canero en cuatro municipios de la provincia de la Habana," 2, 6.

70. *Revista ANAP*, the monthly magazine of the National Association of Small Agriculturalists (1986), 6-7. BNC, "El Credito Bancario a las Cooperativas y a los Agricultores Pequenos," 16. Ramirez, "El Sector Cooperativo en la Agricultura Cubana," 2.

71. ANAP, Asociacion Nacional de Agricultores Pequenos, "Informe Central al VII Congreso de la ANAP," 12.

72. CEE, "Proceso de Creacion y Crecimiento de la CPA, Diciembre 1984" (Havana: Direccion de Agropecuaria, CEE, March 1985), 9.

73. Victor Figueroa, Jaime Garcia, and Elia Serra, "Contradicciones en el Sector Agricola No Estatal de Villa Clara y Expectativas de la Expansion del Cooperativismo," paper presented to the First Scientific Forum on Agricultural Cooperatives, Central University of Las Villas, May 1990, 18. Perez, Cruz, Dacosta, Garcia, and Jorrin "Valoraciones acerca del proceso cooperativo canero en cuatro municipios de la provincia

de la Habana," 9.

74. Stubbs and Alvarez, "Rural Women on the Agenda: the Cooperative Movement in Cuba," 144, 151.

75. ANAP, Asociacion Nacional de Agricultores Pequenos, "Informe Central al VII Congreso de la ANAP," 12, 13.

76. Carmen Diana Deere, Mieke Meurs, and Niurka Perez, "Toward a Periodization of the Cuban Collectivization Process: Changing Incentives and Peasant Response," *Cuba Studies/Estudios Cubanos* 22 (1992).

77. Niurka Perez, Liliana Martinez, and Milagros Cabrera, "Influencia Formativa de las CPA y las CCS sobre los Jovenes Campesinos Cooperativistas" (Mimeo: University of Havana, 1990e), 3.

78. Although Fidel had warned at its initiation that the cooperative movement should not fall into *gigantismo*, promoting ever larger cooperatives, in 1981 the Ministry of Sugar established the minimum size target of sugar cane cooperatives as 806 hectares (Martin Barrios 1987: 149, 155).

79. In the 1983 survey cited earlier it was found that 35 percent of those in CPA leadership positions completed the ninth grade. Also, a higher proportion of the leadership are party members (38 percent) than the general membership (14 percent). PCC-Havana, "Estudios de los Problemas Economicos, Tecnicos, Sociales, Politico de las C.P.A." (Mimeo: Provincial Commission of Havana Province, 1984), 17.

80. Martin Barrios, *La ANAP*, 222.

81. Interview with official of the BNC, Havana, March 1987. Also see Vicente, Enelvis, "Analisis de la Irrentabilidad en las Cooperativas de Produccion Agropecuarias Caneras de la Provincia Habana: Vias de Eliminacion," Ph.D. thesis (University of Havana: July 1990), 20-21, and ANAP, Asociacion Nacional de Agricultores Pequenos, "Informe Central al VII Congreso de la ANAP," 9, 11.

82. Ramirez, "El Sector Cooperativo en la Agricultura Cubana," 14.

83. For a full discussion of the evolution of the Cuban marketing system and, particularly, the free peasant markets, see Deere, Meurs, and Perez, "Toward a Periodization of the Cuban Collectivization Process: Changing Incentives and Peasant Response," upon which this section draws.

84. *Revista ANAP No.6*, the monthly magazine of the National Association of Small Agriculturalists (1982), 13.

85. PCC-Havana, "Estudios de los Problemas Economicos, Tecnicos, Sociales, Politico de las C.P.A.," 5

86. ANAP, Asociacion Nacional de Agricultores Pequenos, "Informe III Encuentro Nacional de CPA" (Havana: ANAP, May 1988), 5. In Havana province, for example, it was calculated that of the 5,350 CPA households, 62 percent were in need of improved housing. By the end of 1983, some 420 homes (13 percent of the projected demand) had been completed, with another 383 under construction. See PCC-Havana, "Estudios de los Problemas Economicos, Tecnicos, Sociales, Politico de las C.P.A.," table 7).

87. ANAP-MINAZ, "Informe sobre la Situacion que Presenta el Trabajo del Sector Campesino y Cooperativo en la Provincia de La Habana al Cierre del Quinquenio 81-85" (Mimeo: ANAP-MINAZ, January 1986), 4.

88. ANAP, Asociacion Nacional de Agricultores Pequenos, "Informe Central al VII Congreso de la ANAP."

89. Martin Barrios, *La ANAP*, 224. Ramirez, "El Sector Cooperativo en la Agricultura Cubana," 15. The party went to considerable efforts to expand its membership among the peasantry in the early 1980s, particularly in the CPAs. In the province of Havana, for

example, the party had only eight base committees and 231 militants among the whole peasant sector in 1980; only five of these with 90 militants were located on CPAs. By 1983 the number of base committees on the CPAs had been expanded to thirty-six and the party counted with 397 militants, approximately 7 percent of the CPA membership of the province. See PCC-Havana, "Estudios de los Problemas Economicos, Tecnicos, Sociales, Politico de las C.P.A.," 19.

90. At the Third Congress of the Cuban Communist Party (December 1985 to February 1986), Fidel Castro announced that the party was commencing a process of "rectification of errors and negative tendencies." This process has been analyzed as Castro's alternative to Gorbachev's perestroika; as an abandonment of the SPDE (System of Direction and Planning of the Economy, which is associated with material incentives and enterprise financial autonomy, a planning system initiated in 1975) in favor of moral incentives; and/or as a response to Cuba's hard currency debt and fiscal crisis. The Political Bureau of the PCC adopted what is known as the *Programa de Medidas* for the cooperative sector in March 1986. See ANAP, Asociacion Nacional de Agricultores Pequenos, "Informe Central al VII Congreso de la ANAP," 1, and ANAP, "Informe Central al VII Congreso de la ANAP," (Havana: ANAP, May 1987): 7-8.

91. The discussions surrounding the closing of the peasant markets are summarized in *Granma*, 19 May 1986 and 20 May 1986. In an interview by Deere on February 17, 1987, Carlos Rafael Rodriguez (then vice president of Cuba) confirmed that the plan was to phase out the peasant markets only after the infrastructure for an expanded parallel market in foodstuffs was in place, perhaps in late 1986. According to him, Fidel Castro was so taken by the demands of the CPA delegates that he decided to close the free peasant markets at once.

92. *Granma*, 20 May 1986.

93. Gloria Valle, "Analisis de los Problemas que Afectan el Desarrollo de las Cooperativas Agropecuarias Cafetaleras: Estudio de Casos en las Provincias Granma, Holguin, Guantanamo y Villa Clara" (Mimeo: Center for Demografic Studies, University of Havana, September 1989).

94. Another "task" resulting from the ANAP Congress was to increase the pace of new cooperative housing construction. The number of new units completed nationally had increased to 2,548 in 1986; in 1987, the number almost doubled, with 4,802 units completed. See ANAP, "Informe III Encuentro Nacional de CPA," (Havana: May 1988): 12. In response to problems in obtaining services and inputs from state enterprises, raised by the CPA delegates at the 1986 congress, two new consultative bodies were also created—CONCA (Consejo de Cooperacion Agricola) and CONCAI (Consejo de Cooperacion en los Complejos Agro-Industriales Azucareros). Each regional consultative body was to be made up of the presidents of the CPAs and CCSs, state enterprise managers, and local representatives of Popular Power. Minag-Minaz-BNC-ANAP, "Cooperativas de Produccion Agropecuaria con Dificultades Financieras, Programa de Trabajo" (Mimeo: BNC, June 1987).

95. Valle, "Analisis de los Problemas que Afectan el Desarrollo de las Cooperativas Agropecuarias Cafetaleras: Estudio de Casos en las Provincias Granma, Holguin, Guantanamo y Villa Clara," 4.

96. Mieke Meurs, "Agricultural Production Cooperatives and Cuban Socialism: New Approaches to Agricultural Development," in *Transformation and Struggle: Cuba Faces the 1990s*, ed. Sander Halebsky and John Kirk (New York: Praeger, 1990).

97. See Carmen Deere, "Cuba's National Food Program and Its Prospects for Food Security," *Agriculture and Human Values* 10, no. 3 (1993) for a detailed discussion of the

effect of the demise of COMENCON on the Cuban agricultural sector and of the goals and accomplishments of the food program.

98. Perez, Garcia, Jorrin, Menendes, Cruz, and Dacosta, "Algunos Aspectos de la Composicion Socio-Economica y Demografica de Campesinos Individuales Caneros en Cuatro Municipios de Provincia Habana," 4, 15.

99. Perez, Gonzalez, Garcia, Cruz, and Dacosta, "Informe del Estudio sobre las Relaciones Politico Economicas del Campesinado con el CAI Azucarero 'Antonio Guiteras' Municipio Puerto Padres, Provincia Las Tunas." Niurka Perez, Ernel Gonzalez, Miriam Garcia, Joaquina Cruz, Caridad Dacosta, and Barbara Jorrin, "Informe del Estudio sobre las Relaciones Politico-Economicas del Campesinado con el CAI Azucarero "Obdulio Morales" Municipio Yaguajay, Provincia Sancti Spiritus" (Mimeo: Research Group on the Sugar Sector CAIs of the Province of Havana, University of Havana, July 1990b).

100. Perez, Garcia, Jorrin, Menendes, Cruz, and Dacosta, "Algunos Aspectos de la Composicion Socio-Economica y Demografica de Campesinos Individuales Caneros en Cuatro Municipios de Provincia Habana," 16-17. A study of 880 CPAs in 1985 revealed that the average income of cooperative members from work in the cooperative was 1,700 pesos. There was tremendous variation in the sample, depending on the principal crop of the cooperative. Income on cooperatives with mixed production was the highest, 2,800 pesos per member, followed by sugar cane cooperatives at 1,800 pesos. The lowest incomes were among the coffee CPAs, 800 pesos per member. See ANAP, "Analisis del Movimiento Cooperativo Hasta Diciembre 31 de 1985," (Mimeo, February 1986).

101. Perez, Gonzalez, Garcia, Cruz, Dacosta, and Jorrin, "Informe del Estudio sobre las Relaciones Politico-Economicas del Campesinado con el CAI Azucarero 'Obdulio Morales' Municipio Yaguajay, Provincia Sancti Spiritus," 8, 9.

102. In 1988 78 percent of the CPAs had electricity, benefiting some 34,000 households. See ANAP, "Informe III Encuentro Nacional de CPA," 12.

103. Perez, Garcia, Jorrin, Menendes, Cruz, and Dacosta, "Algunos Aspectos de la Composicion Socio-Economica y Demografica de Campesinos Individuales Caneros en Cuatro Municipios de Provincia Habana."

104. Perez, Garcia, Jorrin, Menendes, Cruz, and Dacosta, "Algunos Aspectos de la Composicion Socio-Economica y Demografica de Campesinos Individuales Caneros en Cuatro Municipios de Provincia Habana," 42.

105. Perez, Garcia, Jorrin, Menendes, Cruz, and Dacosta, "Algunos Aspectos de la Composicion Socio-Economica y Demografica de Campesinos Individuales Caneros en Cuatro Municipios de Provincia Habana," 16.

106. Perez, Garcia, Jorrin, Menendes, Cruz, and Dacosta, "Algunos Aspectos de la Composicion Socio-Economica y Demografica de Campesinos Individuales Caneros en Cuatro Municipios de Provincia Habana," 30.

107. Perez, Gonzalez, Garcia, Cruz, and Dacosta, "Informe del Estudio sobre las Relaciones Politico Economicas del Campesinado con el CAI Azucarero 'Antonio Guiteras' Municipio Puerto Padres, Provincia Las Tunas," 2.

108. Interview with official of the BNC, Havana, 21 February 1991.

109. Niurka Perez, Miriam Garcia, Caridad Dacosta, Ernel Gonzalez, et. al. "Analisis Comparativo de Algunos de los Problemas que Inciden en la Irrentabilidad de Seis CPA Caneras Mediante el Metodo 'Tormenta de Ideas'" (Mimeo: Research Group on the Sugar Sector CAIs, University of Havana, 1990d), 1.

110. Unfortunately, a consistent time series on the distribution of private sector sales to the state has yet to be constructed. The data cited in the text are drawn from ANAP, "Informe III Encuentro Nacional de CPA," 9, and Nora Cardenas,"Actividad del Seguro

Agropecuario y su Relacion con el Ministerio de la Agricultura," paper presented to the International Symposium on Agricultural Insurance, (Havana, 1991): Annex 1,3, and 4.

111. Meurs, "Agricultural Production Cooperatives and Cuban Socialism: New Approaches to Agricultural Development." Niurka Perez, Liliana Martinez, and Milagros Cabrera, "Influencia Formativa de las CPA y las CCS sobre los Jovenes Campesinos Cooperativistas" (Mimeo: University of Havana, 1990e). Victor Figueroa, "Informe Cientifico Resumen, II Taller Cientifico Provincial acerca del Cooperativismo y el Problema Alimentario" (Mimeo: Cooperative Research Group, Central University of Las Villas, April 1991).

112. Figueroa, Garcia, and Serra, "Contradicciones en el Sector Agricola No Estatal de Villa Clara y Expectativas de la Expansion del Cooperativismo," 18. Perez, Cruz, Dacosta, Garcia, and Jorrin "Valoraciones acerca del proceso cooperativo canero en cuatro municipios de la provincia de la Habana," 18.

113. Perez, Martinez, and Cabrera, "Influencia Formativa de las CPA y las CCS sobre los Jovenes Campesinos Cooperativistas."

114. The advance is somewhat higher on the sugar cane CPAs, ranging from 5.76 to 7.30 in 1988 and 1989 in the CPAs Martires del Moncada and Eduardo Gonzalez, two CPAs studied precisely because they were having financial problems–in one cooperative, partly because of the high level of the advance. In the year that each of these had profits to distribute, such amounted to 0.10 to 0.14 pesos per peso of advance. The total daily income of cooperative members was thus in the range of 6.31 to 8.07. See Vicente, "Analisis de la Irrentabilidad en las Cooperativas de Produccion Agropecuarias Caneras de la Provincia Habana: Vias de Eliminacion," table 8.

115. Perez, Martinez, and Cabrera, "Influencia Formativa de las CPA y las CCS sobre los Jovenes Campesinos Cooperativistas," 11.

116. Life history interview with the chief of production of the CPA Manuel Cordero, Las Parras, Majibacoa, June 1992.

117. The data on the composition of household income is presented and discussed in detail in Deere, Carmen Diana, Ernel Gonzales, Niurka Perez, and Gustavo Rodriguez, "Household Incomes in Cuban Agriculture: A Comparison of the State, Cooperative, and Peasant Sectors," The Hague, Institute of Social Studies Working Paper Series no. 143 (1993).

118. The value of self-provisioning by both peasants and CPAs has been valued at official prices. To the extent that some peasants participate in the black market, where prices are considerably higher, peasant household income levels have been underestimated, qualifying this result. Also, one cannot discard the possibility that peasants underreported the level of their self-provisioning, as happens in most rural household income surveys.

119. An *arroba* is equal to 25 pounds; a *caballeria*, to 13.47 hectares.

120. See Deere, Carmen Diana, Niurka Perez, and Ernel Gonzales, "The View from Below: Cuban Agriculture in the Special Period in Peacetime," *Journal of Peasant Studies* 21, no. 2 (1994) for a description of the changes introduced on the state farms between 1990-1993.

121. ANAP, Asociacion Nacional de Agricultores Pequenos, "Analisis sobre la Actualizacion del Registro de Asociados Correspondiente al 31-12-90" (Mimeo: ANAP, 1991).

122. See the wide range of studies carried out by the Rural Research Group at the University of Havana, and the work of the Cooperative Group at the Central University of Las Villas. See Perez, Cruz, Dacosta, Garcia, and Jorrin, "Valoraciones acerca del proceso cooperativo canero en cuatro municipios de la provincia de la Habana"; Perez, Niurka, Ernel

Gonzalez, Miriam Garcia, Joaquina Cruz, and Caridad Dacosta, "Informe del Estudio sobre las Relaciones Politico Economicas del Campesinado con el CAI Azucarero 'Antonio Guiteras' Municipio Puerto Padres, Provincia Las Tunas," (Mimeo, Research Group on the Sugar Sector CAIs of the Province of Havana, University of Havana May 1990a); Perez, Niurka, Ernel Gonzalez, Miriam Garcia, Joaquina Cruz, Caridad Dacosta, and Barbara Jorrin, "Informe del Estudio sobre las Relaciones Politico-Economicas del Campesinado con el CAI Azucarero 'Obdulio Morales' Municipio Yaguajay, Provincia Sancti Spiritus," Mimeo, Research Group on the Sugar Sector CAIs of the Province of Havana, University of Havana, July 1990b; Perez, Garcia, Jorrin, Menendes, Cruz, and Dacosta "Algunos Aspectos de la Composicion Socio-Economica y Demografica de Campesinos Individuales Caneros en Cuatro Municipios de Provincia Habana;" Perez, Niurka, Miriam Garcia, Caridad Dacosta, Ernel Gonzalez, et. al. "Analisis Comparativo de Algunos de los Problemas que Inciden en la Irrentabilidad de Seis CPA Caneras Mediante el Metodo 'Tormenta de Ideas,'" (Mimeo, Research Group on the Sugar Sector CAIs, University of Havana, 1990d); Perez, Niurka, Liliana Martinez, and Milagros Cabrera, "Influencia Formativa de las CPA y las CCS sobre los Jovenes Campesinos Cooperativistas," (Mimeo, University of Havana, 1990e); Victor Figueroa, "Informe Cientifico Resumen, II Taller Cientifico Provincial acerca del Cooperativismo y el Problema Alimentario," (Mimeo: Cooperative Research Group, Central University of Las Villas, April 1991); Victor Figueroa, Jaime Garcia, and Elia Serra "Contradicciones en el Sector Agricola No Estatal de Villa Clara y Expectativas de la Expansion del Cooperativismo," paper presented to the First Scientific Forum on Agricultural Cooperatives, Central University of Las Villas, (May 1990).

7

Conclusion: Looking Forward

Mieke Meurs

The cases examined in this volume suggest that, under certain conditions, collective forms of agricultural organization may contribute to the growth of agricultural output and rural living standards over what had been possible under existing forms of private production. Under other conditions, however, the results of collective agriculture can be poor or even disastrous. Taken together, the analyses in this volume highlight a number of factors that consistently influence the relative viability of collective and private forms of agricultural organization; these include both local conditions and government policy. The findings have importance today for populations and governments that are struggling to overcome land fragmentation, low agricultural productivity, and rural poverty. But they also have implications for the numerous countries with fairly modern, large-scale agriculture, in which governments are attempting to transform the socialist institutions of centrally planned, collective production toward economic organization based more on markets and private property.

Some Lessons from History

Collective agriculture was thought by its early proponents to offer a means of raising agricultural productivity. In the period prior to World War II, private agriculture in many parts of the world was plagued by technological backwardness, land fragmentation, and rural poverty. Highly unequal land distribution, weak development of resource and credit markets, and low levels of industrialization that kept dense populations on the land all contributed to these problems. Low levels of agricultural productivity, in turn, limited the accumulation of surplus for industrialization. A variety of forms of collective organization were recommended by theorists and organizers to help peasants overcome these problem. Possible forms of collective organization included mutual aid groups, machine-sharing cooperatives, credit cooperatives, and production cooperatives. The authors in this volume, especially Victor Danilov and Justin Lin, discussing the Russian and Chinese cases, suggest that the early, diverse forms of collective organization in agriculture did indeed offer a means of raising agricultural productivity, by helping rural households to overcome a variety of market failures.

The cases as a group suggest agricultural production cooperatives also contributed to raising productivity, but not under all conditions. For collective agricultural production to result in productivity increases, both local conditions and government policy needed to be appropriate. Most important, there needed to be a specific economic problem to which collective production could provide a specific solution. The achievement of economies of scale or the provision of an undersupplied public good are examples of problems to which collectivization of production might provide a solution. If collectivization of fragmented landholdings made mechanization economically viable, and local crop types were subject to economies of scale (as in the case of wheat, for example), then collectivization might contribute to productivity growth. This was the case in parts of East and Central Europe, Cuba, and Russia. Or if the collectivization of individual households into a single production unit allowed collective action problems to be overcome in the building of irrigation infrastructure, as was the case for rice production in parts of China, collectivization of household production might also contribute to productivity growth. But simply bringing poverty-stricken rural households together into one production unit was not helpful if they continued to produce using the same technology as before.

In fact, simply collectivizing poor households into a single production unit can contribute to dramatic and even deadly declines in agricultural performance. This is in part due to incentive problems inherent in some collective forms of production. To ensure adequate incentives for quality work, collective organization, like private organization, must provide strong links between work performance and rewards. Private agricultural producers may achieve such links by working their own land, so that there is a direct link between work and reward, or by closely supervising hired labor on small-to-medium farms and firing workers who do not perform adequately. On a collective farm, of course, problems arise because no one individual's reward depends on his work alone, and this creates a temptation to free ride—to not work hard oneself and not supervise one's fellow workers, while collecting a full share of any surplus created. If these problems are severe enough, or if they are not offset by specific productive benefits of collective organization, output declines will result from collectivization of agricultural production.

As we have seen, incentive problems did often plague collective forms of agriculture in the cases reviewed here. The cases also suggest, however, some specific factors that consistently influenced the prevalence of such problems. Perhaps most important, government policies that made it impossible for even well-run farms to provide adequate returns to labor eliminated all motivation for good work. If inappropriate technologies or crop types were imposed on the farm from outside, for example, undermining performance, or if industrialization policy targeted agriculture as its "cash cow," then good collective farm work could not be rewarded. Rural households responded appropriately by reallocating work effort into other ventures, and productivity on the collectives plummeted. Government policies that protected farm workers completely from the consequences of their efforts, through government-guaranteed wages and soft budget constraints for farms, had a similar effect, reducing incentives for work.

The cases examined here also emphasize that collective members needed an effective means of punishing shirking collective members if they were to preserve their own motivation for work. Lin, in examining the Chinese experience, emphasizes that forced membership in collective farms eliminated the option of casting out uncooperative members, as well as the option of leaving shirkers to fend for themselves on a dying collective. Several authors also note the impact of excessively large farms in reducing the potential for enforcement of work norms, by lowering the likelihood of any one shirker being caught. Finally, the authors of the Hungarian, Bulgarian, and Cuban cases all emphasize the importance of strong social networks among collective members in increasing the means and significance of informal punishment of shirkers.

Perhaps the clearest finding from the cases is that forced collectivization consistently produced substantial declines in agricultural output and performance. Where force was used to collectivize, this often implied a disregard for the logic of local conditions, both physical conditions, as in the case of imposing collective forms of agriculture where no immediate economic benefits would be derived from such forms, and social conditions, where members of the new farms lacked the social networks necessary to ensure adequate collective work. Further, in the Russian and Chinese cases, forced collectivization coincided with limited investment and high levels of surplus extraction from the countryside, which made successful production impossible and further reduced incentives for work in the collectives.

It is also clear from the cases examined here that even where collective agricultural production is successful in raising productivity, by overcoming certain problems of land consolidation and modernization of production, this does not guarantee that this form of organization can continue to offer benefits over time. The gains through modernization may provide a one-time boost to productivity, and once these have been achieved incentive problems in collective production may no longer be outweighed by the continuing benefits of collective organization. In the 1980s, governments in all of the cases examined here moved toward greater degrees of decentralization and quasi privatization of labor-intensive agricultural production, seeking to capture the incentive and informational benefits of private farming in labor-intensive products. In many of these cases, including the Chinese shift to the Household Responsibility System, many private households farmed land with the continued support of collectively provided services, using collectively purchased inputs and then marketing products through the collective.[1] While government regulations were in part responsible for the continued link of producer households to collectives, the combination of private production and collective also recalls some of the experiments of the early years of collectivization. Following the logic of Chayanov's model, these experiments allowed households to collectivize only those parts of agricultural organization where specific benefits continued to be derived—in land preparation, for example, or in marketing.

What this long and diverse historical experience highlights is the impossibility of defining one optimal organizational form for agricultural production. The potential productivity benefits of collective agriculture depend on local physical conditions, social relations, and institutional context, which influence not only the performance of collective farms but also the difficulties faced by private agricultural producers. Other researchers have emphasized a similar point. Daniel Bromley, for example, in his work on institutional change, has emphasized that the link between the relative efficiency of different institutions and the context in which they exist.[2] In contrast to much of existing economic theory, Bromley argues that the efficiency of different institutions arrangements often cannot be ranked in the abstract.

Looking Forward

These findings contribute to a more balanced understanding of the (now mostly concluded) experiment with socialist agricultural collectivization. But perhaps more important, they are relevant to populations and governments weighing the costs and benefits of collective versus private agriculture today. This includes those in Third World countries facing long-standing problems of low agricultural efficiency and rural poverty. Where serious market or coordination failures prevent private farmers from attaining desired levels productivity and income, the evidence presented here suggests that collective forms of agriculture may sometimes provide a means of improving productivity and incomes. Others have certainly made this point—William Thiesenhusen argued that group farms might be used to reduce the costs of directing credit and extension services to land reform beneficiaries in Latin America, and 50 percent of all World Bank-assisted agricultural projects in Africa in a 1986 review involved using cooperatives to raise productivity and incomes.[3] But the cases examined here provide more specific guidance about the conditions under which collective production may be a viable alternative to private production than many previous studies. In addition, the cases emphasize the importance of organizational flexibility—of allowing local populations to choose the combinations of collective and private organization that best solve locally, and historically, specific production problems.

Our reexamination of collectivization also suggests some important lessons for those in formerly centrally planned economies that are currently undergoing a transformation toward market-based organization or that may attempt such a transformation in the future. Given the relatively rapid expansion of quasi-private agriculture throughout the centrally planned economies in the 1980s, many observers expected that collectivized agriculture would be quickly be replaced by private farming throughout East-Central Europe and Russia following the events of 1989. This position was supported by Western observers and advisors, who frequently asserted the universal productive superiority of private over collective forms of agricultural organization.[4]

Based on this argument, some have attempted to legislatively enforce a particular "optimal" form of agricultural organization as part of postsocialist reform. In Bulgaria, legislation was passed to force the universal liquidation of collective farms and to greatly complicate the organization of new cooperatives, to speed the "natural" process of decollectivization into individual smallholding units.[5] In Hungary, the independent Smallholder Party attempted to implement similar legislation, but failed, and in Russia, too, Boris Yeltsin argued such a position, although the eventual Russian legal structure fell well short of enforcing such a uniform reorganization.[6]

Even where one particular form of agricultural organization was not legally prescribed, however, debates about agricultural policy in postsocialist countries often centered on defining the "optimal" form of agricultural organization for the nation.[7] The historical experiences examined in this volume suggest a number of reasons that such notions of a one-size-fits-all solution to the problems of collective agriculture are nearly as misguided as the earlier strategies that forced a single, collective model agriculture on all areas, regardless of local conditions and desires.

As we have seen, collective agriculture initially responded to problems of land fragmentation and technological underdevelopment in agriculture, which in turn undermined rural productivity and incomes and limited potential export earnings from agriculture. Under certain conditions, a strategy of simply breaking up collective farms into individual smallholding units threatens to recreate these old problems. Where limited market development prevents new landholders from consolidating small plots or obtaining needed inputs, credit, or technology, or forces them to pay high monopoly markups on these items, private farmers may be unable to replicate the modern production organization achieved decades ago by the collective farms, which allowed many socialist countries to compete effectively on global agricultural markets.[8] Under these conditions, privatization of production is likely to coincide with a fall in agricultural productivity and incomes.

In traditional grain-growing regions this is likely to be a particularly severe problem for both local populations and governments, since economies of scale may be significant. In other regions, however, scale economies will play a much less important role in ensuring agricultural productivity. In peri-urban areas, for example, farmers holding small plots and using only very limited technology may achieve high productivity and incomes through the production of labor-intensive fruit and vegetables, and private organization may offer returns much superior to those offered by collective forms of production. Or in mountainous areas, where few economies of scale can be achieved under any conditions, smallholders may competitively produce certain livestock products, wine grapes, or tobacco. The rationality of collective or private production thus continues to depend heavily on local conditions, including the physical, social, and institutional factors discussed above.[9]

The parallels between the earlier imposition of universal collectivization and the current attempt to impose private farming are not lost on the local populations. In Bulgaria, one peasant woman complained, "First the communists made us give up our land and now the [government, led by the anti-communist] UDF is making us take it back. It is like getting slapped on both sides of your face."[10] And as was the case during collectivization, local populations have actively resisted such imposed, uniform solutions where they have felt that these did not promote their material interests. Movement toward the organization of private farms has proceeded much more slowly and partially than early observers expected. In Russia, when collective farms were forced to reorganize by Yeltsin-backed legislation at the end of 1992, 92 percent of farms chose to reorganize as joint-property agricultural enterprises or new cooperatives.[11] In Bulgaria, as of 1994, 54 percent of rural households planned to place their restituted land in new cooperatives, while in 1993, 43 percent of privatized Romanian land had been returned to collective agricultural "associations."[12]

Attempts to impose private farming have often led to resistance. In Bulgaria, for example, villagers used a number of quasi-legal methods to preserve cooperative farming from the 1992 legislative attack and even resorted to violence when other methods failed.[13] In Estonia, too, government support for private farming has been met by significant local resistance.[14] This resistance cannot be written off simply as evidence of peasant conservatism or manipulation of local populations by former collective farm managers. Detailed studies of patterns of decollectivization suggest that, although political allegiances do sometimes play a role, rural households adopt private farming much more easily where cooperatives have ceased to offer advantages in overcoming a variety of market failures.[15]

Perhaps telling is the fact that in two countries where no one form of agricultural organization has been imposed or even favored by government policy, a smooth transition to a mix of property forms has resulted. In Hungary, despite attempts by the independent Smallholder Party to impose smallholder farming, government policy provided a relatively level playing field for private and cooperative forms of agricultural organization. By 1994, 36 percent of agricultural land remained in collective forms of agricultural organization. Choice of organizational form initially showed a clear regional pattern, with collective forms of production continuing to predominate in grain-growing regions of Hungary through 1992, and private production dominating in mountainous and peri-urban areas. As markets for land and other inputs developed, however, and private producers could attain the scale economies previously offered only by collective forms of organization, grain production ceased to provide a rationale for collective organization. The prevalence of cooperative farming in grain regions was reduced, and other local considerations, such as the (in)divisibility of local capital stocks, became more important in explaining the choice of organizational form.[16] In the Czech Republic, too, local cooperative farm members and management were permitted to freely choose the future form of agricultural organization. Here, too, reorganization took mixed forms, with cooperatives controlling about 50 percent of agricultural land in mid-1993.[17]

Still missing from the landscape of formerly socialist economies are the more diverse forms of semicollective organization that characterized early experiments with collective agriculture. Credit, service, and marketing cooperatives might help private farmers to overcome continuing market failures caused by limited market development and persisting monopoly power. In doing so, they would permit households to collectivize only those areas of production faced with specific problems that collective organization could address. But whereas new production cooperatives have been able to build on collective farming organizations of the socialist period, more limited forms of cooperation must often start from scratch. Local populations lack knowledge of how to organize such cooperatives, and legislation facilitating the development of such cooperatives may not be a priority for urban-based legislators.

Nonetheless, allowing the widest possible range of flexible mix of organizational forms will permit appropriate adjustment to the widest range of local conditions. To foster such a mix, it is important for policymakers to create the most level playing field possible between different forms of organization. This will likely imply more than simply doing nothing. Cooperatives restructuring out of old collective farms may currently benefit from access to physical capital, land, or credit, which private farmers cannot easily replicate due to limited market development. In this case, the creation of a level playing field may require government intervention in the promotion of competitive markets for agricultural inputs. Specific policies might include the organization of land exchange bureaus, where the multitude of small, privately held plots might be consolidated into larger parcels for rental and where information on land prices and quality could be centralized, or assistance in the organization of bank branches or cooperative banks, which may be better able to evaluate the creditworthiness of small, local producers. These changes, as well as the passing of legislation on credit and service cooperatives, which is still lacking in some countries, could also contribute to a more rapid emergence of a wider range of forms of cooperative.

Further, where production cooperatives continue to predominate due to their ability to resolve coordination problems of individual producers, historical experience suggests that governments may contribute to improving agricultural performance by assisting in the development of more responsive and democratic management techniques in the cooperative sector. Where management is not responsive to the desires of members, neither management nor members will have adequate incentives for quality work. International cooperative organizations, such as the International Cooperative Alliance, may offer support for such extension work.

Finally, the historical experience with collectivization examined in this volume highlights the negative impact that a weak economic context can have on the incentives of producers in any form of economic organization. Where governments have depressed agricultural prices in order to promote rapid industrial development, the artificially low prices have destroyed incentives for adequate work and investment in both the cooperative and private sectors, and production has declined precipitously. Using agricultural surplus to placate urban populations or support industrial investment may appear as an attractive short-run solution to government problems and thus has been pursued as part of restructuring efforts.[18] Propping up the rest of the economy at the expense of agriculture is not a long-run solution, however, since it may lead to permanent distortions in the newly emerging agricultural structure.

This reexamination of the history of socialist collective agriculture provides an important counterpoint to those who would argue that collective forms of agriculture have proven an unequivocal failure. But its more general lesson is the fallacy of single solutions to locally diverse problems of agricultural production and the importance of facilitating accumulation in agriculture if this sector is to eventually serve as a base for accumulation elsewhere in the economy.

Notes

1. Louis Putterman, *Continuity and Change in China's Rural Development* (New York: Oxford University Press, 1993).

2. Daniel Bromley, *Economic Interests and Institutions: The Conceptual Foundations of Public Policy* (New York: Basil Blackwell, 1989).

3. William Thiesenhusen, "Landed Property in Capitalist and Socialist Countries: The Russian Transition," in *Agricultural Land Ownership in Transitional Economies,* ed. Gene Wunderlich (Lanham, Md.: University Press of America, 1995), 36, 39. Avishay Braverman, J. Luis Guasch, Monika Huppi, and Lorenz Pohlmeier, "Promoting Rural Cooperatives in Developing Countries: The Case of Sub-Saharan Africa," in World Bank Discussion Papers 121 (Washington, D.C.: The World Bank, 1991).

4. Karen Brooks, "Decollectivization and the Agricultural Transition in Eastern and Central Europe," in WPS 793 (Washington, D.C.: The World Bank, Agricultural and Rural Development Department, 1991).

5. Robert Begg and Mieke Meurs, "Writing a New Song: State Policy and Path Dependence in Bulgarian Agriculture," in *Privatizing the Land: Rural Political Economy in Post-Communist Societies,* ed. Ivan Szelenyi (London: Routledge, 1998), 245-70.

6. Erik Mathijs, "The Process and Politics of Agrarian Reform in Hungary," in *Political Economy of Agrarian Reform in Central and Eastern Europe,* ed. Johan Swinnen (Aldershot, U.K.: Ashgate, 1997), 253. Don Van Atta, "Agrarian Reform in Post-Soviet Russia," in *Political Economy of Agrarian Reform in Central and Eastern Europe,* ed. Johan Swinnen (Aldershot, U.K.: Ashgate, 1997), 331.

7. Ray Abrahams, "Some Thoughts on Recent Land Reforms in Eastern Europe," introduction to *After Socialism: Land Reform and Social Change in Eastern Europe,* ed. Ray Abrahams (Oxford: Berghahn Books, 1996), 3, 10. Isabelle Lindemans, "Process and Politics of Agricultural Privatization in the Czech and Slovak Republics," in *Political Economy of Agrarian Reform in Central and Eastern Europe,* ed. Johan Swinnen (Aldershot, U.K.: Ashgate, 1997), 180.

8. Mieke Meurs, "Institutional Evolution in East Central Europe: A Comparison of Agrarian Change in Hungary and Bulgaria," manuscript under review, 1998. Thiesenhusen, "Landed Property in Capitalist and Socialist Countries: The Russian Transition," 36, 39.

9. Thiesenhusen, "Landed Property in Capitalist and Socialist Countries: The Russian Transition," 36, 39.

10. Gerald Creed, "An Old Song in a New Voice: Decollectivization in Bulgaria," in *East Central European Communities: The Struggle for Balance in Turbulent Times,* ed. David Kideckel (Boulder, Colo.: Westview, 1996), 37.

11. Thiesenhusen, "Landed Property in Capitalist and Socialist Countries: The Russian Transition," 36, 39.

12. Karen Brooks and Mieke Meurs, "Romanian Land Reform: 1991-1993," *Comparative Economic Studies* (Summer 1994). Meurs, "Institutional Evolution in East Central Europe: A Comparison of Agrarian Change in Hungary and Bulgaria."

13. Deema Kaneef, "Responses to 'Democratic' Land Reforms in a Bulgarian Village," in *After Socialism: Land Reform and Social Change in Eastern Europe,* ed. Ray Abrahams (Oxford: Berghahn Books, 1996). Begg and Meurs, "Writing a New Song: State Policy and Path Dependence in Bulgarian Agriculture."

14. Abrahams, "Some Thoughts on Recent Land Reforms in Eastern Europe," 3, 10.

15. Erik Mathijs and Johan Swinnen, "The Economics of Agricultural Decollectivization in Central and Eastern Europe," working paper 3/1, Department of Agricultural Economics, K.U. Leuven, Belgium, 1997. Meurs, "Institutional Evolution in East Central Europe: A Comparison of Agrarian Change in Hungary and Bulgaria." Brooks and Meurs, "Romanian Land Reform: 1991-1993."

16. Katalin Kovacs, "The Transition in Hungarian Agriculture 1990-1993: General Tendencies, Background Factors, and the Case of the 'Golden Age,'" in *After Socialism: Land Reform and Social Change in Eastern Europe,* ed. Ray Abrahams (Oxford: Berghahn Books, 1996). Meurs, "Institutional Evolution in East Central Europe: A Comparison of Agrarian Change in Hungary and Bulgaria."

17. Lindemans, "Process and Politics of Agricultural Privatization in the Czech and Slovak Republics," 180.

18. Thiesenhusen, "Landed Property in Capitalist and Socialist Countries: The Russian Transition," 36, 39. Begg and Meurs, "Writing a New Song: State Policy and Path Dependence in Bulgarian Agriculture."

Index

agricultural exports, 40, 89, 106, 110, 113, 144, 156-57, 163, 187

agricultural output, 18, 25-27; in Bulgaria, 8, 12, 16, 18, 25, 27, 87, 97, 99, 105, 109-10, 113; in China, 8, 16, 18-19, 22, 25-26, 152, 160, 163-65, 170, 178; in Cuba, 8, 19; in Hungary; 8, 16, 18, 21, 26, 126-27, 139, 141, 145-46; in Russia, 8, 13, 16, 18-19, 21, 25, 39, 73-76

agricultural productivity, 37, 40, 76, 88, 90, 105-06, 109-10, 113, 137, 139, 145-46, 171-74

agricultural proletariat, 190, 210, 218, 222

Agro-Promishleno Komplex (APK) 111-14

All Union Communist Party Bolshevik (AUCPB), 46, 52, 54, 56, 62, 68, 70

Asociacion Nacional de Agropequarios Peqenos (ANAP), 196-201, 203, 206, 208-09, 211, 213-14, 220, 223, 225

Berov, Liuben, 112

Boyd, Michael, 113

Bulgarian Agrarian National Union (BANU), 92-93, 102

Bulgarian Communist Party, 97-100, 104, 106, 114

Bulgarian Workers Party, 14, 94

Carter, Michael, 7

Castro, Fidel, 196-97, 200, 213, 216

Chaianov, A.V. *See* Chayanov, A.V.

Chayanov, A.V., 4, 10, 29, 43-52, 61, 78, 240

collective farms: consolidation of, 14-15, 22-24, 60, 88, 106-07, 141, 143, 201; independence of, 16, 22-24, 73, 95, 101, 108, 111, 115-16, 139, 141-42, 214, 216-17, 225; land share of, 14-16, 87, 96, 98, 100, 102, 104, 137-38, 141, 144, 203; share of peasant farms, 50, 60, 63, 68-69; size of, 14-17, 98, 100, 106, 111, 137-38, 141-42, 160, 162, 201-03, 211

collectivization: benefits and costs of, 6-7, 25, 104-06, 109-17, 139-42, 176, 206-09, 215-17, 224; coercive measures and incentives and, 1, 9-10, 13-17, 22-24, 47, 59-72, 94-104, 136-44, 159, 200, 209, 213-14, 225; defined, 4; factors in success of, 3, 5, 7-8, 18-25, 145, 186, 210-13, 218-22, 226, 237-44; and free-riding, 7, 22-24, 28, 108, 173-74, 238-39; ideological and agricultural objectives of, 1, 4-5, 94, 107,

About the Contributors

Victor Danilov, senior researcher, Institute of History, Russian Academy of Sciences, is the author of Rural Russia Under the New Regime and is currently co-editing a volume of documents entitled *The Tragedy of the Soviet Village, Collectivization and Dekulakization.*

Carmen Diana Deere, professor of economics and director of the Center for Latin American, Caribbean and Latino Studies at the University of Massachusetts, Amherst, is the author of a number of books and many articles on Latin American agricultural development and gender issues, including the co-edited volume *Transition and Development: Problems of Third World Socialism.*

Veska Kouzhouharova, senior research fellow and assistant director of the Institute of Sociology of the Bulgarian Academy of Sciences, is the author of numerous articles on Bulgarian agriculture, as well as the books *Bulgarskoto Selo, 1878-1944* (1993), *Seloto Sotsiologischesi* (1989), and *Bulgarskoto Selo prez Vekovete* (1985).

Imre Kovach, senior research fellow, Institute for Political Science of the Hungarian Academy of Sciences, is the author of many articles on Hungarian and East Central European agriculture and the co-editor of *Actors on the Changing European Countryside* (1998).

Justin Lin, professor of economics, Hong Kong University of Science and Technology and Peking University and director of the China Center for Economic Research, is the author of numerous articles on Chinese agriculture and on problems of labor incentives in farming institutions.

Mieke Meurs, associate professor of economics at American University, has published numerous articles on collective and centrally planned agriculture, issues of gender equity in East Central Europe, and problems of transformation in formerly centrally planned economies. Recent work has appeared in journals including *World Development* and *Politics and Society.*

Niurka Perez, professor of sociology in the Faculty of Philosophy of the University of Havana and the founder and director of the Rural Studies Team at the university, has written extensively on rural and gender issues and is a co-author, with Carmen Diana Deere, of *Cuba Agraria: Transformaciones Locales en el Siglo XX*.

Rositsa Stoyanova, researcher at the Institute of History, Bulgarian Academy of Sciences, is the author of numerous articles on political parties and political power in Bulgaria in prior to World War II. A recent article appears in *Charity and Charitable Foundations in Bulgaria 1878-1951* (Sofia, 1997).